Instruments of Social Research

Instruments of
Social Research

JASPAL SINGH

RAWAT PUBLICATIONS
Jaipur | New Delhi | Bangalore | Hyderabad | Guwahati

ISBN 978-81-316-0429-8

Published by
Prem Rawat for **Rawat Publications**
Satyam Apts., Sector 3, Jawahar Nagar, Jaipur 302 004 (India)
Phone: 0141 265 1748 / 7006 Fax: 0141 265 1748
E-mail: info@rawatbooks.com
Website: www.rawatbooks.com

New Delhi Office
4858/24, Ansari Road, Daryaganj, New Delhi 110 002
Phone: 011 2326 3290

Also at *Bangalore, Hyderabad* and *Guwahati*

Typeset by *d'lines* DTP SERVICES, Jaipur
Printed at Chaman Enterprises, New Delhi

जिनि खोजा तिन पाइआ
गहरे पानी पैठ
तिनि बपुरा क्या पाइआ
जो रहे किनारे बैठ

—कबीर

Contents

Foreword

The study of sociology was introduced in India during the waning period of the British rule by eminent scholars who were trained in anthropology – a discipline suited to the study of simple societies with traditional social behaviour. Although India was a large country, its culture and society was, by large, of the traditional kind in which behaviour patterns of people tend to be ossified. People lived in close communities of kinship groups such as caste and tribe, and integrated in the larger society as groups rather than as individuals. Sociological studies in that context were centred on a satisfactory understanding of such topics, as any other. Understandably a major publication brought out by reputed sociologists in India in 1979 was entitled *The Fieldworker and His Field: Problems and Challenges in Sociological Investigation* which dealt with problems of the sociologist/anthropologist collecting information firsthand from the community he/she is studying. Emile Durkheim's conception that the individual's behaviour is determined by the group seems to have underlined most of the studies of Indian sociologists.

There has been a radical change in Indian society and culture since independence and the introduction of the republican form of government. The individual has become the unit in the society instead of the group in the past. The hold of the traditional groups has loosened and the individual is now able to join or leave many voluntary groups. Such a situation enables the individual to take more independent decisions. In other words the individual behaviour instead of being oriented by the group as in the traditional societies now becomes more subjective, depending upon one's own consciousness, which renders society more complex. Society now can be regarded as the network of inter-subjective relationships among individuals. The changed situation calls for the method of sociology suggested by Max Weber, which is termed *verstehen* or interpretative understanding as rightly assumed by Professor Jaspal Singh, the author of this volume.

The science of sociology according to Weber attempts to understand the meaning of an action and also seeks to explain it causally. Such a method calls for on the part of the sociologist to get acquainted with the problem and the field, and with one's own sociological insight and intuition draw hypotheses which could be the possible solutions of the problem. Hypotheses are still the subjective understanding of the investigation. They have to be confirmed or rendered objective by obtaining the requisite information from the individuals themselves who compose the society under investigation. The instruments of social research presented in this volume are the devices used by sociologists to design the ways of collecting and processing information from the individuals under study until the writing of the final report. In my opinion this book could be taken as a reliable research guide for postgraduate scholars conducting sociological research in a complex society such as the modernising societies of India and its neighbourhoods. It would be a handy reference book for research guides in sociological studies in designing recipes of research works for their projects.

Professor Jaspal Singh has not merely collected the instruments of social research from various volumes and arranged them systematically but has also enlivened them with his interesting way of writing and by giving his sage advice to budding scholars for avoiding pitfalls in the use of some of the complex devices. A lifetime of study, teaching and research of the author is reflected in this work. I have great pleasure in welcoming this volume.

Victor S. D'Souza

Preface

"Methods, methods, methods! I will give a punch on your nose and methods will come out of it. Go back to your field and do not return until you have collected the data!" Thus spoke an eminent professor to his brilliant research scholar. He wanted him to stop thinking and do his research. The assumption was that the data speak for themselves. These days it is well-recognised that data collection is different from a fishing expedition.

The task before a research worker is to gather new facts and/or to interpret the already available facts in a new way. He himself designs his tools of research. He gathers, processes and analyses the data collected by him in an innovative and creative manner, making his own way all the time. Traditional sociologists in India tend to be social philosophers or ethnographers. They somehow gather a large mass of data, hoping that somehow something will come out of them at last. The need for preparing fully thought-out research designs and proceeding systematically throughout is not adequately recognised. Psychologists in India tend to fall back upon scales constructed by others. Sociologists hardly ever make use of scales. It is high time that we went beyond descriptive identification of configuration of variables with participant observation and case study methods. The survey method is supposed to make use of representative samples and reliable scales. The goal is to ascertain the magnitude of variables and their precise interrelations. A survey is as good as its sample. Beyond that, the experimental method is best suited for pinpointing the cause-effect linkages. However, unlike the natural sciences the social sciences have not gone far enough to fully utilise the potential of more advanced methods of research. In this book we have focussed our attention on important aspects of empirical social research.

I am thankful to Erwin K. Scheuch, Ute Scheuch, René Koenig, Helmut Petri, Anthony D. King, Victor S. D'Souza, P.P. Singh, Ekkehard Mochmann, Karl Heinz Reuband, Eric Tannenbaum and Joerg Blassius for valuable discussions. Thanks are due to Narinderpal Singh for preparing subject index and author index. Thanks are due to Maninder Singh for typing the manuscript and to Pranit Rawat for publishing the book. My audience here consists of postgraduate students and young research scholars of universities in SAARC countries.

Jaspal Singh

List of Tables

List of Figures

1

Instruments of Social Research

The subject matter of sociology is society. A number of academic disciplines are interested in it. Empirical sociology makes use of the method of science (based on experience rather than spirituality or speculation) for finding new facts, understanding the same ourselves, and logically explaining the already available facts in a new way. For this reason, we become creative, and go ahead methodically, using various techniques of data collection and data analysis. How do we proceed? Instruments of research help us to gather and analyse valid and reliable data, with an assured degree of certainty for theory construction. Validity means that the data are sound enough to maintain what they claim. Reliability means that repeated measurements yield identical results with a degree of certainty like a line carved on stone.

Creativity

How do we exercise our sociological imagination to create something? We do not know exactly what creativity is, and how it works. Factor analysis on empirical data has brought out at least four factors of creativity. These include elaboration, flexibility, fluency and originality. For our purpose here, creativity means the ability to discover new facts and/or to interpret the already available data with a fresh approach. Great minds do this, among others by fiddling with, analysing (piecing apart), synthesising (reconstructing) known facts/ideas in an ingeneous manner. Robert Michels put forth his iron law of oligarchy. Einstein's theory of relativity created a radically new understanding of space, time, matter and energy. Gunnar Myrdal put forth his theory of cumulative causation.

Becoming creative. That is the problem. But how? First of all, we use our sociological imagination, imbibe the spirit of creativity, and generate fresh ideas. There are three types of creativity: (1) Exploratory creativity identifies facts in space and time. (2) Combinational creativity puts them together in an alternative way. (3) Transformational creativity alters some dimensions of structure and ideas, for generating new patterns. A researcher makes use of his creative imagination for generating innovative ideas and or interpreting whatever is available, in an original mode. He tries to make some sense out of the chaos under study, with a view to understanding and explaining its structure and functioning. Preliminary explanations are critically analysed (taken apart, dissected). These are compared and contrasted, with a view to discovering their interrelationship. For instance, Darwinists have analysed evolution in five parts: reproduction, mutation, selection, isolation, and cooperation. The outcome is simplified and systematically restructured (synthesis). Creative and innovative persons generate their own high quality novel ideas with hard work, ingenuity and precision.

One of the ways to becoming creative is to look at the matter with our own senses, and give words to our experience. This is a mental process. Our brain has vast potential, and multidimensional qualities. These have been acquired during the course of evolution. We keep it in working order, because disuse of organs retards them. Formal education, informal socialisation and intensive utilisation sharpen our brain. We provide adequate opportunity to explore, generate or transform something into something else. We apply our mind to the matter. We try to understand it intuitively and explain it to others in a way they can grasp the matter. When we have something to say (message), we say it in the best manner we can (medium). For this purpose, we proceed systematically. There is method even in madness.

Creativity proceeds by dint of mental ability. This can be analysed into five levels. These are shown in Table 1. We build upon the basis of already existing knowledge. We learn it by heart and recall it when needed. Depositary education is based on memorisation alone. Beyond that we proceed ahead and analyse, synthesise, and apply meaningfully. Everything cannot be useful everywhere. All judgements are subjective. But these are to be based on material facts rather than speculation. Try to understand the social, organic and inorganic evolutions in terms of each other. Comprehend the rise, stabilisation and entrenchment of democracy in a Third World country in terms of **alap, jor** and **jhala** of an

Indian musical instrument, say, sitar. Social structure can often be understood in terms of the rhythm of dance. Something can be explained in terms of something else. We apply our mind without breaking it down. Reflect. Present linear structure in a cyclical frame. Split known structures and processes into their significant elements. Depending upon the task before us, these are reversed, inverted, mixed up, systematically rotated in order to get a better fit. These are pieced together, realigned and reintegrated in another way with a view to producing effects. We refrain from thrusting our favourite pigeonholes on the matter under consideration, overlooking mismatch. We carefully examine what holds and what does not hold under the given conditions. The outcome is put to use for solving problems. Action without reflection leads us nowhere. Critical judgement is the highest mental ability.

Table 1
Five levels of mental ability

	Term	*Example*
1.	Recall	Memorisation and reproduction of religious books
2.	Analysis	Splitting Marxist class into Weberian class, status and power
3.	Synthesis	The spiral of a Hegelian thesis and antithesis merging together
4.	Application	Explaining democracy in India with Michel's iron law of oligarchy
5.	Critical judgement	Evaluation of arguments for and against value-neutrality in social research

This does not mean that you go on finding fault all the time. That impedes realistic action. Criticism can be constructive as well as destructive. Capacity is utilised at a proper place and time with a sense of proportion. We examine the matter systematically. We accept, reject, clinch the matter. Those with high mental ability are able to simplify complications, and come out of difficulties. Those with low mental ability get entangled in thorns while plucking flowers. They are not able to take care of themselves, and their dress gets torn. How do we use our mental ability to become creative? Apply your mind. Place the problem in proper perspective. Explain. What is the matter? What do you want? Act promptly. A stitch in time saves nine.

Creativity is hardly ever instant. You apply your mind, and go on doing so. This is a time-consuming activity. Serendipity pattern intuitively emerges, as if suddenly, while an observer grasps the Gestalt and develops insights into the matter, as a result of prolonged exposure, in addition to deep thought. The gestation period for excellent performance is often long.

Creativity Circles

Judgements are always subjective. These are inter-subjectively verified. Like-minded persons come together on assorted occasions. Experience of togetherness and intense interpersonal interaction in such circles promotes creativity. Members come into contact with each other. They keep company with one another and share a productive atmosphere with mutual stimulation, fruitful vetting and constructive criticism.

It is not enough that they effectively register their social presence there. They get involved in the matter under deliberation, and apply their minds together. They provide the context for one another's attitude and behaviour. They communicate without any let or hindrance. They ensure that they can depend upon one another. Their mutual trust and confidence facilitate spur-of-the-moment teamwork. They boost one another's morale. They share what they know. They exchange their experiences. Bickerings over differences are avoided by maintaining privacy in interstitial spaces. Those who exercise alternative choices are not classified as enemies. Intellectual differences are not personal differences.

Figure 1
Tasks before a creativity circle

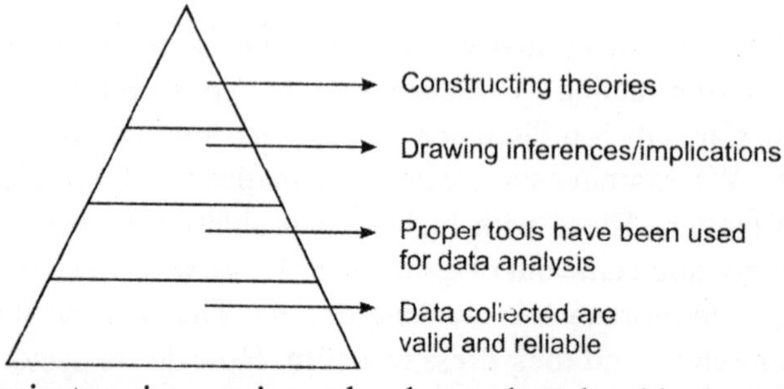

In brainstorming sessions, they have a long hard look at the matter together. They let their brains reel. They carefully listen to what others want to say. They enter into discussions, and stimulate one another to come out with valuable insights into the matter. They offer constructive suggestions for surmounting hurdles in the way of viable and workable solutions for recognising realities and coming to terms with problems in different situations. Points are checked up with counter-points and collateral evidence. They say so. But did anybody see or smell a rat? Sometimes they are happy to agree. Sometimes they beg to differ. Unnecessary controversy or annoyance is tactfully avoided. However, by bringing out points and counter-points, the discussion warms up. The matter gets clarified. Blanks are filled in with supplementary information in order to facilitate convergence of registered perceptions. They put two and two together, without asking somebody higher in the pecking order how much that should be. The matter is fitted into some symmetry, pattern, or a beautiful design. Knowledge comes from recall of repeatedly memorised existential experience. Had it not been like this, it would have been like that. Had it not been like that, it would have been like that. Had you not been like this, you would have become that. What would have happened if he had been absent from duty without leave? Interacting individuals communicate this to one another. They apply it to the solution of problems confronting them in a variety of situations. The outcome is critically evaluated. Flaws are thereby removed. Formulations are tested and verified. In the absence of its supporting culture, a creativity circle fails to yield fruitful results.

Coordination is the key to the functioning of such a cluster. The coordinator *(khalifa, guru)* with thorough knowledge and great insight is a working member of the group. He is a mastermind. He possesses sharp antennae and far-sighted vision. We can say super-consciousness. He knows what exactly he is doing. He sets the agenda. He creates congenial atmosphere for fruitful interaction. He guides his disciples, and brings home subtle nuances. He awakens their creative skills. The disciple yields results. He rectifies distorted perceptions. He sees to it that they do not go off the track or mix up issues. He can function effectively only so long as he continues to be acceptable to his group. He does not give imperative orders. He is a promoter.

Seminars, conferences, joint meeting grounds, enable creative persons to share their encounters and experiences. While constructive criticism facilitates creativity, demoralising atmosphere retards it. Moreover, in the absence of a supporting culture, such facilities are allocated on *quid pro quo* basis, or altogether grabbed by tub-thumpers of head clerks on one pretext or another. These are usurped by dilettantes and charlatans for meeting together in vanity fairs at home and abroad, eating sumptuous food, and cheating one another for one-upmanship.

There is an ever-increasing tendency to carry on electoral campaigns, sales promotion drives and publicity stunts in the name of seminars and surveys. Trade union activities are often carried on in the name of academic workshops. Participants make use of such opportunities to hunt around for affable clients or convenient patrons. Such re-functioning of collective resources for private use pillarises goal displacement.

Figure 2
Building enduring relations

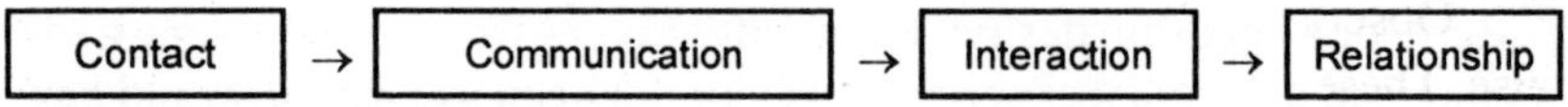

Methodology

Methodology is the theory of method. Empirical theories are based on sense impressions obtained through experience. How is this done? Our brain does it. It possesses vast potential and multidimensional qualities. These are acquired during the prolonged process of evolution. Formal education and informal socialisation sharpen it. Shall we look at the matter in detail?

From our point of view here, sociology is possible only as the continuous practice of empirical social research. How do we pursue our subject matter? For this purpose, we rely upon our senses. We can hear, see, smell, taste and touch. Senses can be sharpened with instruments. Empiricism sidetracks traditional beliefs, emotions and sentiments as well as *a priori* knowledge.

Research means finding new facts and/or presenting already known facts in a new way. How do we go ahead? Keenly observe and discern. Sensations coming from outside impinge upon our mind/consciousness. Our nervous system identifies relevant signals. In contrast to affection (feelings) and conation (will), this is an ultimate mode of conscious life. Human consciousness acquires these qualities during the course of evolution. Cognition (knowledge) includes perceptions, memory,

Figure 3
Giving words to experience

reasoning, and so on. Intuition (instant understanding, obtained while observing) is kept under control. Signals are methodically interpreted and organised. In this way, sensations become perceptions. Perception is functionally selective. State of mind affects it.

A snob arrogantly asserts: "It is true, because ***I*** (The Great) say it is true!" Statements like: "Truth is not altered by the opinion of the vulgar, or the confirmation of many", are laudable. These unravel the courage of conviction as well as the willingness to suffer for it. But intuition is hasty. It is far from being scientific. This has got to be checked up and verified. Empiricists use the method of science for finding facts and their linkages.

Observed facts are verified or falsified. These are neither true nor false. These are just there. Our job is to understand ourselves, and explain the matter for others. For this purpose, we become creative, proceed methodically, and use proper techniques of data collection and data analysis.

Data Collection

Data are recorded observations. Primary data from surveys, etc., are used for the purpose in hand. These days the same are not discarded after use. These are stored in data archives. These are retrieved later on for cumulation, simulation, comparison and similar other purposes. Secondary data are used for a purpose other than that for which they were originally collected.

For data collection, we observe attentively. Sensations coming from outside impinge upon our mind. These are systematically interpreted and organised. In this way, sense impressions become perceptions.

We do not go on collecting huge masses of data beyond the needs of our research design. It is in vain to hope that something will come out of them later on somehow. Data gathering is costly. It is a time-consuming activity. A lot of money has to be paid to field investigators on account of salary, TA/DA. The researcher is expected to submit his report by due date. Somebody may be waiting for the project report, or for him.

Example 1: Data Collection is not Hanuman's Tail

Do not go on hoarding everything, hoping that something will somehow come out of it all at least one day. Data collection is not a hunting expedition. One has to be methodical and goal-oriented. It is not necessary to carry the hillock with *Sanjivani booti* from Simla to Lanka by air. Do not allow data collection to become Hanuman's tail, which goes on extending endlessly. After some time, one has to call it a day.

No duplication. Fill in the interstitial spaces in between. Apart from avoiding overlaps and filling in the gaps, systematically throw away redundant materials. Data analysis is even more important than collection of valid (measures what it purports to measure) and reliable (consistency of results) data. These days, emphasis is shifting from the latter to the former. One reads the lines and what lies in between the lines in order to draw logical inferences as well as their necessary connections or implications for decision-making.

Example 2: Decision-making

Three teachers were travelling in a small car on a lonely road in a beautiful forest. By chance, a low-flying bird tried to cross the road, in front of the car. The car driver took note of the flying object and slowed down his vehicle, with a view to preventing an accident. The apprehensive bird dithered for a moment and tried to fly back. He struck against the car and died on the spot, there and then. The travellers felt sorry for the pheasant, but took the dead body along.

Paul removed the feathers, and cut the meat into eight pieces. Jeff found out a recipe. Marga cooked it in a pot in her modern kitchen. They enjoyed the sumptuous dinner, and mused over the happening on the dinner table. They were not sure whether it is a cognisable offence. It infringed animal rights. It is a loss to the already diminishing diversity in the natural environment. Better keep quiet about the matter. But why did the bird have to die? He could not take a timely decision! A stitch in time saves nine. Indecisiveness due to fear is the cause of the death.

Data may be interpreted and re-interpreted in a variety of ways, depending upon the purpose at hand. Identify the variables and their configurations. Ascertain their magnitudes. Pinpoint their exact relationships. Are these relationships causal? Make out the trends. In which way is the wind blowing? Concentrate. Let loose your sociological imagination. Do not be in a hurry. In other words, combine empirical evidence with logical reasoning. Interpret the matter in your own way. Try to make some sense out of it all. The analyst recognises the points of contact. He traces the links, records interactions, and notes down relationships. He recognises symmetry and pattern (shape, style, design). Processes consist of their flows and dynamic. The findings are put together with what others in the field have said in this regard. Avoid over-generalisation. On the other hand, we cannot go very far with inadequate interpretation. When somebody asserts that so and so is good or bad, it need not necessarily be so. This reveals the former's attitude towards the latter. When a respondent asserts that bride price is not given in their community, this may indicate that the practice is not considered well and proper. When a political leader claims that there is no infighting in their party, he may be concealing this reality. A researcher has to apply proper checks and balances. Statistical significance is helpful. But it is not enough to draw inferences about association between variables. We have to go beyond statistical significance to their theoretical importance. Experience of surface reality is not enough. There is a throbbing heart beneath a *choli*. Illustrations, even if based on a single deviant case, may bring home a point. Unverified assumptions must be appropriately checked up and verified. Otherwise, the researcher would have to hear that some people know a lot about sociology, without understanding what society is.

Example 3: Atro and Chatro, Double Meaning

It so happened that Atro and Chatro went to an island of cannibals for ethnographic fieldwork. They became popular there, being jolly good fellows. Soon Chatro fell in love with the king of cannibals. She politely asked him, "May I offer you my hand?" "I have already had my breakfast", he replied!

Often there are gaps between subjective (in the mind of the actors in a situation) the objective (factual) and conventional (dictionary meaning) intentions of various terms. In case of speech like irony, the opposite of what is said is correct. In such cases, inverse or opposite inference is justified.

Figure 4

Ageing impairs mental faculty

Ageing → Cognitive decline → Dementia

Example 4: Domestic Pattern of Authority

Who is dominant at home, husband or wife? Surveys on domestic pattern of authority indicate that husbands make decisions. Refined analysis reveals that certain type of decisions are invariably made by women, so long as they make it appear that their husbands would like them to act that way. She would be a loser in domestic politics if she cannot resist the temptation of bragging that she is the man in the house, and wears pants, not *ghagra*. In that case, the authority delegated to her for this purpose would be withdrawn. The husband would react with counter-self-assertion, and put her back into her place. Effective exercise of authority is a cultural accomplishment. On the whole, the husband-wife relationship is asymmetrical.

Western critics repeatedly assert that researchers in India unnecessarily gather large masses of data. They say that data analysis is a weak point with research workers in this country. Often they are bent upon linking their findings with what famous persons have already said in this regard. They make hasty generalisations with a view to saying what the sponsors of their work would like to hear. The conclusions are not adequately scientifically justified. Thus, boys and girls without family encumbrances are hardworking research assistants. They are not well-versed in flexibility, imagination, initiative, originality and other factors of creativity. Is it so? In any case, traditional knowledge is a fair component of discoveries. However, it is often counter-productive to thrust the data into traditional theoretical pigeonholes. The brain possesses multidimensional qualities by dint of the long process of human evolution. Apply your mind. Cautiously interpret the data in your own way. Misinterpretation, e.g., by ignoring a smirk, yields flawed results. Clear concepts smoothen the progress of reasoning. A concept is

Figure 5

Bringing variables under common names

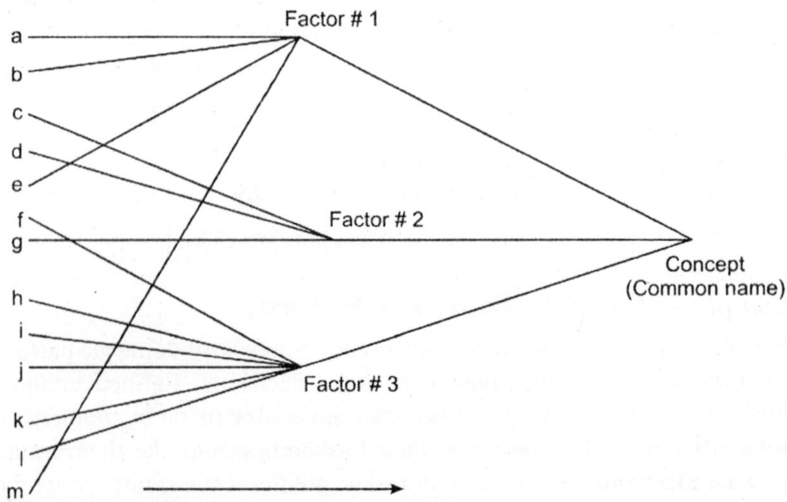

an abstract idea that stands between a concrete object and the word and phrase representing it. A definition pinpoints the contents of a concept. A nominal definition asserts that henceforth a concept will be used in that sense. (For instance, a successful wife is one who can spend more than her husband earns, while a successful husband is one who earns more than his wife can spend.) A real definition shows that a concept contains this and that empirical referents.

Conceptualisation

Conceptualisation is a delicate task. We seek pearls from the heap of mud. For this purpose, we look around for indicators. An indicator reveals other than itself to the knowing power. Thus, if a respondent says, 'Sunday comes every other day', this indicates his commitment to work. Conceptualisation involves bringing together significant relevant facts. Red threads from the data are brought together. These are tied up at their ends with knots. Knots are given names, depending upon the purpose in hand. Proper nouns are replaced with the names of the underlying variables. Critical concepts are called categories. Conceptualisation is done in order to derive abstractions from observation of particular concrete facts. Abstraction demands higher mental ability. We are interested in making generalisations across space and time. A perceptive observer exercises his brain and creates concepts that enable him to give some sort of form to the content under observation. Concepts serve as building blocks for theory construction. Over-generalisation may be based on false assumptions. Thus, a depressed person becomes a victim of his own categories of thought based on one-sided imagination, e.g., negative thinking and fuzzy ideas. Similarly, beautiful theories constructed on the basis of excessive conceptualisation cannot stand confrontation with ugly facts.

Example 5: Conceptualisation, Bringing Words Under Common Names

In a panel discussion on a vision for the 21st century, five scholars were asked to put forth their views before an audience of learned scholars. They filled the knowledge of five oceans in five pitchers. Somebody in the audience brought the red threads together and tied these up at their ends. Thus, he identified a single salient feature of the contents in all these pitchers. He gave it a common name. Globalisation is the name of the game, he asserted.

Chalak, clever, bright, quick and smart have different conventional, objective and subjective intensions. Religion, religiosity and religious organisation are only partially overlapping terms. One man's terrorist may be another's freedom fighter. Liberators can be invaders. Hindi word *'ninda'* can be translated as condemn or deplore. Kali Mai showing the tongue may mean 'put them to shame' to some persons, and 'lay off' to others. Panchayati Raj signifies empowerment to some persons, and corruption to others. In case of "I am firm, you are obstinate, he is a pig-headed fool", the three terms have a dissimilar register. Otherwise, they mean one and the same thing. Devotees across national and religious boundaries refer to the same person as Bhai Mardana or Hazrat Baba Mardana.

Data become information when their significance becomes known. Information consists of isolated events in time and space. Theories are large pieces of knowledge. These are explanations, generalisations, and theoretical frameworks. Hypothesis, theory and law differ from one another in terms of their degree of certainty. Routine data collection and analysis can be left to teams of middle-level research assistants. But only well-trained, highly educated, talented scholars can do research designing and theory construction. They understand how to identify the gaps between what people think, say and do. They know when they have to go beyond statistical significance to theoretical connections that are already well-known. Pythagoreans asserted that mathematical patterns are coterminous with social relations. But there are exceptions to this rule.

Figure 6
Information and knowledge

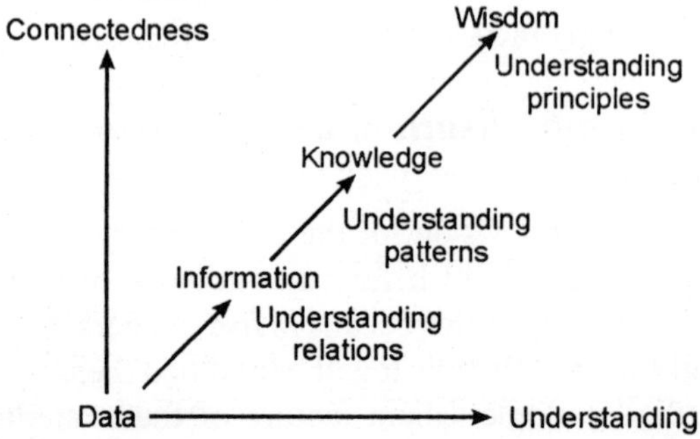

Source: O.K. Hussch, "Reusable Data ...", *Journal of Knowledge and Management Practice*, 9(3) 2008, p. 3.

Knowledge (a large body of theories) of the totality consists of isolated events in time and space (information) as also the linkages between these pieces of information. Scholars have put forward many theories from place to place and time to time. Knowledge is exploding with great speed these days.

Knowledge is more than information, and less than wisdom. This means the ability to make use of knowledge, exercising discretion. It includes street smartness and situational competence. Wisdom puts knowledge to proper use. 'What will I get out of it right now?' is the question before a sophist. A wise man is not self-centered. He is a far-sighted person. He does something for his own benefit, and something for betterment of the world.

Sophism means pretensions to knowledge. This is a logical fallacy, and deliberate error in reasoning. Misuse of knowledge in disregard of ethical considerations for the achievement of one's goals is called sophistry. Subtle and crafty sophists are eager to construct theories that bring them benefits, in disregard of their being actually true or false. They tilt the results of opinion polls in a way that helps them to profitably sell more goods or get more votes. This is a refined form of hypocrisy and cant. While wisdom is benign, sophistry is malignant.

Sophists are inclined towards constructing theories with a view to safeguarding their own interests. With the passage of time and change in the conditions of existence, unintended consequences of their intended action may boomerang on them. Wise scholars call a spade a spade. Eventual mistakes can be rectified by finding new facts or interpreting the available facts in a new way.

Example 6: Sophism, False Claim

In the late 1950s, an African student in Germany worked hard and submitted his doctoral thesis in time. Before his *viva voce* examination, one of his friends lodged a complaint with the university authorities. He accused the candidate of having made false claims for getting admission to the university. The enquiry committee sent his school certificate (in Swahili language) to his country's Embassy for verification. They wrote back saying that it is only a licence for killing a wild elephant!

There were few foreign students in Germany those days. They were keen to improve their relations with foreign countries. His supervisor assured the enquiry committee that otherwise the candidate was intelligent and well-behaved, and had done good work. The committee took a lenient view of the matter, and let him off scot-free. He got the degree sought by him. At last he had killed an elephant with that licence!

Example 7: Data Cooking, Unscientific and Unethical

A critic accused the government of persistently manipulating, distorting, exaggerating, suppressing or tilting scientific data to serve its own purpose, and to protect the interests of its supporters.

A power holder, a sophist, arrogantly replied that they know best what is to be done. They themselves look at facts and review the misleading statements of unwanted scientists. They reformulate their findings in the light of what is good for the people of their country. Read : Interests of power holders.

Example 8: Data Cooking, in a Centre of Excellence

In the 1960s, IIT Delhi was established as an institute of national importance, under an act of Parliament. The institute employed some highly qualified teachers, and admitted the best available students. They got plenty of funds for establishing state of-the-art laboratories. The main building was still under construction.

A brilliant research scholar worked day and night. He promptly submitted his Ph.D. thesis. The examiners reported that even though the data have been meticulously collected and presented with charts and diagrams, the scholar had failed to apply his mind. The data had not been adequately scientifically interpreted. The candidate was bent upon forcibly fitting his observations into the theoretical frames known to him. His knowledge of recent developments was not up to the mark. However, in view of the fact that he had already learnt to do research work on his own, the thesis may be accepted and the degree may be granted.

During the course of his open defence and *viva voce* examination, a professor raised certain doubts. The candidate was asked to produce the data sheets with readings. The candidate got jittery. He admitted that being in a hurry to accept a foreign assignment he had extrapolated the trends, without taking further readings. He had cooked up the data. Extrapolation is based on neglective fiction, assuming that everything will keep going on in the same old fashion. The authorities took a serious view of the matter. Toleration of data cooking in a centre of excellence would have shattered its reputation. He was immediately rusticated and removed from the hostel the very same day, lest other students should agitate about the 'harsh' treatment meted out to one of them. The authorities there were powerful enough to be able to do so those days.

The soundness and consistency of research reports from universities in India have become doubtful in recent times. In the absence of supporting norms, partial democratisation hinders organisational effectiveness. A leisure class goes on justifying its existence by showing off its status, instead of performing socially useful productive functions.

There are limits to empiricism. Human mental apparatus cannot do everything. It has vast potential, but restricted span. Cognition is imperfect. Perception is functionally selective. A vamp's perceptions are different from those of a heroine. One analyst's brain drain is one beggar less for another. Dogs, with a keen sense of hearing, can hear some sounds. Dog-whistles are available in the market. Radha could take note of Shyam's flute from far away. Only sharp-eyed eagles can see some sights. A large part of reality is beyond the reach of the human mental apparatus. Watching television and computer screen for several hours a day further diminishes the capacity to receive optical and acoustic signals. Environmental pollution alters flavours, smells and tastes. Gone are the days when we could read a religious book for *akhand path* in moonlight or with a *jyoti* (earthen lamp) in dark nights. Besides being functionally selective, our perception can become blunt. A large part of reality is beyond our comprehension. We cannot observe phenomenon beyond fragmentary details and epiphenomenon (surface reality), what to speak of noumenon (mysterious, unknown, unknowable), with or without scientific devices. Our explanations do not go beyond the explainable.

All explanations are more or less subjective. Objectivity boils down to inter-subjectivity. Different scholars looking at the matter from their own points of view come to the same conclusions. There are ways of thinking, feeling and acting other than those of empirical sociologists. We can derive the benefit of tempering empiricism with other approaches, say, critical rationalism. Thus, perceptions are placed within the overall framework. We place the manifest symptoms within the situation of their underlying latent causes. The present is interconnected with the remnants of the past and seeds of the future. Relevant facts are separated from insignificant noise. In this way, the study of empirical sociology becomes the study of society. Interestingly, some people know a lot of sociology without having an inkling into what society is. Everybody does not and cannot know everything. There are limits to sociology. We know that we do not know. An important point may be noted here. In a liberal-democratic society, governments, journalists, scholars are expected to play their own roles. All governments have to protect themselves and justify their existence. All journalists have got to earn a living for themselves. Those who pay the piper call the tune. Journalists are servants of power. Media of mass communication are doing business in the field of mind management. They administer the pills prescribed by their advertisers/owners. They keep an eye on their employers' intentions, covered with the readers'/viewers' wishes. They attract their attention, entertain them and bring home the message sent through them. They spread words that enable the powerholders to manage the minds of their voters and supporters. While a journalist justifies a policy that has already been made, a scholar is supposed to call a spade a spade. He provides critical inputs for policy-making. Scholars avoid over-generalisation. They are expected to be objective as well as responsible. They fall back upon their experience in the light of their intellectual background. Their vigorous training makes them well-conversant with cultural subtleties. Role-mix becomes problematic sometimes.

Example 9: Sexing up and Playing Down

All governments have to protect themselves. Obtrusive observation by their security agencies selectivity tilts what they observe. This distorts their reports. Often, reports from a single, uncorroborated source are manipulated and forcibly fitted into a favourite pigeonhole. At the time of their assessment, such reports are sexed up (exaggerated). These are manipulated with a view to throwing dust in the eyes of the target group. These are spiced (not straightforward) in order to justify decisions already taken. A dog is given a bad name before killing him on the basis of such defamation. Governments play down (understate) the impact of pollution on environment in general and green house effect in particular, denying global warming. Thus, data presented in the dossier and their summaries at the end as well as abstract in the beginning stand in contradiction with one another. On being pointed out, discrepancies are rebutted as unintentional clerical mistakes. In this way, public relations men are able to say what they are asked to say by those at the helm of affairs. Companies are able to sell their wares. Politicians are able to get votes. Definition of the situation becomes a self-fulfilling prophecy.

Bush and Blair accused Saddam of possessing stockpiles of nuclear and biological weapons of mass destruction as well as a prompt delivery system. UN observers certified that this is not true. Bush and Blair refused to accept this certificate as valid. Their security services told them what they wanted to hear. Then they launched pre-emptive (going at the threat before it materialises) attack against that country with their full might. Thus, they justified the impending flow of oil money in their own pockets, under the pretext of democratisation. Five centuries ago, Spain, the great civilise, had colonised Latin America and justified the flow of silver stream in the name of missionary activity. Life is like that. But times are changing at a tempo as never before.

Value freedom is the point under reference here. Thus, values and interests are kept apart from dispassionate analysis. A value-free scholar is not a player. He is a referee. He maintains proper distance from his subject matter. There are conventions for providing protection to all scholars against harassment and victimisation of the type done by contending factions against Socrates in Athens. These days, intellectuals like Noam Chomsky and Asthma Jahangir can raise audit objections. Scholars explore ideas in a freewheeling way. They are permitted to sort out controversies. Thus, e.g., universities become dreamlands for fresh ideas and contending theories.

A scientist is not a propagandist or a make-up man. Image-building is not a rightful function of research. He calls a spade a spade. He refrains from labelling something as good or bad from his own point of view. He takes the definition of their situation into consideration from the people under study for understanding and explaining their conditions of living. He places his subjects within their own nets of signification. A value-free researcher is a matter-of-fact scholar. The point is that of what is rather than what ought to be.

Techniques

Methodology is the theory of methods. Techniques refer to their actual practical applications. Various techniques are used for different purposes at different times under a variety of circumstances. No technique can do everything.

How do we go about it all? To begin with, think of a viable problem for study. It should be theoretically important as well as practically significant. It should be feasible with the time, money and effort at our disposal. It must be worthwhile. Research for the sake of research is a futile pursuit. Divide the problem into parts, factors, dimensions, components or aspects. The factors are broken into variables with values.

The case study method is eclectic. It can be combined with several other methods, depending upon the situation and our resources. It helps experienced analysts to intuitively identify the configuration of the relevant variables. It provides us anecdotal evidence for bringing home certain points. Provides illustrations. The results are hardly conclusive like a line carved on stone. Experienced persons find the case study method very helpful. We can understand the structure of an organisation by going through it for getting something done. We go on watching carefully how it functions. A case analyst moves up and down the hierarchy. He talks to the persons concerned. The process, the flow, the bottlenecks, the pecking order becomes clear during the course of encounter and experience. The researcher conceptualises. He frames up. He explains everything in terms of everything else.

We may also use participant observation for identifying the configuration of variables. An observer lives with those under study over a prolonged period of time, say, 18 months. Often 4 to 5 years. He participates in their day-to-day activities. In a way, he could be one of them. He thinks, feels and even acts like them. He is one of them. This does not mean that you have to become a prostitute in order to do fieldwork on prostitutes. Avoiding the danger of going native, he observes what they do, say and think. He inspects the muddle without getting bogged down into it. The material is arranged in a viable order. He understands and explains his data. He formulates hypotheses and places them within a viable theoretical framework. This is a flexible and dynamic technique. Participant observation yields a list of variables and their configuration as well as hypotheses, which need further testing. Off and on he returns to

Figure 7
Total social phenomenon

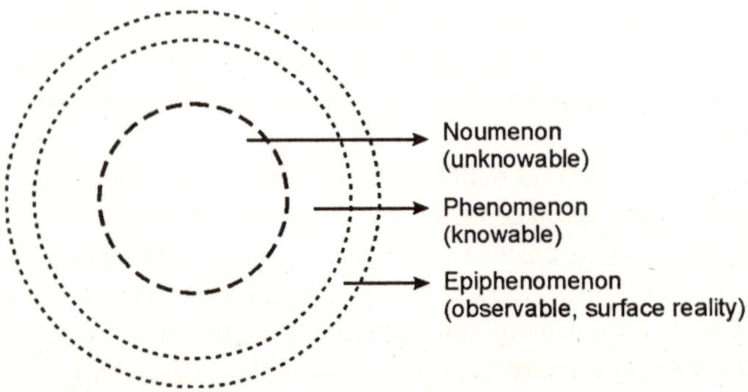

his field with a view to noting down the ongoing changes and emerging trends in structure and functions.

Example 10: Observing Participation, Like Mirza Ghalib

As a drunkard entered the door of a liquor shop, he was amused to witness a pious teetotaler coming out. He wondered how come that the man could throw his weight around that door, thus missing up the sacred with the preface. Further, observation revealed that he had just inaugurated a pub owned by his godfather. A wine merchant.

When we have obtained a list of relevant variables, we go ahead and design a social survey with accurate scales and a representative sample of the population under study. This enables us to ascertain the magnitude of our variables, and their interrelationships. Large surveys are beyond the capacity of individual researchers. Teams, using standardised procedures, carry these out. Application of statistical procedures, without ignoring their underlying assumptions, ensures a higher degree of certainty. Reliability (repeated measurements yield the same results) and validity (measure what they claim to gauge) of their outcome can be established. For instance, if computerised content analysis of a paragraph written by a candidate shows a larger frequency of verbs over adjectives, this indicates something other than itself to the knowing power—his positive attitude towards work.

Table 2

Items for constructing a scale (Saddam Hussain)

How would you describe your initial reaction towards news about Saddam Hussain's capture?

- Reluctance to believe the news
- Revision of doubt
- Mixed feelings
- Subdued reaction
- Disappointment
- Satisfaction
- Outright joy
- Shock over pathetic passive figure
- Elation
- Godly justice
- Vindication

Survey method is the Grand Trunk Road of sociological research, i.e., its most important method. A survey is as good as its sample. Experiments are conducted for finding out the exact cause-effect relationships between variables. Statistical applications like log-linear method are useful for getting results with large sets of data.

Figure 8
Cause-effect relationship

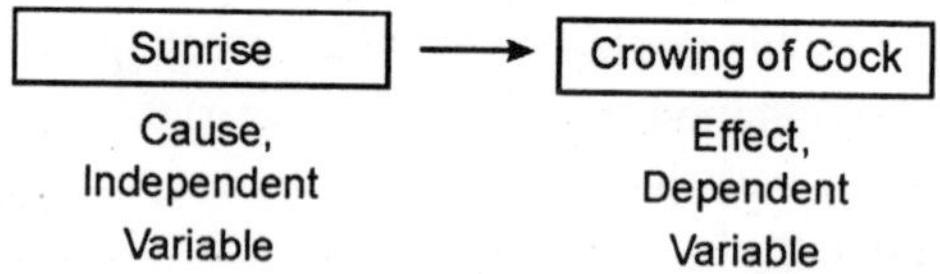

Electronic data processing has facilitated content analysis. This is a technique for objectively and systematically quantifying the manifest content of communication. Once the words have been counted and tagged together, these are linked with relevant aspects of their context. Thus, for every word in Adolf Hitler's book *Mein Kampf*, 125 persons died in the Second World War (1939-45). For every page of this book, 4,700 lives were lost. For every chapter of the book, the number of dead persons was more than 12 lakh. After counting the key words in a certain context, we go ahead to draw logical inferences and their implications for a purpose at hand. Hitler tried to realise the programmatic theoretical statement thrown up by him by mongering the Second World War, producing tragic consequences.

Figure 9
Causal chain

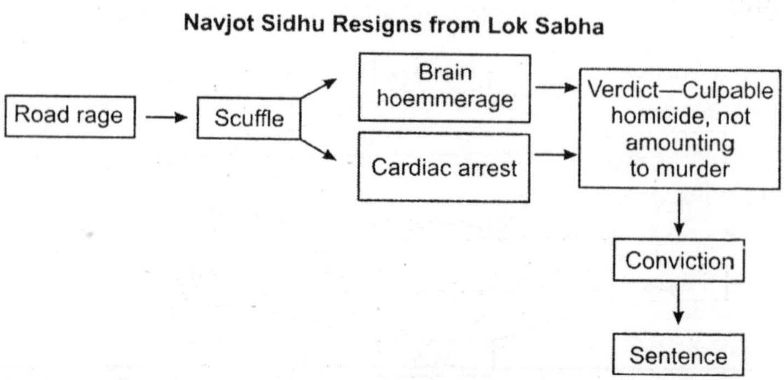

Let us take up another case in point for consideration. Content analysis of India's films would reveal that singing, dancing, and escapism (make the viewers forget their worries) is the essence of Indian films.

The point is that the findings of such techniques are made use of for theory construction. A theory disturbs the disorder. It puts everything in its place. There is place in it for everything. As a matter of fact, various techniques are steps at different stages of research work. We cannot pin down cause-effect relationships until and unless the significance and strength of the relevant variables, and before that their configuration, have already been ascertained.

There are two things here, content and form. In essence, the task before a researcher is to have something to say, and then go ahead to prepare his report as systematically and precisely as he can. Read your project report again and again, with due concentration. Go on revising meticulously, like a goldsmith or a watch repairer. Keep it pending for unconscious incubation for some time. At the end, wrap up the issue. Read again. Do not rush to send it for publication. Haste makes waste.

In Search of Excellence

Let us pass on to McKinsey's 7-S framework for the pursuit of excellence. This shows that open-minded and goal-oriented intense interpersonal communication leads to friendly environment, which makes the operation of organisations smooth. They sit together in brainstorming sessions. They spend a lot of time together, and remain in touch with one another without barriers. There are seven variables in this process.

Figure 10

McKinsey's 7-S framework for organisational effectiveness

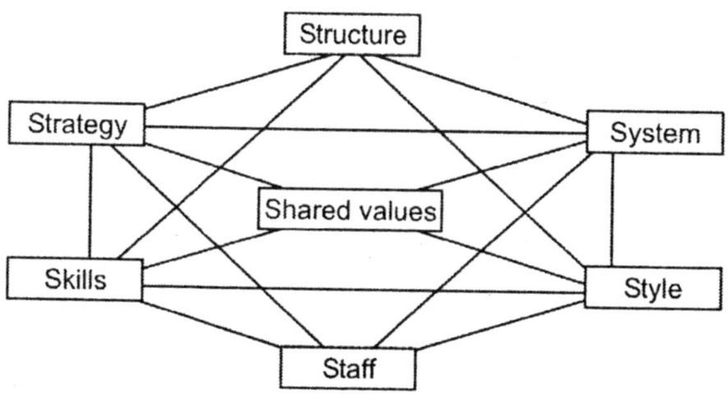

Elaboration

1. **Structure** : Who decides what is to be done? How are tasks put together? Who reports to whom?
2. **Strategy** : Broad long-term view consisting of tactics for manoeuvering and attaining advantages.
3. **Shared values** and guiding culture are accepted throughout an organisation. Often these are the values of the power holders enjoying apical dominance.
4. **System** : Orderly arrangement of parts and procedures for the attainment of common ends. Systems are networks of structures.
5. **Skills** : Trained capacity to perform tasks.
6. **Staff** : Teams of persons with required qualifications, age-mix and experience.
7. **Style** : Peculiar way of solving problems, saying and writing.

Intensively interacting individuals talk to one another. They stimulate one another, and do whetting. They call attention to lacunae, fill in the blanks, and come out together with a useful solution to the problem under consideration.

Example 11: Arjuna and Dronacharya, Concentration

How do we construct theories? This question can be answered with a story from Mahabharata. In their final examination, guru Dronacharya asked his students to hit a target with an arrow. Except Arjuna, all other candidates found this question to be vague and tough. They were at their wit's end to make out the target, what to speak of hitting the same. How did he do it? He applied his mind to the matter, with single-minded devotion, without annoyance or nervousness. He monitored in a vague sort of way what lay around. His social background, mental ability, education, training, and socialisation stood him in good stead. He thought of nothing else. He found a small bird perched amidst the leaves of a tree. What could be a more suitable target? He took a mental note of the matter, and narrowed the focus of his attention. He saw nothing except a black dot in the centre of an edge. Arjuna slowly raised his bow. He took aim, shot at the bird, and pierced through its eye with his sharp arrow. He did it! He got through the examination with flying colours.

Mind is a monkey. It moves around at a speed faster than light. Resist the temptation of allowing it to wander too far away. If properly harnessed, it has vast potential. This is even more necessary when you are performing multiple tasks simultaneously. Beyond routine repeated operations, divided attention distracts from creative mental tasks. This produces anxiety, and makes it difficult to selectively focus attention on one thing at a time.

Concentration within a context, single-minded consideration with an activated mind, is a magical formula for all creative activity. Hurry makes curry.

Example 12: Tapasvi Marx, this-Worldly Asceticism

Even when he was a schoolboy, Karl Marx (1818-83) was well known for his ability to comprehend a vast amount of matter, organise the same systematically, and put it in plain words. He did *tapasya*, sitting on a hard wooden chair for sixteen hours a day in the library of the British Museum. There was no central heating there. He carefully focussed his attention, and persistently went deep into the matter under study. His mind fermented fertile ideas with unconscious incubation. He drew abstract generalisations. The intellectual giant called forth his creative imagination slowly and deeply, without distraction. He went on more or less uninterruptedly for as many as twenty-five long years. Even after that long, the third volume of his book *Das Kapital* remained incomplete. He needed more time to accomplish this task. He passed away before he could see even the second volume of his book in print. Creative writing is a time-consuming ascetic activity.

Conclusions

Let us grasp the matter firmly. We can explain the explainable by carefully examining the reality from within and grasping it from outside with the help of our senses. Search engines and instruments of research sharpen our ability to do so. This enables us to construct hypotheses, theories and laws. These differ from one another in terms of their degree of certainty. Their validity and reliability must be verified/falsified. Attentiveness with persistence and imagination helps us to do all that.

Let us not forget that nobody ever does research by way of others telling him how to go about it. Research work is a science as well as an art. A researcher has to devise his own skills and means for achieving this goal. Do not feel restricted by set parameters. Enter into conversation with great scholars and their ghosts. Critically evaluate their life and works. Have something to say and say it in the best manner you can.

References

Boden, Margret A.,"Links Between Machines and Creativity", *Guru Nanak Journal of Sociology*, Vol. 19, No. 1, April, 1998, pp. 1-9.

de Vaus, D.A., *Surveys in Social Research*, Sage, London, 2002.

Goode, W.J. and P.K. Hatt, *Methods of Social Research*, McGraw Hill, New Delhi, 1990.

Kalton, Graham, *Introduction to Survey Sampling*, Sage Publications, New Delhi, 1984.

Mayntz, Renate et al., *Techniques of Empirical Sociology*, Penguin, Harmondsworth, 1976.

Mills, C. Wright, *The Sociological Imagination*, Oxford University Press, London, 1976.

Singh, Jaspal, *Methodology and Techniques of Social Research*, Kanishka, New Delhi, 2000.

2

Max Weber

Interpretative Sociology

Sociology is possible only as the practice of empirical social research. Nevertheless there are methods of research other than those of empiricists. Let us have a cursory look at same of them.

Interpreting 1857*

"When my grandfather, a priest of the Mar Thoma Syrian Church, passed away while he was in his forties, the burden of supporting his mother, two brothers and an unmarried sister suddenly fell on my father's slender shoulders. As no call centre jobs were available those days, he decided to join the Army, which utilised his services in the Burmese sector during the Second World War.

There was nothing special about what my father did as similar reasons compelled hundreds of thousands of Indians to enrol in the British Army and serve in all the theatres of war. Today, 60 years after independence, it seems there are some people who think it was improper to work for the British Raj.

What prompted the thought is the success the cultural police in Lucknow achieved in thwarting the attempt of a group of 19 British officers to visit the Lucknow Residency. Theirs was a tour of all the major centres of 'Rebellion', organised by an enterprising tour operator to cash in on its 150th anniversary.

The ferocity of the protest was such that the mortally scared group preferred to skip the Residency, where many of the British officers were buried. For the UP government, their decision was a blessing in disguise

*Philip, A.J. : "The Rebellion, Warts and All", *The Tribune*, Chandigarh, 28 September, 2007, p. 11.

as it averted the need to provide protection to the group from the hot-heads, who expended their *shaurya* by destroying a few British graves.

Amazingly, all this was done in the name of nationalism and by a group, which supposedly believes in *atithi devo bhava* (guest is god), one of the loftiest tenets of the Indian ethos. Instead of protesting against the visit, they should have invited all the descendants of those who served in British India to come and see what their forefathers had done to this country. At least, the tourism industry would have benefitted.

At the root of it all are many misconceptions about the 1857 uprising, described by the British as 'Sepoy Mutiny' and by Veer Savarkar as 'the First War of Independence'. In recent days, it required the courage of the Deputy Speaker of Lok Sabha, Charanjit Singh Atwal, to question the wisdom of describing 1857 as the 'First War'. He wanted to use that term for the war Punjab, under Maharaja Ranjit Singh, fought against the British in 1854. However, historically, it was Tipu Sultan (1750-1799), who fought the British the first time.

Also, 1857 was preceded by several mutinies, the most famous being at Vellore where the Indian soldiers revolted and liberated a fort from the British control. This happened 50 years before 1857. The Vellore revolt threatened the foundations of the East India Company. Of course, the Rebellion in 1857 represented the greatest of all challenges as it was spread over a vast area and it even dislodged the British from power in Delhi for a while.

Alas, freedom was not the main objective of those who joined the Rebellion. They were guided by rumour mongers. The British decided to 'introduce the Enfield rifle into the native service. This involves the use of greased cartridges, the ends of which must by bitten off by the soldier'. Word spread that the grease contained beef and pork tallow.

Hindu and Muslim soldiers were told that using the cartridge would reduce them to the status of the low castes. So they revolted.

Jawaharlal Nehru describes in his book that the landed gentry, who felt threatened by the British strengthening their own system of administration, supported the revolt. The feudal lords could no longer collect taxes. They, therefore, supported the rebellion. While reading up on the 1857 records, I came up with a fascinating document where one of the rulers involved in the rebellion wonders why the British were building roads, bridges and canals, instead of providing employment to the people.

There are extant records to show that on their way to Delhi from Meerut on May 10, 1857, the mutinous soldiers looted and plundered. After all, they had no idealism to guide them. Nor did they have any nationalist feelings. They were guided by the desire to protect their religion and seek vengeance. And when they reached Delhi, They did not have any leader to put on the throne to give constructive leadership to the country.

So they turned to Bahadur Shah Zafar, the last Moghul. Bholanauth Chunder in *The Travels of a Hindoo* describes the Moghul : 'He was then past his eighteenth year—it matters little whether of solar or lunar months. His physical condition may well be imagined when we know that he had become decrepit, and weak, and quivering...But age and infirmities had not quenched his thirst for power, so sobered his views with the conviction of the futileness of human greatness and when a charged over spirit of his dream, and there glowed a bright kingdom in his vision, he identified himself with the cause of the rebellious sepoys.'

Most commentators have praised the Hindu-Muslim unity witnessed during the time. But allowance has to be made for the fact that the low caste Hindus and the educated were not among the mutinous lot. They did not spare any Europeans they saw on the way. Nor did they spare even the Christians of Indian origin. Chaman Lal, who taught in Delhi, was shot, 'because some good people of the city took the mutineers to his house and told them that he was a Christian.'

In the name of Emperor Bahadur Shah, they issued a declaration. It shows that one of the complaints against the British was that they were giving freedom and equality before the law to every Indian. This freedom was unacceptable to the mind set of the leaders of the Rebellion as these lines from the declaration bring home :

'The people of Hindostan, both Hindoos and Mohammedans, are being ruined under the tyranny and oppression of the infidel and treacherous English...the British Government in making zamindari settlements have imposed exorbitant *jumas,* and have disgraced and ruined several zamindars, by putting up their estates to public auction for arrears of rent, in so much, that on the institution of a suit by a *common Ryot, a maid servant, or a slave,* the respectable zamindars are summoned into court, arrested, put in goal and disgraced...' In other words, the Rebellion was not for the benefit of the common man.

Small wonder that it did not have mass support. In many places, the intelligentsia of the period organised prayer meetings in support of the

British. They saw in the Rebellion the return of the old feudal system. A majority of the soldiers also remained loyal to the British. In addition, a majority of the Indian Maharajas supported the Company Raj with men and money at a moment when their own independence seemed within sight.

Among the sepoys themselves a great proportion remained loyal to the Raj. Delhi was retaken by 1700 British and 3200 Indian soldiers! 'The task force that blew up the Kashmere Gate in Delhi, facilitating British victory at great personal risk, consisted of only six British officers and 24 Indian soldiers (10 from Punjab and 14 from Agra and Oudh)'.

These facts contradict the modern assumption that all the Indians who actually experienced colonial rule saw it as inherently exploitative at least at that time. In any case, modern standards cannot be applied to the events of the past. It is also not proper to gloss over the imperfections of the Rebellion in our enthusiasm to celebrate the 150th anniversary of the 'First War of Independence'." Let us look at the issue from Max Weber's point of view.

Life

Karl Emil Maximilian Weber, was born at Erfurt in East Germany in 1864. He was the son of an advocate, a leader of the national liberal party in Germany, and a prominent member of the erstwhile 'parliament' of his country. Many visitors, intellectuals and political leaders, used to come to their house. At the age of 29, Max Weber got his doctorate from the University of Berlin, and became a professor in the University of Freibourg. Later on, he moved on to other universities. However, most of the time he remained in the University of Heidelberg. He was the live wire behind a number of voluntary scholarly associations. He visited several countries in Europe and America. Max Weber was a member of the constituent assembly for drafting the constitution of Germany after the First World War (1914-18). He was also an unsuccessful candidate for getting the sponsorship ticket of the liberal party for the presidentship of his country. Weber was neither a leftist nor a rightist, but in between the two. His work shows that his own political orientation is right liberal. Weber suffered from pneumonia, and breathed his last at the age of 56, in 1920.

Max Weber was a highly intelligent person. He had systematic and thorough knowledge with varied detailed historical depth. He had a sharp intellect. His style is clear, uncomplicated, direct and lucid. However, he possessed an explosive temperament, and entered into unnecessary litigation towards the last years of his life.

Research Methodology

(a) Verstehen

This is a German word. It means interpretative understanding. Weber's methods of research have come out to be very useful. He has combined the methods of the natural and the cultural sciences. Natural sciences explain facts by finding out their causes. Cultural sciences understand the meanings of facts. To understand means looking at the course of action with a view to ascertaining its real meaning. This may neither be the conventional meaning, nor the objective meaning. It is the subjective meaning in the mind of the actor himself. Such a meaning can vary from person to person. This can be clarified through empathy between the actor and the researcher. While doing so, the researcher has to desist from projecting his own meaning onto the minds of the acting individuals. Weber's method of research involves grasping the facts from outside and interpretatively understanding from within, the inside story. Apart from using the method of *Verstehen,* meanings can be understood by constructing ideal types.

Nowadays, in hindsight, we can say that *Verstehen (samjhna)* is a psychological process. It involves consciousness, concentration, intelligence, imagination, learning, motivation and so on. Understanding means that an observer meets those under observation on their own terms. He internalises the inner meanings by recognising the outer signs. Understanding creates a condition of mind for distinguishing between the subjective and the objective. The quality of one's subjective judgement plays a part in understanding. Perception is functionally selective. For a starving beggar, 2+2=4 *rotian.* Some have eyes, so to say, while some others have no eyes. Some possess trained capacity for comprehension, while others are marked by incapacity in this regard. Common sense is not very common. To err is human. Intuition is not always reliable. Trained observation is required.

Erklaeren (*samjhana*) is a logical process. It is a third person perspective. Explaining, clarification, description, saying with reasonable arguments what it signifies. This provides evidence for bringing the matter home to others. The researcher provides the reasons, or shows cause, why it is like that. One explains by grasping the context from outside, in terms of impersonal natural conditions. The researcher tells others about the matter by putting up precise evidence. The conditions under which something can be taken as granted are specified.

While understanding from within, inside story (*ander ki baat*), is a subjective process, explaining from outside is an objective process. Weber combines the two. Thus, understanding and explanation are two complementary processes. In this way, the observer can take account of the meanings and motives in causal explanations. One's causal explanations are based on the socio-cultural conditions of existence under which certain forms of meaning can become effective.

Verstehen does not permit direct explanation and verification. This technique is useful for getting feedback from the field under study in participant observation. It produces hypotheses for further testing. These have to be tested before formulating theories. *Verstehen* + *Erklaeren* take care of two different contexts, that of discovery and justification.

At the outset, we translated the German word *Verstehen* as interpretative understanding. Interpretation means bringing out meanings that are not immediately obvious.

Example 1 : If X says that Y is a good man, this does not mean that Y is good or, for that matter, bad. The statement reveals that the attitude of X towards Y is favourable.

Table 1

Distinguishing empathy from what it is not

	Emotion	*Example*
1.	Apathy *(udaseenta)*	I don't care. *Koi mare koi jive, Suthra ghol patase peeve.*
2.	Emotion *(bhavna)*	Feeling sad. *Tatta hanjhu shagan pa sanun, birha tali dharo.*
3.	Emotional contagion *(Sansaric bhavna)*	Catching others' emotions.*(sansarik bhavna)*
4.	Empathy *(Samvedna)*	Sharing others' experience from within. The wearer knows where the shoe pinches. Emotional resonance.
5.	Pity *(daya)*	It seems you need help. *Abla jeevan hai tumhari yahi kahani, anchal mein hai doodh, aur ankhon mein pani.*
6.	Sympathy *(sahanubhuti)*	Helpful attitude. Love thy neighbour as thyself.
7.	Telepathy *(dooranubhuti)*	Reading somebody's mind, without being told about it.

Example 2 : If a person says that every day is a Sunday, we cannot conclude that the remaining six days of the week have been abolished. We conclude that his attitude towards work is favourable. Hasty generalisation from concrete to abstract must be avoided.

Example 3 : If the signboard says that sex determination test is not done in a hospital, this does not necessarily mean that the test is not available, at least under the table. It means that the test is illegal and or is considered somehow improper, something to be kept concealed from others.

Example 4 : While studying the social background of diabetes, replace Khatri and Arorà castes with sedentary lifestyle. Avoid conclusions that can give rise to stereotypes, prejudice and discrimination.

What is the point? Draw broad generalisations. Move over from concrete to abstract and from narrow to broad, broader, broadest. Replace proper nouns with the names of relevant variables underlying a set of conditions giving rise to the problem under study.

Sociology has made rapid strides after the Second World War. However, so far perhaps nobody has done as much for the subject as Max Weber. In order to understand contemporary sociology, one has to acquaint oneself with Max Weber's contributions.

(b) Ideal Types

Ideal types are used for finding out the meanings as well as causes of social facts. These are also used for comparing complex events or processes. For constructing ideal types, one has to define certain salient features of the situation as essential. These are brought out, accentuated, exaggerated, maximised. The remaining aspects are understated, minimised, left out of view for the time being. These ideas are used to construct word pictures or to abstract models. These models are based neither on averages nor on proportions. These are not exact replicas or photographs. They indicate limits. They are like cartoons. We can construct a number of different ideal types of the same phenomenon. All of them are correct.

While constructing ideal types, we take care that there are sufficient reasons for their being possible in actual life situations. An ideal type is neither true nor false. It is pure. It is clear. It is a hypothetical construct, to be used for understanding the reality. Ideal types are constructed for use from time to time, depending upon the purpose in hand. Then these are kept aside. May be we can find some use for them later on too. They help us to bring home a point. Ideal types are tools for gaining knowledge. By themselves alone they are not knowledge. Empirical reality appears in mixed forms. Pure forms are rare.

For instance, let us take up Weber's ideal type of the 'spirit of capitalism' for consideration. He included the following elements in it—freedom of occupation, profit motive, accountability, rational enterprise, and organised markets, among others. Individuals are units of production in this model, not families. Weber knowingly excluded usury, adventurism and colonial exploitation from this ideal type. Weber's capitalism is a rational means for earning profit in a disciplined way. We will discuss soon hereunder how Weber used ideal types of the protestant ethic and the spirit of capitalism for understanding and explaining the process of social change.

(c) Value Freedom

In the interest of rational understanding, Weber's sociology keeps values apart from social facts.

What is a value? Value is that which is set down as somehow desirable or worthy of being followed, in disregard of whether we go after it or not. Beliefs regarding truth, beauty, wealth, honour, prestige have values attached to them. Values are based upon beliefs, not rationality. Clashes for choosing between different values, and between what is valuable and what is not, go on from time to time in societies and in the minds of individuals for choice between alternatives. Values are what people acknowledge as precious.

Weber favoured value freedom. He exhorts sociologists to keep their roles as scholars and as citizens apart from each other. That they would not think in a prejudiced manner. They would not thrust their own values on the categories of thought of the people being studied by them. With his emphasis on value freedom, Weber wanted to make sociology a science indeed.

Science and ethics differ from each other insofar as science does not praise or condemn anybody. Science does take into consideration our motivation and our ability. But it does not lay down for us what we should do. Science looks for the course and causes of reality without arbitrariness. Values may be based on non-rational beliefs. Weber clearly saw values as separate from scientific facts. He highlighted that science deals with *what is*. It does not deal with *what ought to be*. Weber's doctrine of value-freedom does not mean that a scientific researcher may give up values from his own conduct. On the contrary, he stressed that values are windows of understanding of human society. The social act does not become intelligible until and unless we understand values. Value freedom involves keeping our own values aside while studying society and culture. What are the meanings that the people under study themselves attach to their actions? How do they themselves interpret their own actions? These questions can be answered only when the researcher exercises value neutrality. While doing research, a researcher has to be impartial. The people under study cannot be understood without taking their own categories of thought, their own nets of signification, into consideration. While doing so, the researcher must look at the facts of observation without superimposing his own values on them. He has to study them in terms of their points of view, not his own.

Figure 1
Induction

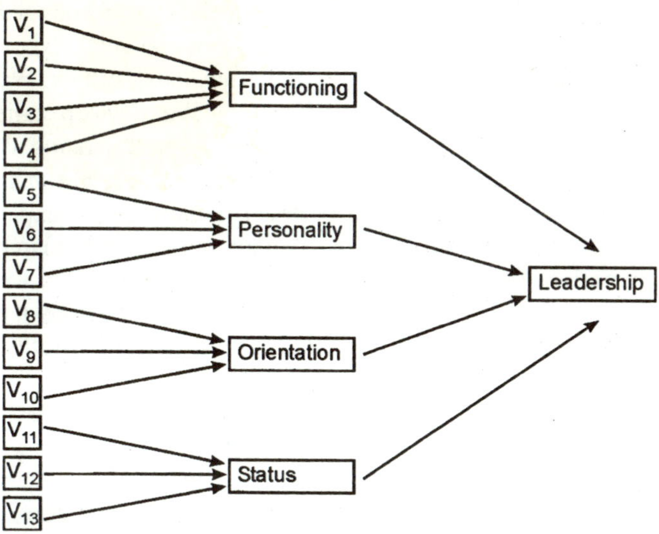

Example 5 : Weberian scholars assert that bias, ideology, preconceptions, prejudice deflect our observation and understanding, just like a straw, or even a beam in our eyes. They are in favour of value neutrality. Marxists deny that it is possible for us to proceed in this way. They look at society and history with their declared partisan attitude in favour of the working class. It is our being that determines the consciousness, they say. We cannot be value-neutral. It is not the consciousness that determines the being. Value freedom is a myth that hides an ideology.

(d) Explanations

Let us now try to understand what is an explanation. An explanation is different from understanding or discovering. Discoveries and justifications belong to different contexts. The context of discovery is based on imagination or inspiration. It is more than mere guess work. Here we intuitively come to think of an appropriate solution for the problem under study. Our mind wanders here and there. We dream. We freely associate things with other things. We try to think of meaningful patterns underlying a process. To discover means to grasp and understand, or to represent the matter to oneself. One gets an idea. One comprehends something without expressing it, getting angry, or telling others about it. Such knowledge is directly experienced. It involves understanding as a psychological process. It generates hypotheses.

On the other hand, to explain means to make plain or intelligible, to unfold and illustrate the meaning, to expound or to account for something, or to clear it from obscurity. We clarify it in such a way that others understand it. Explanations are based on reasoned elaboration of experience. Such knowledge can be communicated to others. We call for explanation in the context of justification. We develop criteria for inter-subjectively verifying the matter. Thus, different persons using that procedure will arrive at the same conclusions. We present valid proof, evidence, logical arguments. We perform demonstrative experiments. We make others accept our findings without any doubt. Explanation is a logical operation. We demonstrate the truth of the premises as well as the validity of the argument. Even if the justification is not enough, it does not mean that the conclusion is false. In that case, we provide another justification for the same conclusion.

The point is that it is not one and the same thing to understand the matter oneself, and to explain it to others. These are two different operations. We come to know of something in the context of discovery. In the context of explanation, or justification, or presentation, we communicate it to others.

An explanation answers the question : How? or Why? It clears up obscure matters by upholding and illustrating them. It makes them plain. The matter becomes understandable. We untangle chaos and the links. We organise our findings in a meaningful way. Facts follow logically from it.

An explanation consists of two parts. That to be explained is called *Explanandum*. That which explains is called *Explanans*.

A scientific explanation must be relevant, true and general. Relevance pertains to cogency, pertinence or suitability. Truth refers to neither being false nor half true. Generality means its applicability to a broad range of cases. It is not limited to a specific instance. A scientist does not dogmatically stick to an explanation. There is always some scope for improvement. He does not defend an explanation on the basis of old habits, revelation or authority. A scientific explanation is based on proper clarifications and adequate evidence. Therefore, it is stated in such a way that it can be critically tested and systematically verified. A scientific explanation is even more acceptable if it is simpler (more natural), possesses considerable predictive power, and is compatible with previous well-established explanations.

We may divide explanations into three types:

1. *Descriptive explanations* give an account of the procedures or structures. They state various criteria, facts, purposes, steps. For example:
   (i) Explaining the structure of a university.
   (ii) Describing how peasants adopt agricultural innovations.
2. *Interpretative explanations* clarify the meanings of certain terms. They tell us in what sense they are being used. For example:
   (i) Defining acculturation, cultural reproduction, or organisational effectiveness.
   (ii) To *explain away* means to modify the force of an argument by tilting or distorting facts.
3. *Reason-giving explanations* account for why something leads to something else. For example:
   (i) Why are there ethnic tensions in so many parts of the world?
   (ii) Show cause why action should not be taken against you for absence from duty without leave.

Nagel's four-fold typology of explanations is discussed hereunder.

(e) Induction and Deduction

These are two types of explanation. As already discussed, to explain is to clarify, to say what it is all about, to point out the reasons for something. It helps us to put our findings in a proper way. An explanation may describe a process, interpret its meaning, or show cause why it is like that. First of all, we have to understand the matter ourselves. After that we have to explain it to others. Scientific explanation can be given in four different ways. These are discussed below:

1. *Genetic explanation :* This explains the present-day events, and what is going to happen in future in terms of the chain of events in the past. This may be done by narrating a story about how something started, or by finding out the historical events that gave rise to it. For example, W.H. Morgan (1818-81) classified the evolution of human society in three stages—savagery, barbarism and civilisation. Similarly, depending upon the ever-widening exclusion of blood relatives from marriage, Friedrich Engels (1820-95) identified the following five stages of evolution of marriage and family— promiscuity, consanguinal family, punnaluan family, pairing family, and monogamy. One more example, G.H. Hutton has discussed various theories of the origin of the caste system in India in the traditional magical and religious beliefs, occupational distinction, race and colour, etc. All these instances show that the present has been explained in terms of the past. All these are genetic explanations. *Criticism* : Do not impose your own present-day standards on the past, or on other cultures. Others cultures, other ways.

2. *Structural-functional explanation:* It explores in detail the interconnection between the various parts of a system or a package of

Figure 2
Induction and deduction

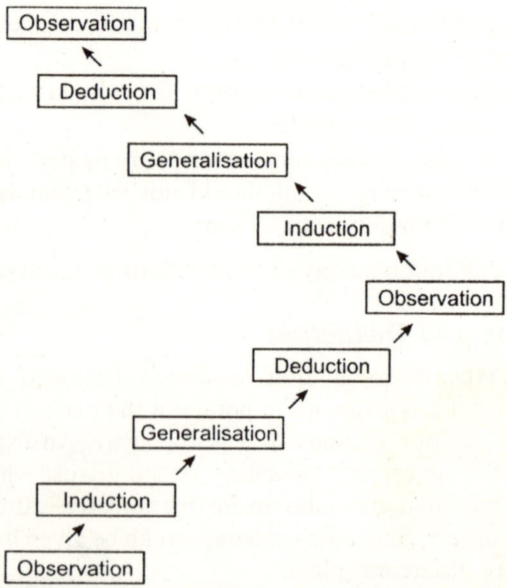

Figure 3
Induction

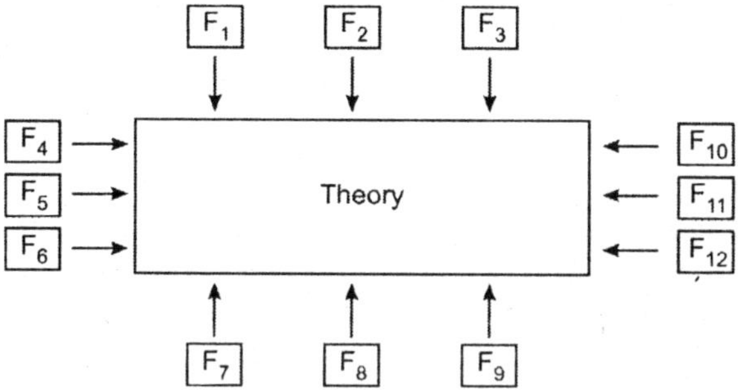

practices and draws conclusions about what they do for one another, how they fulfil each other's needs. These are explained in terms of each other. It offers plausible rationales about elements doing something useful for a given totality. Such rationales are flexible, not rigid. A structural-functional explanation is not a causal explanation. In fact, what is a cause for one purpose may be an effect for another purpose. *Criticism :* Do not confuse the objective with the desirable.

For example, Davis and Moore's explanation of social stratification, of incentives for occupying positions for performing socially useful tasks. Deprivation in the past, with a view to acquiring the required qualifications, justifies gratification later on.

3. *Inductive explanation :* The task of induction is to find unity in diversity. It brings together important points under a common name. Induction proceeds from particular or single observed instances to general or universal conclusions. It abstracts concepts and makes generalisations. This is done by observing specific instances and then summing up the results. The specifics meet in a comprehensive all-engulfing generality. The basic unity of an entity holds it together in diversity. Induction may suffer from defects like mal-observation and non-observation. We fail to perceive properly. We seem to observe without having observed.

Induction can proceed in various ways. We can intuitively try to find similarities in the known instances of a phenomenon. We can even undertake, where possible, exhaustive enumeration or summation of all the elements in a class.

However, this is not always possible. In that case, we have to be satisfied with something less. We do induction by simple or incomplete enumeration. We do this when we can reasonably assume without complete enumeration that in general something can be accepted as true on the basis of repeated similarities of experience. It is expected that the remaining cases would also be the same. We resort to such a procedure when it is not possible to count all the cases. Uniformity of nature is assumed. It is taken for granted that the unobserved instances, and the conditions in which they exist, are like the observed ones. When this is so, even a representative sample of the population can be taken for study. If the universe is homogeneous, the study of even a single case would be enough for drawing inductive inference. In case the universe is large or unlimited, exhaustive enumeration is not possible. Then we make probablistic conclusions, hoping all the time that somehow or the other, the known cases are like the unknown ones. Induction can also be done by comparing the observed instances in analogous situations elsewhere, and giving them a common name. However, we have to avoid over-generalisation beyond what is justified by the underlying data. We have also to avoid jumping to conclusions on the basis of incomplete evidence.

Induction is not a perfect method. It cannot guarantee the truth of its results. These can be falsified even with a single negative observation. This point can be aptly illustrated with a story from Bertrand Russel. Once upon a time, there was a turkey. He found that on the first day at the turkey farm, and on all the subsequent days, he was fed at 8 a.m. He made these observations under a variety of circumstances—days of the week, months and seasons. Thereafter, he inductively arrived at the conclusion that he is invariably fed at 8 a.m. However, on a day before Christmas, instead of being fed, his throat was cut. Consequently, his inductive career came to a sudden end! The point is that even an inductive inference with true premises can lead to false conclusions. Induction can be erroneous. However, without being skeptical, often we can reasonably assume that there is sufficient reason to believe something. Then we go ahead and generalise.

4. *Deductive explanation :* Induction proceeds from facts to theory. Deduction goes from theory to facts. Deduction is the process of drawing valid inferences from a given theory or hypothesis. It infers from premises or propositions representing the already known facts. Let us keep four points in view. Conclusions flow from the premises. There is complete internal consistency. We are working with a closed system. All the relevant circumstances are before us, or are implied in the premises.

A deductive explanation begins with a general statement and draws out its consequences for particular instances. Let us take some examples into consideration:

Example 6: All bees are hard-working.
Maya is a bee.
∴ Maya is hard-working.

Example 7: If a country exercises surplus repression on its people, it is economically underdeveloped.
Country C_1 exercises surplus repression on its people.
∴ Country C_1 is economically underdeveloped.

Unlike induction, which involves a lot of creative thinking, deduction is a rigorous logical procedure. The inference is contained in the premises. The conclusion flows from the premises. In case the premises are true, the inference would also be true. However, logic does not guarantee the truth or falsity of premises. These are assumed. These assumptions are verified empirically. For this purpose, observation, survey, experimentation, and other methods are made use of. Such a procedure is by no means automatic or mechanical. Right decisions have to be made. For instance, let us take 'horned syllogism'. Here, one has to accept one of the two alternative propositions. Each of these is inconsistent with the original contention. Both the courses are undesirable. The victim is in a predicament. Both the choices are tricky. Such predicaments have to be resolved in time. Practice makes a man perfect.

Biologists often make use of the inductive method. Mathematicians often use the deductive method. Induction and deduction can also be combined together in an argument. Observe. Generalise, proceeding inductively from particular instances to a general statement about them. Move back from the general to its particular instances. Thus, check up your generalisations by confronting them with particular facts. Inductive and deductive instances can be checked up with each other by shuttling back and forth between the two types of arguments.

Let us call it a day and finish here by referring back to the start of this chapter. Sociology deals with the present, while history deals with the past. Social scientists try to interpret the available evidence by asking themselves how it must really have happened. Other researchers, places and times, other findings. We cannot explain the past in terms of the present-day standards. What is good for the cow need not be so for the calf. Other people cannot be properly understood by imposing our own standards on their ways of thinking, feeling and acting. They have to be sufficiently scientifically understood and explained in terms of their own nets of signification. Weberians try to be as dispassionate as humanly possible. Objectivity is a laudable goal. In practice, it boils down to inter-subjectivity. Interpretation means bringing out the meaning of the facts under observation and giving them some sense. It can also take the form of serendipity, as a result of naive observation by a trained observer by dint of his sagacity. Thus, linking up of apparently innocuous facts yields useful conclusions.

References

Boudon, R., *The Logic of Sociological Explanations*, Penguin, Harmondsworth, 1974.

Koenig, René, *Handbuch der Empirischen Sozialforschung*, Ferdinand Enke Verlag, Stuttgart, 1967.

Singh, Jaspal, *Methodology and Techniques of Social Research*, Kanishka Publishers, New Delhi, 2001.

Weber, Max, *Wirtschaft und Gesellschaft*, JCB Mohr, Tuebingen, 1976.

3

Social Research

Meaning and Characteristics

What is Research?

This means looking out. Answers to questions. Investigating with a view to discovering or inventing. Clarifying. Justifying. Trying to create new knowledge. Finding out some need that can be profitably fulfilled, and so on, depending on the purpose in hand. Research consists of procedures for meticulously looking for, and clearly presenting, knowledge on different aspects of something under study.

Why is it Conducted?

Research is a goal-oriented activity. Social research is pursued for three reasons :

(a) Theoretical importance : Describing the nature and scope of the matter under investigation. Bringing out the essential features of the field. Identifying their similarities and differences. Classifying and reclassifying facts with a view to understanding and explaining their relations. Outlining the set of conditions under which these exist. Ascertaining the cause-effect relationships. Theoretical research broadens and deepens our perspective. This provides us deeper insight into the problem under study, and beyond that it improves the quality of our judgements. Theoretical research is often pure research (see further hereunder).

(b) Practical significance : This helps us in solving economically meaningful and socially important problems facing us. Practical research performs diagnostic (identification), therapeutic (remedy) and pedagogic (educational) functions. Such research is often applied in nature (see further below).

(c) Image-building : Such research performs cosmetic functions. It shows the wonder that is our village, or our great cultural heritage, etc. Image builders conveniently ignore some aspects of the problem under inquiry, while highlighting others. This suits their purpose. Local and regional elites are glad to finance such research (or something of the sort). Exaggerated attempts at image-building are often a response to the challenges posed by dominant forces from outside. These are a reaction to acculturation. In the long run, the impact of such advocacy may be counter-productive. Image-building is not a legitimate function of empirical social research. A scientist is supposed to call a spade a spade. Scientists refrain from labelling something as good or bad. They are matter-of-fact people in search of excellence.

How to Do Research?

This can be done in a number of ways. Sociologists prefer the method of science for this purpose. Sociology is possible only as the practice of empirical social research.

Sociology is not only a science, but also a creative art. It is a science insofar as it uses the method of science for deriving abstract principles. It is an art because it makes use of high level skills for creativity. The role of intelligence, imagination and smartness in all innovative ventures cannot be denied. One learns to do what others have never done before by putting in a lot of effort for acquiring skills and painstakingly cultivating certain bents of mind. One goes on improving these through learning by doing. This means observing others' experience by talking to them about it, and gaining from what they have to say in this regard.

Whether research is done in the field or in a laboratory, a lot of money and effort are needed for this purpose. Before embarking on such an expedition, it is advisable to chalk out the outlines of the project being undertaken. This is done by dint of extensive reading of books, current and old periodicals and unpublished sources, and surfing on the net. This is done in order to find out which aspects of the problem being studied remain unexplored. Catalogues, abstracts, bibliographies are used for this purpose. A researcher gains by taking pains to find out what others in the field are doing. Then, he examines the various types of the universe under investigation. He meets the persons concerned, closely observes them, talks to them. Rising above their nets of signification he tries to ascertain the invariable sequence of events in their lives. Concepts, definitions, hypotheses and theoretical frameworks are put to use. Data are collected systematically and thoroughly without missing their connecting linkages. A researcher bewares of collecting large heaps of data without knowing what is to be done with them later on. He desists from becoming a frog in the well. He explains facts in terms of other facts. He does not unnecessarily stick to the already available techniques and well-known theories. Those who do research work dare to look out for alternatives. They innovate. They put forward logically consistent arguments with a view to constructing new theories and adding to the existing body of knowledge.

Researcher

A researcher is a special person. He cultivates several qualities in himself. He acquires maturity and depth by rubbing shoulders with like-minded persons in an atmosphere congenial to creativity, in a centre of excellence. He goes all the way to make the impossible possible. He is supposed to be able to simplify complications and implement the results in his own way. For this purpose, he tries to understand the matter from within, and grasp it from outside. This requires focussed attention on the task being performed. Concentration is a magical formula for all creative activity. Gaps in the form and content are filled up by looking around for fresh data. One who is always complaining *ad miseracondiam* about personal handicaps and adverse circumstances is unfit for becoming a researcher. The same is the case with one who is inert. The world is not interested in the storms you encountered, but did you bring in the ship? A researcher makes it possible to get what is not available by stretching himself. What can be had is sufficiently utilised. He practises mental hygiene. He keeps his mind free of unnecessary thoughts. Without forgetting where he has to go, he chooses the best possible means for arriving there. The capacity to disentangle the seeming chaos, to make something out of the prevalent disorder, to find unity in diversity, are the tasks before a researcher.

While a single individual can be more creative and can work with speed and efficiency, the type of research work we do these days requires effective teams. Members of a team are carefully brought together. They learn to have trust and confidence in one another, so that they can enter into meaningful cooperation. It is not easy to set up a compatible team with heterogeneous mental levels, motivation and needs of those who can be recruited. Politics of scarcity and politics of passion stand in the way. Those interested in setting up centres of excellence identify a capable team leader. He is then given freedom to establish a working group around himself. Work culture is promoted by bringing together individual needs with organisational goals. These are clearly stated.

It is not possible to go very far in search of excellence in any field without a team of persons having proper skills and work values, capable of giving critical stimulation to one another. They are provided well-equipped and well-managed research institutes as well as other provisions for the pursuit of excellence. Proper mechanisms have to be devised for encouraging initiative, dissent as well as mutual understanding. Let us also not forget that systems and techniques are means for achieving certain ends. The man behind the methods and techniques of research is even more important. A social science researcher is above all a human being.

What is to be Done?

Gather relevant facts. On being properly recorded when their significance becomes known, data take the form of information. Information consists of isolated events in time and space. When various pieces of information are linked together into a viable frame, we get a theory. Knowledge consists of a large body of theories. Conversely, a theory is a chunk of knowledge. Beyond that, wisdom means the capacity to make use of knowledge, exercise discretion, using situational competence, and proper training. What is the need for all that? Scientific research is a means for achieving specific goals. In a liberal democratic society, its objective is rationalisation of social life.

Figure 1
What is to be done?

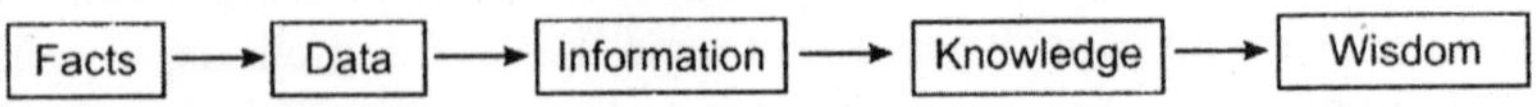

Types of Research

Here, we may classify research work into two types—pure and applied. What is the difference between these two?

(a) Pure research creates basic or fundamental knowledge. It does so by looking for the laws underlying the forces of nature and society. Pure researchers engage themselves in such activity out of curiosity. This is an esoteric pastime. We do not know what is to be done with the findings right now. These may perhaps be of some use for somebody later

Figure 2
Types of research

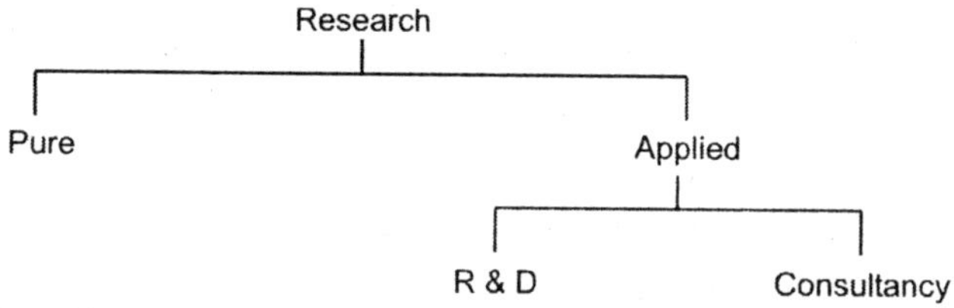

on one day. This is an endless pursuit, motivated by intellectual challenge. Pure researchers possess extraordinary creative genius.

The following illustrations would help us to understand what basic or pure research is.

Example 1 : A tiny atom is structured like the universe. It consists of three parts—neutron, proton and electron. Electron revolves around the first two. The former is negatively charged, while the latter two are positively charged. These are the conclusions of pure research.

Example 2 : Discovery of the structure of DNA made a scientific breakthrough. It opened the way for advancements in fundamental research in molecular biology, microbiology and genetics. These were used for applications in biotechnology and genetic engineering. Hybrid seeds with higher yield, disease-resisting cattle, effective medicines, etc., came out of such painstaking endeavour.

(b) Applied research : It uses the results of pure research for solving meaningful practical problems. Its findings help us to raise industrial and agricultural production. Applied research is cost-effective as well as socially relevant. Over the years, lag between the availability of the results of pure research and its applications has decreased. Shortening of space and time between laboratory, factory and market has made efficient companies with smart managers competitive, while the laggards have been outsmarted. Profits of mass-produced and widely distributed products have gone up.

The following illustrations should be helpful in understanding what applied research is :

Example 3 : Knowledge of the structure of atom has been applied for manufacturing radio valves, transistors, computer chips, printed circuits, etc. Applied research in electronics, with huge inputs of money and highly qualified manpower, has led to the development of advanced versions of computer hardware and software, micro-processors, robots, internet and various new branches of information technology. These have opened up new possibilities never dreamt of earlier.

Example 4 : Discovery of DNA was a breakthrough. Applied research in pharmacy made processes and products based on extractive chemistry outdated, and produced new medicines. It opened new avenues for polytomous (fibres, food, fruits, flowers, fragrances) diversification of agriculture.

Example 5 : Take up a scale for measuring attitude towards work in USA. Improvise it for use in the Indian situation. For this purpose, use the local idiom, and functional equivalents. Then put the new scale for use on a representative sample of comparable population. The result should be useful for pedagogical (teaching) purposes.

Example 6 : Put the concepts and theories of sociology to use. Do a survey for identifying the factors facilitating and hindering agricultural innovations in Himachal Pradesh. Publish your findings. Policy makers and executive officers are supposed to make use of this publication with a view to raising agricultural production. For instance, they may use the price incentive, taking for granted the willingness of peasants to adopt the improved practices.

(c) Research and Development (R&D) : R&D is a variant of applied research. It builds bridges between science and industry. Prototypes are prepared by making adjustments here and there. Ground is prepared for assembling imported components with local screw-drivers. These are given local brand names with a view to appeasing the protagonists of *swadeshi*. Improvisations adapt the imported stuff making it suitable for local conditions—climate variations, unreliable power supply, affordability, fashions, etc.

The following illustrations should bring home this point :

Example 7 : Results of applied research are made use of for manufacturing television sets, voltage stabilisers, invertors, etc., to suit the local requirements.

Example 8 : Applied researchers make a radar. This is used for identifying flying objects. Teams of researchers work together to modify the radar to identify low-flying aircrafts.

Example 9 : Advancements in geology, botany and other basic sciences have enabled scientists to develop new applied disciplines—environmental studies and remote sensing. R&D in this field can prepare designs for greening the desert in Rajasthan by utilising the underground water resources, constructing dams on river Brahmaputra, and a grid of canals for navigation and irrigation.

Example 10 : Henkel is a multinational firm in soaps and detergents. It carries on research for improving the emulsifying property of its detergents. The results are put to use for manufacturing a new version of its products (Ariel, for instance).

Its publicity department designs advertisements in mass media with a view to improving its sales. Before they do so, they conduct public opinion research about who makes decisions in a family—husband, wife, or somebody else—about which brand of detergents is to be purchased, and for what reasons. This is R&D.

Its marketing department does research to find out in which corners of different types of shops Ariel packets are to be displayed so that these attract potential customers' attention. This is R&D. It improves salability and profitability.

A student of sociology learns how to do research. S(he) improves her/his employability and chances of upward mobility, income, and marriageability. R&D is beneficial in a number of ways.

(d) Consultancy : This is another variant of applied research. A consultant is a subject-matter specialist. He provides advice and guidance on what is to be done in a particular situation in order to achieve optimum results. For this purpose, he collects data, interprets the same, and prepares a report. A consultant is a man of business in the garb of a researcher.

The matter can be clarified with the following illustrations:

Example 11 : An astrologer calculates the configuration of stars. He advises a minister on which auspicious moment he should lay a foundation stone, or cut a ribbon in order to get votes and support for himself in the next general elections. A financial consultant in USA is the functional equivalent of an astrologer in India. He advises his clients on how to make money, subject to the condition that they already have money. For tendering such advice, he takes their needs for security, liquidity, profitability as well as the capacity for taking risk into consideration.

Example 12 : A professor gets a contract for improving organisational effectiveness of a firm making huge losses. He makes use of his theoretical wherewithal, practical experience, and talent to understand the local situation. He carries out a detailed investigation on what is going on. Then he prepares a report. The manager makes use of the professor's recommendations for sorting out its difficulties.

Example 13 : A sociologist is asked to write a report on the role of caste in voting behaviour. The findings are used by a political party to work out strategy and tactics for getting more votes in the next general elections.

Let us clinch the matter. Pure research is a romance, or even an obsession. Findings of pure research are intended to enlighten. A researcher earns respect for his achievements. He is great. Applied research yields apt solutions for pressing problems. Findings of applied research are the intellectual property of those who discover or invent them. The results of such research can be patented. Patents can be bought and sold in the market. These earn profits for their owners. Consultancy is money-making. Consultants become well-to-do.

Linkage between Pure and Applied Research

Let us come to our own country. For us, pure research is an expensive luxury. It needs highly qualified and motivated scientists, large financial backing, infrastructure (books, journals, laboratories, organisational aids, proper atmosphere). In any case, the results of pure research are not patented. These are international property. Everybody can use it. We can utilise it to our own advantage. In our own country, we can profitably focus on applied research, which is economically viable and socially relevant.

Figure 3
Bridging the gap

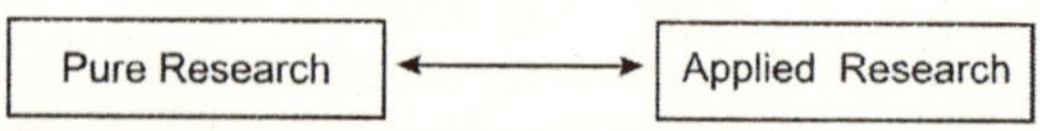

Bridging the gap between pure and applied research means establishing linkages between bookish knowledge and its effective utilisation. Scientific knowledge enables us to bring land, labour and capital together, with a view to achieving substantial improvement in our standard of living and quality of life.

Example 14 : A CSIR laboratory in Himachal Pradesh signs a memorandum of understanding (MOU) with a distillery in Poona. They are asked to look out for a formula for manufacturing beer with tea leaves.

Table 1
Objectives of different instruments of social research

	Method	*Objective*
1.	Case Study	Illustrations, anecdotal evidence for identifying variables
2.	Observation	Identifying configuration of variables
3.	Social Survey	Ascertaining the magnitude of variables, and their relationships
4.	Experiment	Cause-effect relationships
5.	Content Analysis	Intentions of senders and wishes of receivers of communication (by counting the manifest content (e.g., counting words)

Steps in Social Research

There is no uniform set of steps for all types of research. Panacea for curing all problems does not exist. Each problem has to be tailored according to its specific needs.

Let us say at present:

1. Choice of a topic for research
2. Survey of available literature
3. Formulation of hypotheses
4. Sampling
5. Scaling
6. Data collection
7. Data processing and analysis
8. Deriving conclusions
9. Report writing

Social Surveys

Times are changing fast. Those days are gone when a few sycophants carried tales about 'what the people say' to a king or a feudal lord. This method led to a lot of miscommunication and enabled some people to serve their own vested interests. With increasing rationalisation of social life, it has become necessary to do surveys for gathering full facts about the socioeconomic situation and for carrying out polls for ascertaining public opinion. That is why a large number of social surveys are being conducted every year. Students of social science research methods have to learn to conduct such studies. This involves acquiring the necessary skills for gathering the required data about their subject matter, analysing the data meaningfully, and writing reports about the work done. Social surveys can be about various aspects of society, culture, economy, politics, organisational behaviour, and so on.

In contemporary society, no administrator or manager can collect all the required facts himself. He can no more afford to get lost in what a few flatterers around him have to say. He has to understand the broader social milieu. It can be costly to make decisions without ascertaining all the facts before-hand. Increasing technological development, division of labour, planning, bureaucratisation, and similar other reasons, are making it necessary to conduct social surveys at regular intervals. It becomes easier to implement decisions if those effected by these decisions are given a voice in making them, or at least their opinions are properly ascertained. That is why it is becoming common to take representative samples of the population and consulting the people by interviewing them. In order to be able to do so, students of social science research methods have to be well-versed in the survey method.

A social survey is different from a census. In a census, important details about all the inhabitants of a country are noted down. In India, census operations have been conducted every ten years, since 1871. Now in 2010 it is under process. A large number of enumerators is mobilised for this purpose. Most of them are government servants. Everybody is required by law to provide the required information to them. Census operations cost a lot. These have also become unmanageable. In addition to the decennial census, a lot of data are being collected through sample surveys now and then.

A social survey is also different from investigative journalism. Reporters hastily file their reports by gathering whatever can be had from whosoever is at hand. On the basis of such information, which may not be representative, they decide which way and how fast the wind of public opinion is blowing. In contrast, data for social surveys are gathered systematically by administering well-thought out questions to representative samples of the population. Thus, the conclusions obtained are based or entrenched in a solid database. It is true that all conclusions are not applicable to each and every individual. Surveys enable us to understand the forces and structures underlying the universe being studied.

Some research scholars grab all the material they come across, hoping that something or the other will emerge out of the large mass of data collected. However, later on they realise that they are unable to decide what to make out from all the data they have collected. Facts do not speak for themselves. These have to be interpreted. Therefore, it is helpful that before starting a survey we should identify the variables underlying the various dimensions of the phenomenon being studied. This can be done through a review of the available literature in the field, and collection of data with case history and participant observation methods. The survey method is to be used for ascertaining the magnitude of these variables, and their interrelationships. The survey data also enable us to choose one out of a number of alternative hypotheses. Recent developments in constructing log linear models have facilitated the use of survey data for determining cause-effect relationships. However, the experimental method is the surest way to causal analysis.

Money for doing surveys is provided by sponsors. A sponsor agrees to grant the financial resources when the topic of research is of interest to him. Sponsors are only interested in getting the results. They are convinced if the researcher submits a viable proposal, and completes his project in time. Repeat projects are sanctioned if the previous reports are satisfactory. The report of the research project is written primarily for the sponsors. But the entire input or the survey does not come from the sponsor. Research institutes have long lives. They are there to serve everybody. Surveys are done by interviewing the general public. A large number of respondents give their costly time free of charge for answering all sorts of questions. So the findings of a survey are not somebody's private property. It is the moral responsibility of the researcher to make proper arrangements for disseminating his findings widely. This will prevent their utilisation by some power holders for safeguarding only their own interests.

Research Design

How do we design a survey? The design of a social survey is different from consultancy. A research worker is free to design and control his own study. A researcher is interested in constructing theories about some phenomenon. A consultant's problem is oriented to the needs of a client. The latter exercises due control on the former. Consultants provide recipes to their clients, who give them the money required for this purpose. Consultants focus their attention on immediate practical goals. They are required to stick to their assigned tasks. If they are unable to satisfy their customers by giving the right answers to the questions placed before them, they may not get another project or assignment. On the other hand, a researcher is free to change the focus of his attention during the course of his work. A consultant's reports are confidential. These are meant for restricted circulation among his clients who have paid for them. The findings are not open to the general public. Sponsors of research are interested in generating deeper and long-term findings with a broader perspective, and methodological rigour. A consultant makes use of whatever method is handy for the time being. A consultant's findings are internally evaluated by the sponsoring organisation. Research findings are evaluated by the scientific community. A research design is prepared for collecting and analysing new data, or for interpreting the already available facts in a new way.

Preparation of a research design involves making proper arrangements for systematic research work. The researcher plans the various operations, keeping the theoretical framework and the availability of the required resources in mind. A research design is the outline of a plan for collecting and analysing data. For this purpose, hypotheses are set out. Concepts are refined. Operational definitions are formulated. Scales are chosen. Reliability and validity are taken into account. One decides which tools are to be used and which statistical tests are to be applied. Preparing a research design involves deciding the appropriate means for achieving the targets laid down ahead of time, with minimum expenditure of time, money and manpower.

Stages of Survey

New knowledge is something not known to others. We have to devise our own procedures and in our own special way. We have to avoid taking a beaten track. However, acquaintance with how others perform such tasks enables us to orient ourselves properly. In a design for survey research, various operations are carried out in a sequential manner. Usually, this task is performed in two stages. Firstly, introspection and analysis of the material and secondly, empirical verification.

Introspection

This is a subjective process. This means self-examination. One gets an inside view of one's consciousness. The result is organised and articulated. It is checked for defects.

It is well and proper to proceed systematically, not haphazardly. Research is done for saying something new. There is no point in rediscovering what is already known to others. Therefore, we have to acquaint ourselves with the available literature in the field. For this purpose, we have to get access to, and make optimum use of libraries, archives, documentation centres, museums, computer centres, and so on. We have to consult books, current periodicals, back volumes of journals, bibliographies, documents available in files, unpublished manuscripts, exhibits, and everything else that is useful and can become available.

For preparing an outline of the study, we go on recording our impressions in a file. In this file we keep our book notes and bibliographical references. We summarise taking due note of the relevant points. We accept, refute or modify other scholars' interpretations, giving reasons. Their arguments are not to be brushed aside lightly. Great minds possess sharp antennae. They seldom make mistakes. We have to critically appreciate what they have said.

However, it is not enough to stop here. We observe ourselves in a systematic way. Our own observations are supplemented with those of the concerned persons, and those around them. Gather as many details as you can. Know the pros and cons of the matter under study. We apply our mind to the subject matter. Brainstorming, meditation and concentration simulate creative thinking. A creative person is often absent-minded. If he fails to notice what is going on around him for the time being, this may mean he is inattentive. What is he doing? He is busy thinking about the problem under study.

Creative imagination enables us to gain insight into the matter. This makes it possible for us to think of original ways of putting things together. We explore our data. We mark out noise from information. Available facts are then organised into a meaningful whole according to some purposeful criterion. These are then rearranged according to some other criteria. Try and try again. Be flexible and move from one set of plausible solutions to another. Soon it may appear that you have reached a dead end. You cannot proceed further. Sleep over the matter for some time. Let things drift along. Sooner or later a solution will strike you. Something will emerge. Try to understand the pattern. Critically judge the outcome. Arrange the material in a systematic way. Read more. Discuss and proceed.

Intuition promotes creative imagination. The human mind is capable of observing, perceiving, and organising by virtue of simple inspection. Concentration, memory, the ability for permutation and combination promote creative thinking. Try to systematise your facts. Think. Reflect. Try to find some sense in the seemingly unconnected facts. Watch for the missing links. Think of different ways of ordering the matter. Carefully apply your mind to the various aspects of the matter under investigation. Cautiously weigh the pros and cons. Note the elegance, the beauty and the symmetry. Set aside the matter for a few days. The mind comes up with ideas slowly and steadily. Suddenly one fine morning you will find a solution to the problem. New ideas spring up spontaneously. Put two and two together. When you become absolutely certain about the matter, connect the isolated facts with each other. Arrange everything into a viable framework. Consider alternative ways for putting the matter into some shape. Arrange and rearrange them into a meaningful perspective. Classify into types. Cross-classify and check up their mutual relations. Gain additional insight by thinking up the converse, contrary and contradictory. Compare and contrast them with each other and their equivalents at other places and times. Explain them in terms of each other. Gradually, the matter becomes clear. Elaborate. Use your methodological training and theoretical repertoire for refining and polishing the matter. Present your findings before others with perception. Discuss them intensively. Get feedback from your colleagues. Consider their criticisms. Reformulate. Clinch the issue and connect it with the introductory remarks in your project report. Link the findings with available theories in the field.

Empirical Verification

This is better done in five stages. These are discussed below:

Formulation of the Problem

A problem for research work is not just picked up from anywhere. It is chosen carefully. It is placed in a frame. Obstacles are foreseen and provided for. What considerations are to be kept in mind while choosing a problem? There is no action without motivation. Motivation comes from within the researcher or in the form of inducement from outside. Competition, incentives, career advancement, availability of facilities, and other reasons, prepare the researcher for taking up certain projects. Every age and every country has its own requirement. It is too much to hope that we can create at home the conditions prevalent elsewhere. There are several reasons for taking up a problem for study. These include needs of the people concerned, popularity of the topic, interests of the sponsor, own goals, availability of resources like money, staff, computer, institutional support, and so on. Generally, researchers enjoy the freedom to find a suitable corner for themselves. If the project needs a task force, the interests of the members of the team have to be kept in mind. The elite anywhere do not like outsiders to interfere in their affairs and create problems for them. Even the researchers themselves have their own conscious and unconscious biases. The problem is formulated in such a way that the task in hand can be successfully completed.

Sponsors of a research project can prescribe the goals, ideological direction, and procedural details. They can interfere by virtue of their say in granting or withholding scholarships, grants and project proposals. Remember, who pays the piper calls the tune. Nobody spends money for nothing. What to speak of the choice of a topic for research, the sponsors' declared and undeclared interests influence the choice of techniques and conclusions. The sponsors will spend their money only if the project fits into their priorities. At the time of sanctioning research grants, the funding agencies take into account the reputation, previous record, disposition and potential of the research manager and his term. His personal networks at home and abroad as well as his approach to the higher-ups are helpful in this regard. Those who share access to financial networks can pull strings. They can get things done the way they like. If one sponsor has loosened his purse strings, the other will also cough up something. The sponsors look for seemingly contradictory qualities of head and heart in researchers. The latter must possess scientific skills as well as appropriate values. Look around for possibilities. Speak to the people concerned. Convince them that you will competitively deliver the goods well in time. Go on applying again and again. If you cannot become a research manager for the time being, find a good man who will lead you, and follow him.

If a financer has offered a scholarship to a young person for doing Ph.D., or a person is otherwise interested in doing so, the place has to be wisely chosen. The research institute should possess the required infrastructure—well-stocked library, well-maintained computer centre, goal-oriented administration, facilities for interaction with productive scholars, creative work culture, and a lot more. A research supervisor with appropriate specialisation should be available. He should be willing to guide the candidate. The topic should interest the student. It should be manageable within the limited time available (3 to 4 years).

Do not conduct a survey unless it is justified by theoretical as well as methodological considerations. It is costly, time-consuming and laborious. Before we embark upon the search for new knowledge, we must ascertain that somebody else has not already worked in the area. We have to consult journals and unpublished dissertations in a good library. Material in data archives can be useful for secondary analysis. Reports by official agencies and investigative journalists are often useful. Abstracts and documentation of the available material in the field are available in print these days. Computerised bibliographies of books and articles can also be ordered. One can order these materials on inter-library loan. Photocopies can also be obtained from within the country and even from abroad by post. Internet has opened up vast possibilities. The point is that before we start doing our research work, we must thoroughly go through the available resources in the field.

Figure 4
Untouchability hinders development

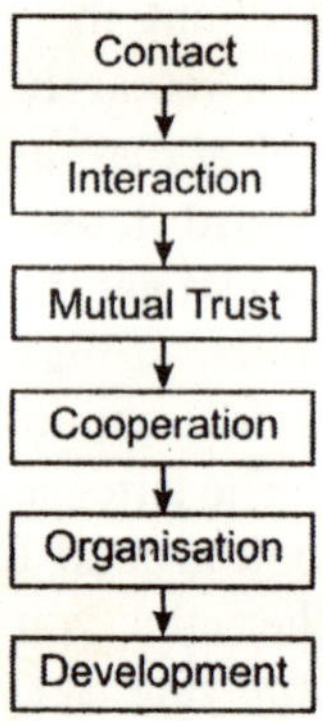

Outlines of Research

The problem under investigation has to be placed in a theoretical framework. This is done with reference to a perspective. If we know our goals well, we can look for appropriate means to achieve these goals.

Figure 5
Some effects of population density

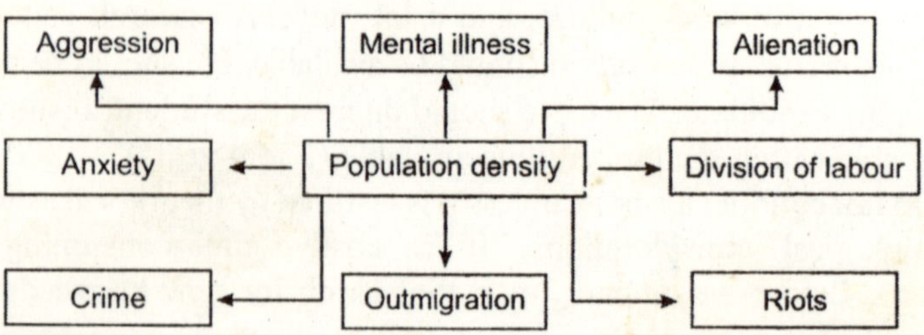

After pinpointing the objectives, we have to state a particular problem and specify its various aspects. We have to limit the space of our study to a few manageable aspects of the problem in hand. Within this orientation, we have to choose certain hypotheses. We have already discussed in a previous chapter how this is done. The point is that we have to think of a framework or a model or a flow chart for properly arranging the facts we are going to collect. For example,

Various steps have to be carefully taken. We have to conceptualise at strategic points in a framework. These concepts are to be connected together with statements specifying their mutual relationships. For example, McKinsey's 7-S framework of managerial excellence has seven strategic points. While preparing a questionnaire, we have to take care of the relevant variables for these concepts.

Figure 6

Prediction of life satisfaction among the rural elderly

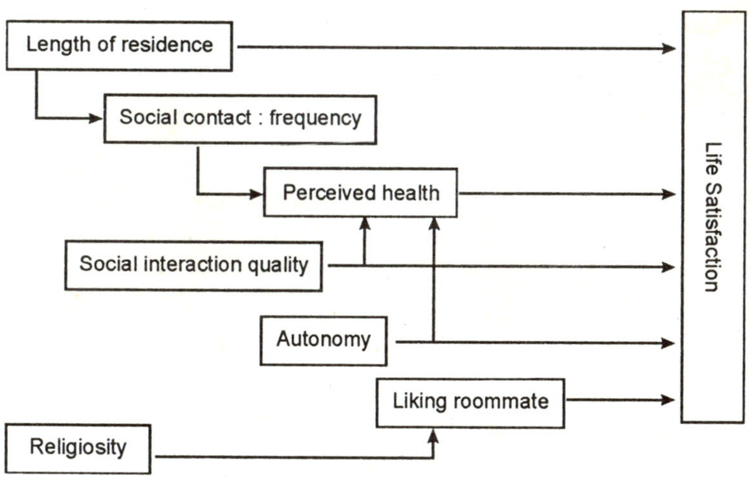

Source : Avtar Singh and Harsharan K. Singh: "Predicting Life Satisfaction...", *Guru Nanak Journal of Sociology*, 6(1), April 1985, p. 70.

Items are operationally defined so that data collection is made easy. For instance, authoritarianism is what a scale for authoritarianism measures. Creativity is given by the creativity test. Intelligence may be operationally defined with reaction time. Analytical ability is what the embedded figure test measures. Various concepts are operationally defined in such a way that their observation, measurement and

Figure 7
In search of excellence

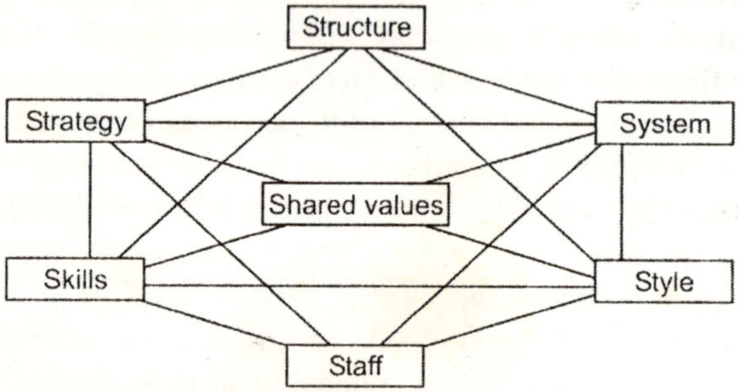

Source : Peters, T.J. and R.H. Waterman Jr.: *In Search of Excellence*, Harper & Row, New York, 1982, p. 10.

verification are facilitated. Measurement is done with scales or indications. These are included in our questionnaire.

The data collected with the questionnaires are analysed. These are confronted with the hypotheses. The outcome of such a confrontation decides whether we are going to accept, reject or modify our hypothesis.

Figure 8
Flow chart of a research design

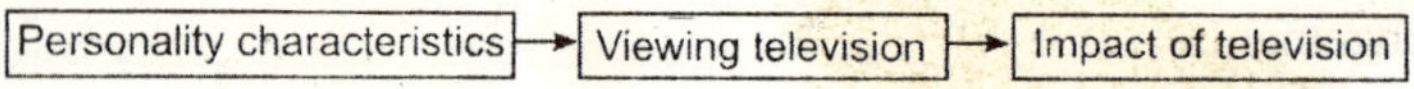

The problem has various aspects, dimensions or factors. Factors are made up of variables. At the time of constructing the theory, proper names are replaced with the name of variables behind the names. A variable has values, which may increase or decrease. The configurations, relations, causes, are abstracted. We are not interested in what a single person does, but in what most persons of the same category normally do. For example, we are not interested in writing the personal biography of Anita or Fauzia or Linda. We are curious about the relevant latent variables. So we make generalisation about how unemployed girls like them are likely to behave under similar circumstances. An outline of our research work will give us models like Figure 6. It is advisable to present the outlines of our research work before our colleagues in a seminar etc. Such dialogues would identify the gaps, clarify the concepts, and refine our strategy and tactics.

Various stages of a research design do not follow each other in a mechanical sequence. Tasks are organically connected with other tasks. Their performance at one stage falls back upon other stages of the assignment.

After finalising our research design, we go ahead and gather our data.

Data Gathering

The procedures for gathering data are decided upon after taking into consideration the goals of the research and the resources available for achieving the ends. Techniques and tools sharpen our perceptions and save us from making mistakes. These are chosen according to the situation. Participant observation, surveys or experiments may be made use of from time to time. A lone researcher cannot complete a survey all by himself. This is a team job. The choice of specific tools is made after we have decided which techniques and tools are to be utilised. For example, observation inventory, sampling procedure, code design, dummy tables and so on.

Before embarking upon such an endeavour, we ought to have selected our field of research, sampling frame, etc. Research material is collected from the field : a region, a village, a factory, a colony, etc. The field is selected in such a way that it represents a broader universe. Arrangements include financial support, time-schedule, access to the filed, and recruitment of assistants. For this purpose, one has to contact prominent people and establish rapport with them. Arrangements for

Figure 9

Variables, factors and theory

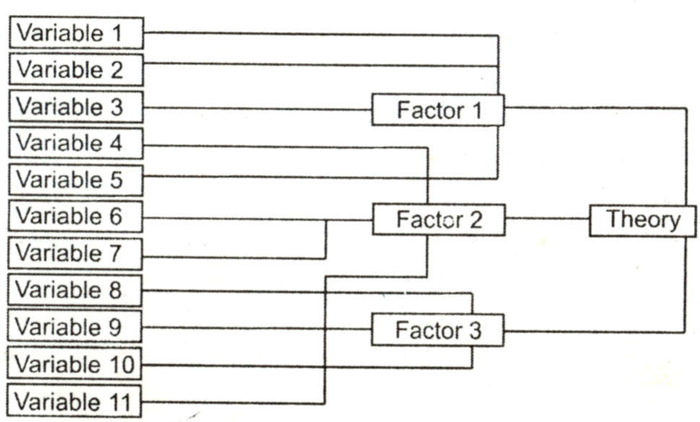

travel, stay and meals have to be made. Before getting an interview schedule printed, it should be pre-tested. It should be checked for question-wording, item sequencing, and proper spacing. If required, translate the interview schedule into the local dialects/languages. On-the-spot instant translations impair standardisation. Carefully check up the translation by re-translating the same. Beware: "Out of sight out of mind" translated into German may come back as "invisible idiots".

Data Analysis

First of all, the data are reduced to a smaller amount. Tables can be prepared manually, and electronically. Qualitative data are converted into quantitative data with the help of a code design. These are recorded on cards, tapes, discs, etc. If a computer is accessible, tabulation can be done and statistical operations can be performed quickly. Tabulation makes it easy to draw valid inferences, think out their implications and interpret the data. In this way, abstract general statements can be made. Statistical tests, logical reasoning and creative imagination are made use of for drawing reliable and valid conclusions.

A researcher finds out the underlying patterns, systematically arranges the available material, and organises the same in a meaningful way. Simple counts, ratios, percentages, bivariate tables, correlation coefficients and other statistical operations facilitate interpretation. We are interested in making statements which explain a large chunk of the given data. We want to construct theories. For this purpose, the given variables are brought under common names. The material is classified. Invariable sequences, structures, types changing trends are noted down. This facilitates testing and verification of hypotheses.

Report Writing

A report reproduces what has been done from the start to the finish. Methodology, description, analysis, and all other steps are described. There is a simple formula for writing a report—Have something to say, and say it in the best manner you can. A research report is written for professionals. A brief newsworthy summary may also be prepared and widely circulated through mass media such as newspapers, radio, television.

Preparation of a synopsis in the beginning facilitates the performance of premeditated strategy and tactics. It also gives experience in writing. First of all, choose an appropriate title for your research report.

This may be different from the title of the original research project at start. If necessary, make it specific and extend it in a desired direction by providing a sub-title. Formulate the problem. Place it within a theoretical framework. Point out the theoretical importance and practical significance of your study. Review the available literature in the field. Specify the gaps you intend to fill in with your study. Describe the sampling procedure, the universe, the type of sampling, the type of sampling framework as well as sample size and its representativeness. Some committees for appraising the research schemes also insist upon attaching copies of questionnaires with the proposal. Inform them about which procedures are being used, how the data are to be analysed and interpreted. Why? State this briefly at the outset.

As far as style is concerned, be brief and to the point. Do not use big words. Do not write emotionally. Scientific writings are for intellectuals. The scientific language is not ornamental. Write like one writes in science practical notebook. Understand the subject-matter. Explain it for others. Write down the references in a standard format. While submitting articles for publication, first of all decide the periodical to which you wish to send your article. Use the format prescribed by the journal. Often the format is explicitly specified inside the front cover, or near about. Attach a summary of your article in, say, 200 words with the article. Type the manuscript in double space on good quality paper. Leave a 4 to 6 cm. margin on the left side of each page. The title, headings, and sub-headings should be appropriately bold. Letters which are to be given in italics in print ought to be underlined while typing.

The various stages in a research design are shown in Figure 10.

At the end, it must be emphasised that the preparation of a research design begins with asking the right questions. As Rudyard Kipling says:

> I keep six honest serving men.
>
> (They taught me all I know);
>
> Their names are what? and why? and when?
>
> And how? and where? and who?

Then we go ahead and look around for the right answers to these questions. Briefly: What is to be done at the time of preparing the research design?

Figure10
Stages of a research design

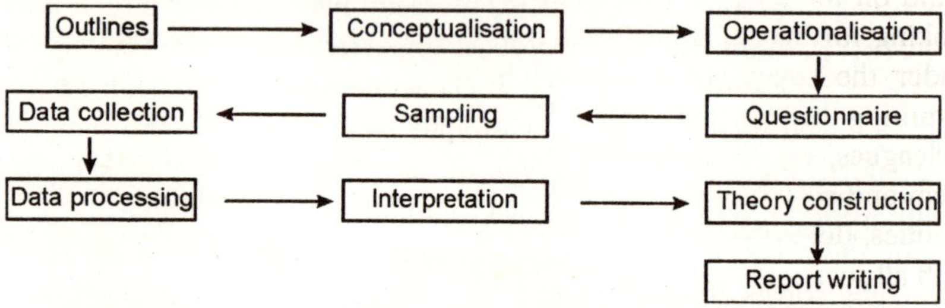

Observation provides data. A research design helps us to collect the data in such way that we can make use of them to construct our theories. Which facts are to be collected and which ones are irrelevant for the time being and, therefore, to be excluded. Available theory decides what were require and what we do not need. Theories are empty forms unless suitably supported with data. For this purpose, we identify their similarities and dissimilarities. We find out the set of conditions which promote and hinder them.

How are the data to be interpreted? While preparing the questionnaire, we ask 'why' after certain items and scales. This provides us insight into the respondents' motives, the depth of their replies, and their significance. The researcher's intuition helps him in analysing the meaning of facts and their correct interpretation. Ask yourself such questions as: What does this mean? Does it make sense? Can it somehow mean something else? How can it be connected with some existing theory? Sometimes a scientifically trained observer is looking for something and unexpectedly comes across something else. This is called serendipity. This provides us fresh insights. It yields surprising results. Serendipity sharpens our antennae. It enables us to grasp the significance of strategically important data the moment we come across them. Thus, relevant thoughts do not get lost. The ability to capture such ideas comes through our theoretical clarity, training and experience. This enables us to make hitherto unsuspected discoveries, without preparing a specific research design.

In addition to a formal research design, on-the-job experience of working under the personal supervision of a master researcher is very useful for transferring skills. Research supervisors provide encouragement, guidance and inspiration. They impart practical training. They correct silly mistakes. They transfer tacit knowledge for coming to terms with intricacies. They also show the way out when a learner is unsure of the next step to be taken. Everything is not written in books. One can stand on the shoulders of great masters and take clues from them for looking further ahead. There is no doubt about it that apprenticeship under the supervision of experienced researchers is very useful for acquiring the required competence. Apart from research supervisors and colleagues, one can also learn from one's own mistakes. Ponder over them and correct them next time. In this way, one gradually recognises realities, develops the knack of dealing with others and comes to terms with all sorts of brass tacks in research work.

Conclusions

Research is done in order to discover something new or to interpret already known facts in a novel manner. The survey method is becoming popular these days. Preparing a research design for a social survey involves working out the necessary steps for constructing theories. First of all, we formulate the problem. Then we use our skill to choose suitable concepts at strategic points in a theoretical framework. These are operationally defined. Suitable items are constructed for measurement of the underlying variables. These are knitted together into a suitable tool, say, interview schedule. This is used to collect data from a representative sample of the population. The collected data are statistically treated. These are interpreted and confronted with various elements in the theoretical framework. The outcome may, thus, be accepted, rejected, or modified accordingly.

Research Route

Example 15 : Before a drug is introduced in the market, it has to pass a lengthy approval process involving a series of clinical trials. That process is called clinical research. In the next few years, many key patents will expire and major pharmaceutical companies (i.e., Pfizer, Eli Lilly, Merck, Apotex, Glaxo, SmithKline, etc.) will be looking to bring new pharmaceutical products off the laboratory bench and onto the pharmacy shelves. In order to accommodate this, the pharmaceutical industry is going through transition from pre-clinical research and development (R&D) to large-scale clinical trial work. As such, the industry will witness a sky-rocketing demand for CRPs (clinical research professionals).

According to a McKinsey Report, global clinical trial outsourcing to India will reach about Rs 5,000 crore by 2010, with the industry requiring about 50,000 clinical research professionals. Although many clinical research institutes enrol science graduates, they essentially end up doing data management work. Medical professionals are best suited for going into actual CR work (*The Tribune*, "Jobs & Careers", 29 August, 2007, p. 2.).

References

deVaus, D.A., *Survey Research Design*, University of Chicago Press, Chicago, 1991.

Singh, Jaspal, *Introduction to Methods of Social Research*, Sterling, New Delhi, 1991.

——, *Methodology and Techniques of Social Research*, Kanishka, New Delhi, 2001.

——, "Pure and Applied Research", *Kerala Sociologist*, Vol. 30, No. 1, June, 2002, pp. 83-88.

4

Scientific Methods

Meaning and Characteristics

Knowledge is exploding these days, with bang after bang. As much knowledge was generated during the last four centuries as during the entire course of human history. It is bloating day-by-day. The number and size of research institutions and the amount of funds at their disposal is going up and up. New disciplines are emerging. The scope of their applications is mind-boggling. Knowledge is now recognised as the fourth factor of production, and the most important one. The other three factors are : land, labour and capital.

Globalisation

Globalisation, with broader horizons and contested loyalties, *Udarcharitanam vasudhaiva kutumbakam,* is changing the structure of our needs. It has made it necessary to manufacture better quality wares, and to sell them far and wide, before other competitors are able to do so. Creativity and innovativeness are in greater demand. Their price has gone up. Research work in social sciences has become more paying than ever before.

Knowledge

Knowledge is not a heap of information. Isolated facts in time and space are systematically collected and adequately analysed for their proper linking together. Knowledge = facts + their interconnections.

Science

A popular slogan is going around : *Jai Jawan, Jai Kisan, Jai Vigyan.* Soldiers defend their country. Farmers grow more food. But what is so

Figure 1
Information and knowledge

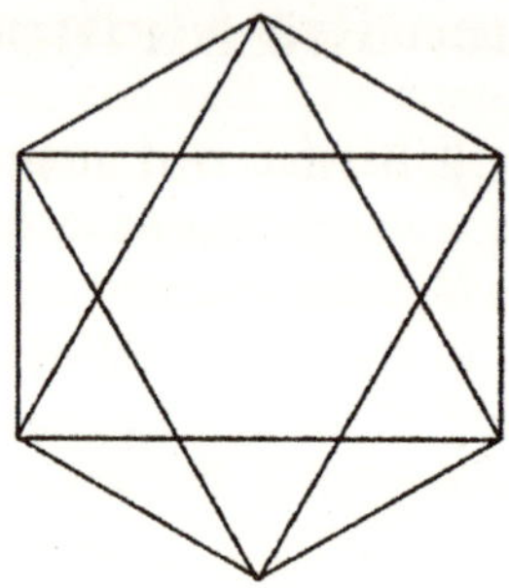

special about science? Its method of research for creating new knowledge.

A scientist knows that he does not know everything. But this does not mean that anybody else does so. Science is a systematic body of knowledge that is formed of components placed together or adjusted into a regular and connected whole. It is an orderly arrangement of parts according to rules. It is systematically built up, using proper methods. The scientists are not supposed to do everything. They become specialists in various disciplines. These disciplines can be classified into branches. The number of disciplines is increasing these days. The rate of growth is the highest in their interstitial spaces. New disciplines are emerging in border areas of sciences.

Technology

Application of science with a view to achieving certain goals. The purpose is to benefit somebody or all concerned. Technology makes science more useful.

Figure 2
Branches of science

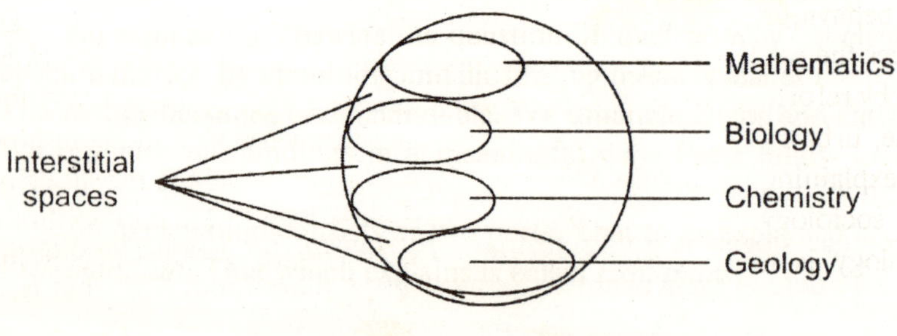

Scientific Institutions

Traditional universities were *associations*. Those who came together, formed a community, and enjoyed their togetherness. Status was more important than functioning.

Modern universities are *organisations*. Their members concertedly act together for achieving their goals. Emphasis shifts from examinations to teaching, and from teaching to research.

Table 1

Institutions for academic work in India

Existing Institutes of Higher Education	
Category	***Number***
Government Departments of Science	6
IITs, IIMs, etc.	20
Universities/Deemed Universities	231
National R&D Laboratories	400
Private Sector R&D Units	1300

The Government of India had set up a Knowledge Commission to reorganise the system of higher education. Its report is being widely circulated for implementation.

Sociology

Several academic disciplines deal with society. *Social philosophy* does not use the scientific method of research. It places greater attention on the desirable rather than the objective. *Social anthropology* has four aspects : physical anthropology, archeology, linguistics, and socio-cultural anthropology. Sociology is interested in the last one. The former focuses its attention on our primitive contemporaries. *Social psychology* studies the behaviour, motivation, consciousness of individuals. *Sociology* studies the relationships between individuals and systems. *Social work* is used by reformers to solve social problems like juvenile delinquency, drug abuse, urban poverty, etc. Sociologists are interested in understanding and explaining. Sociology is present *social history*, whereas the latter is past sociology. Sociology without history is blind. History without sociology is mute. Social change cannot be understood without its historical dimension. Sociology of economic life deals with the means and modes of production, distribution and exchange.

The point is that all these and some other disciplines deal with the social aspects of their main body. Their subject matter is also the subject matter of sociology. However, the instruments of research and concepts of sociology are different. Sociology is possible only as the practice of empirical social research.

Table 2
Sociology is different from ...

Dimension	
Social anthropology	Social economy
Social history	Social philosophy
Social psychology	Social work
Social policy	etc.

Unscientific Methods Theology

Pre-empirical methods, theological and metaphysical, are unscientific. *Theology* is marked by firm belief in the existence of supernatural powers (gods, God). Life and death are in their hands. (*Patta bhi agar hilta hai to Allah ke hukam se !*) All knowledge comes from them. *Rab ik gunjhaldar bujhart, Rab ik gorakhdhanda. Kholan lagiyan pech esde kafar ho jae banda. Kafar honon mool na darda, khojon mool na khumjhin. Sau lai lag bhagtan nalon ik khoji kafir changa.* (Mohan Singh, *Sawe Pattar).*

Mysticism falls back on the belief that we can arrive at the essence of truth, through meditation. Truth lies deep down under the surface of reality.

Metaphysics

Metaphysics talks of abstract forces behind concrete facts. It talks of the spirit behind matter. It searches for essences. For example, white colour and sweetness are the essence of sugar. It asks such questions as : What is the meaning of existence? What happens in the other world, before birth and after death? (*Yeh masaile tassawuf, yeh tera byan Ghalib!*). Metaphysics searches for totality, not piecemeal but as a whole.

Figure 3

There are more things in society than are known to sociologists

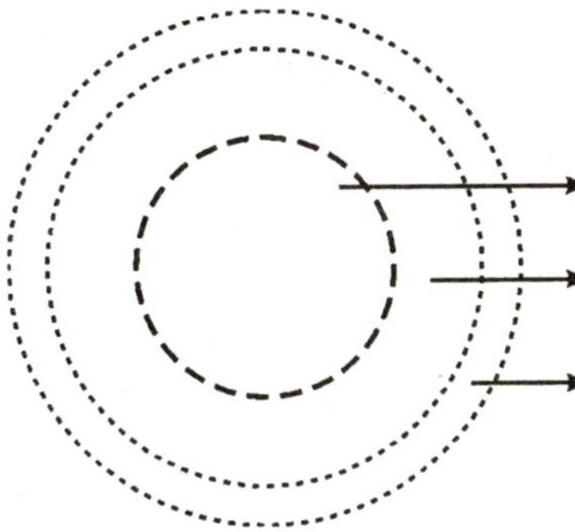

Pseudo-scientific Methods

Astrology

Theology and metaphysics are unscientific. But astrology and ufology are based on cock and bull stories, flights of fancy, superstitions. Astrologers and ufologists are dillettantes and charlatans. Their business flourishes upon the insecurities of their *guelible* clients. They make hay while others are easy to deceive. They claim that they are using the scientific method. But scientists do not agree with them. Astrological predictions are based on the assumption that stars and their configurations affect the conditions of our living in specific ways. (*Meri qismat mein tu nahin shayad !*) Astrologers carry on meticulous calculations, prepare horoscopes, and speculate about future events. They prescribe remedies against bad luck, in return for suitable fees. They promote superstitions, and irrationality.

Critics point out that an astrologer has no access to God's computerised data archive. Such a thing does not exist. His predictions are based on his subjective judgements. Their being true or false is a matter of his own wisdom. We cannot depend upon astrological predictions or what the stars are supposed to foretell.

Ufology

Like astrology, ufology is a pseudo-science. Media of mass communication and science fiction books spread sensational rumours. These claim that so and so has watched unidentified foreign objects at such and such place and time. They claim that strange alien beings visit the planet earth in their spacecrafts. They leave some signs behind them. As a matter of fact, ufologists are swindlers, who arrive at erroneous judgements with fallible evidence of optical and auditory illusions. At best, ufology may prepare the way for extraterrestrial adventure in the future.

Positivism

Method of science falls back upon the assumptions behind positivism and empiricism. These are more or less overlapping terms. Positivists are of the view that we can have no knowledge except that of phenomena, and the knowledge of phenomena is relative, not absolute. For our purpose here, positivism and empiricism are mutually overlapping terms. British philosophers prefer the second term (empiricism), while their French and German counterparts like to be called positivists.

Empiricism

This is a rigorous method. It asserts that all knowledge is obtained safely through sense-experience. *A priori* reasoning (before experience), intuition, revelation (*ilham, dhur ki bani*) are rejected. Reality is observed in fragments. Appearances are meticulously combined.

Neo-positivism

Minute observation of concrete facts. Data are collected methodically. These are analysed, using statistical tools. Concepts are adequately defined, and operationalised. These are measured with scales. Proper nouns are replaced with the names of the underlying variables. Hypotheses are accepted, rejected, or modified, giving reasons. Variables are combined into factors and factors into models.

Table 3

Production of knowledge by empiricists

Observation	Encounter and experience.
Sensations	Hear. See. Smell. Taste. Touch. Identify and differentiate signals from outside.
Perception	Reason-based analysis and organisation.
Meditation	Concentrate. Focus your attention.
Reflection	Find unity in diversity.
Articulation	Formulate. Express.
Consciousness	Awareness.
Knowledge	Interconnected pieces of information.
Wisdom	Use of knowledge, without its misuse.

Rapid advancements in electronic data processing have faciliated the use of statistics for social science research. Neo-positivism has become popular, even indispensable.

An important point must be noted here. We can make serious errors in data analysis by ignoring the philosophical background of data collection and analysis. Understanding of the philosophical background gives breadth and depth to the analysis.

Dialectic

Some methods other than the empirical also claim to be scientific. The dialectical method is one of them. It has several variations.

Socrates (469-399 BC)

He cleverly used the method of dialogue. He was a stone-cutter, and the son of a stone-cutter. His mother was a midwife. He entered into conversation, and asked relevant questions. He pointed out contradictions in the matter under consideration. He constrained the discussant to apply his mind. Like his mother, he helped in producing ideas. Like his father, he chiselled out beautiful figures.

Hegel (1770-1831)

Practised dialectical idealism. He was of the opinion that thought proceeds by contradiction (thesis-antithesis). These are reconciled by fusion of ideas. Thesis conserves. Antithesis abolishes. Synthesis combines the two. Hegel was a dialectical idealist. Marx was a dialectical materialist. The latter turned the former upside down, and made him stand on his feet.

Marx (1818-83)

Dialectics proceeds in spurts from thesis to antithesis. These contain the seeds of their own destruction, or contradictions. The same are opposing tendencies, or internal problems that withhold progress. For example, action and reaction, feudalism and capitalism, life and death. With the passage of time, these become ripe, and interpenetrate each other. These enter into struggle, give up their contradictions, and become one. Thus, tensions between thesis and antithesis get resolved after coming into conflict. The two together form a synthesis. This is a new thesis. Thesis conserves. Antithesis abolishes. Synthesis combines the two. The dialectical process goes on and on like that. There is no beginning and no end in dialectics. *Kahan shuru kahan khatam?* Nowhere!

Characteristics of the Method of Science

The method of science does not enable us to understand everything. There are more things in heaven and on earth than are known to sociologists. Much beyond that is out of its reach. It does not enable us to understand the total reality. But whatever it does is well-done. Scientific knowledge is authentic. It has a large degree of certainty.

In order to understand what the scientific method is, let us distinguish it from what it is not. Science is not mere commonsense.

Common Sense

This method is based on generally prevalent opinions, guess-work, sensible dealings, and so on. Common beliefs, proverbs, sayings are accepted as such. However, these are covered up with guesstimates, official handouts, prejudice and perceived credibility. This can yield erroneous results. For instance, we observe everyday that the earth is flat. But scientific observation and experiments by geographers refute that and tell us that the earth is more or less round. Even otherwise, common sense is not very common. We cannot rely upon it.

Tenacity

We go on believing in the same old ways of thinking, feeling and acting, just because it has always been like that since times immemorial. For instance, not allowing those belonging to a scheduled caste entry into a temple. However, tradition does not mean that this practice is legal and legitimate. Such customs have always been enforced in order to safeguard the interests of the erstwhile elites, and have continued thereafter. Moreover, the content of practices goes on getting altered with time, place, and conditions of living. Definitions of situations go on changing from time to time. What was sacrosanct once upon a time may have to be given up with broader horizons and contested loyalties.

Authority

The method of science does not depend upon the intention of some power holders to be regarded as infallible. The method of authority regards the orders of those in regulated positions of power as legitimate. For example, the orders of a traffic constable have to be obeyed, because he occupies a position of authority. He is powerful enough to get his orders obeyed. Those subject to his authority do so, more or less willingly. Subordinates have learnt to act upon the instructions given by their superordinates. As a matter of fact, always bowing before authoritarian structures (*Sarkar ka hukam hai !*) differs from the method of science. Often, authorities differ in their opinion on a particular matter. They can move in contrary or contradictory directions. The method of science prevents its followers from becoming henchmen of those occupying positions of authority.

Intuition

Designers, painters, poets pursue their creative activities more or less intuitively. Their intuition is a function of various factors that affect their memory and the flight of their imagination. There is something in them that tells them to apply their minds in particular ways. Their insight moulds the matter accordingly. (*Kabhi kahin mere dil mein khayal aata hai !*) It appears that this is the only solution and there is no other way out. But later on they may realise that other alternatives were available. Our training, discipline, sympathy, old records incline us in a certain direction. Intuition does leave some room for error. On the other hand, the method of science helps us to get sure-shot results. The matter under consideration is firmly grasped from outside and thoroughly understood from inside before one comes out with an adequate explanation.

Experience

The method of science is based upon experience. (Sahir Ludhianvi : *Duniya ne tajurbat o hawadis ki shakal mein jo kuchh mujhe diya tha, woh lauta raha hoon mein!*)It is free of pre scientific and ascientific restrictions. It enables us to proceed rationally, without passions. Scientific knowledge is expanding day-by-day. Traditions are becoming outdated. The structure of authority is getting transformed. Common sense and intuition have become outdated. Science and technology have become more important than ever before.

We can safely assert that the method of science is valid as well as reliable. Of course, it is different from the methods of common sense, tenacity, authority, and intuition. What are its characteristic features? The method of science consists of the methodology and techniques of investigation. It enables us to gather evidence systematically, to arrange the same in a viable pattern, and prepare the same for drawing conclusions. It provides us appropriate means for constructing theories.

Earlier, we distinguished the method of science from what it is not. Now we have come to a point where we can count its characteristic features. Here these are:

Objectivity

This means the inclination to perceive the facts under observation as they are. In contrast to that, subjectivity involves intuitive assessment. We have to observe how the subjects under observation think, feel and act. While doing so, we come across a number of problems. What appears clear to a cow need not be clear to a calf. Often we fail to understand the difference between the subjective, objective and conventional intentions.

Commonly prevalent ideas have their after-effects. Once a statement has been made, it may become true just because somebody has said it (self-fulfilling prophecy). A scientifically trained observer has to give up short-sightedness and closely inquire into the matter under investigation, one has to learn to look at the matter with a cool head, and construct arguments. Events are explained in terms of other events. The scientist observes the direction and intensity of various currents. He notices the drift, the tilt, the way the wind is blowing. Often people act without understanding why they are behaving that way. We have to see facts as they are by rising above intuition, opportunism, wishful thinking and apprehensions. We have to pinpoint the gaps and overlaps. But the scientist is a human being. He is not a machine. Then, how can he ensure objectivity? This can be done through inter-subjectivity, i.e., through dialogue among interacting scientists. Scientists do not go on insisting that something is true, because they say it is true. They rely on cool calculations with facts and arguments. Others can replicate the results at other places and points of time by using the same methods. When formulating scientific statements, we ensure that the same are verifiable/falsifiable. Even then, in actual practice, objectivity boils down to inter-subjectivity. It may also take the form of *serendipity*, i.e., naive observation by a scientifically trained observer. However hard we may try, subjectivity enters our scientific work in one form or another. Especially in case of socio-cultural sciences, our procedures do not completely rule out subjectivity. In order to minimised the chances of error, scientists have to exchange their findings through mutual discussions. We have to be as objective as is possible for us.

Quantifiability

This is another feature of the scientific method. As far as possible, we have to convert the various qualitative aspects of our subject matter into measureable quantities. This makes it easy for us to ascertain their magnitude, interrelationships and causal connections. For this purpose, we are required to gather our facts, arrange them systematically and find out their underlying patterns. Specifying in quantitative terms makes our conclusions firm. Data become comparable. Clear, reliable and valid scales are utilised for increasing quantifiability. While it is true that everything cannot be measured, insofar as this is possible, use of mathematics and statistics increases objectivity. There is no doubt about it that the use of computers for social science research has further opened up the possibilities of quantification.

Theoretical Orientation

We prepare the outlines of recurring events with a view to explaining them. We link up facts with ideas. We think of a viable theoretical framework and fit the outlines therein. Proper nouns (Sahir Ludhianvi) with the names of the underlying variables (poet, Indian). Gradually, we go on broadening our concepts and frames. In this way, we build up a generalised body of knowledge. While constructing theories, we encounter a number of problems. These have to be solved. As already pointed out, one of the problems faced is that a large part of the reality is beyond our grasp. In order to circumvent this hurdle, we try to understand the unknown in terms of the known.

Table 4
Theoretical orientation

Theory	*Orientation*
Structural functionalism	The part that elements play for the whole.
Conflict theory	Ability of some to dominate others, or to resist such domination.
Rational choice	Interaction of utility-maximising individual benefits.
Social construction	How social phenomena develop in particular social contexts.

Universalism

The method of science is not unique to a particular group or region. It belongs to the entire world. It is firmly rooted in research work carried on in various countries. The findings are exchanged all around. Science does not restrict itself to circles of power and influence. It grows through arguments between people representing different points of view and from various directions. It is not stationary. It is dynamic. It is liberal as well. The entire world is a family for science. Science belongs to everybody. Indian science, Islamic science, Brahmin science are all misnomers. If properly drawn, scientific conclusions are free from time and space. They are reliable all over the world.

Summary

The method of science is the most appropriate method of arriving at conclusions that enjoy a large degree of certainty. Scientific research helps us to raise productivity. In order to understand what the method of science is, we have tried to distinguish it from what it is not. We pointed out that the method of science is different from common sense, tenacity, authority and intuition. Objectivity, quantifiability, theoretical orientation, universalism are main characteristics of the method of science. It is founded on the assumptions behind empiricism. Sociology is possible only as the practice of empirical social research.

Now, let us call it a day. You are cordially invited for a swim in the vast ocean of sociology. It is a science. It is possible only as the practice of neo-positivism. You are always welcome !

References

Cohen, M.R. and E. Nagel, *An Introduction to Logic and Scientific Method*, Allied, New Delhi, 1984.

Mills, C. Wright, *The Sociological Imagination*, Oxford University Press, London, 1976.

Singh, Jaspal et al., *Data Collection and Analysis*, Workshop for Young Writers, Indian Sociological Society, Chennai, 2006.

Singh, Jaspal, *Introduction to Methods of Social Research*, Sterling Publishers, New Delhi, 1990.

——, *Methodology and Techniques of Social Research*, Kanishka Publishers and Distributors, New Delhi, 2001.

——, *Samajik Khoj Kee Hai?* Department of Sociology, Guru Nanak Dev University, Amritsar, 1991.

5

Observation

Several methods are available for doing research on a topic. Different techniques are used in different situations. Problems have dimensions. Dimensions can be broken down into variables. Experiments are done in order to find out cause and effect relationship among variables. Surveys are done with a view to ascertaining their exact magnitude. This means that the units under observation possess this much value with respect to the given variables. Surveys are done before conducting experiments. Before conducting a survey, we identify the relevant variables. We see whether they are interconnected in any way. We also ascertain their configuration. Participant observation is a useful technique for achieving this goal. This method is often employed by social anthropologists and ethnologists.

Those who use the method of science can understand the world through observation with their sense organs, with or without instruments. This is done in a systematic way. We sharpen our sense organs by observing attentively and repeatedly. Sensations from outside transmit nervous impulses to the brain. These are organised and become known as perceptions. The reliability and validity of what we have understood in this way is checked by applying due controls and verifying the supporting evidence. Reliability means that repeated observation by various persons, at different places and times, will yield the same results. Validity means that what is being observed is really the same and not something else.

Sensations and perceptions about the material under study are made use of to build up concepts. Indicators from the concepts enable us to think out viable patterns about their underlying regularities and structures. Thus, the concepts can be arranged into suitable frames for constructing theories. One observes in the light of lessons learnt in the past. Theoretical orientation shows a proper way, and leads scientific observation.

Naive or simple-minded observation is an adventure like a fishing expedition. However, if it is undertaken by a scientifically trained observer, it may unexpectedly yield strategically important patterns. Robert Merton called it serendipity.

Various overlapping typologies of observation are available :

1. *Uncontrolled observation* is based on intuition, common sense, pragmatic introspection. It is naive and prescientific. *Controlled observation* uses preplanned strategies for prolonged intense inspection. The observed facts are duly verified. It is done systematically and scientifically.
2. *Field observation* is done under natural conditions. For example, crowd behaviour, traffic intensity at an intersection, a street corner gang, may be observed. In this case, the controls are not sharp. *Laboratory observation* is systematically carried on under controlled conditions in a laboratory or a hospital.
3. In *overt observation,* the observer, e.g., an ethnographer, is known. All that he does is open and above board. A *covert observer,* e.g., an intelligence agent, conceals himself from those being observed.
4. *Non-participant observation* is carried on from an arm chair, a vantage point or an ivory tower. The observer maintains critical distance from the observed. A *participant observer* mixes up with those under investigation. He grasps the matter under study from outside and understands it from inside. He partially identifies himself with those under observation, without going native, e.g., avoiding over-participation. Let us deal with the method of participant observation in greater detail now.

The method of participant observation finds out facts about socio-cultural life and explains them. Observation gives a firm basis for producing knowledge. Participation reinforces the findings with common sense as well as theoretical understanding. Those under study are intensively observed in their social milieu at close quarters. This is done with a view to catching the meaning of their ways of thinking, feeling and acting. While doing so, due care is taken that the subjects and objects of research are kept apart. Thus, it is ensured that the researcher does not project his own prejudices on to the people under study. If this is so, he discovers what he wants to find, jeopardising objectivity. The observer need not be a barefoot researcher. Those being studied know that he is not one of them even though he lives with them. He watches them systematically. He tries to understand how he feels, by putting himself in their place. Thus, he comes to know where their shoe pinches. He takes part in their day-to-day life. He listens carefully to what they have to say about each other. He notes down how they celebrate their festivals. He watches how they deal with each other and with outsiders. He comprehends how they come to terms with the problems confronting them. While doing so, he does not disturb them. He does not interfere with what they are doing. He is an observer, not an interventionist. He does not interfere with their way of doing things. He does not praise or condemn them. His research material is made use of for abstracting general statements about their social and cultural life.

Definition

What exactly is participant observation? Let us try to understand what it is by distinguishing it from what it is not. Participant observation is not investigative journalism. A journalist visits the area of his interest. He meets the people concerned. He talks to them. He acquaints himself with what is going on. He understands each and every aspect of some urgent matter of pubic interest. He files a report with his newspaper. When a dog bites a man, a journalist is hardly bothered. But when a man bites a dog, this is news for him. In contrast to a journalist, a participant observer is a social anthropologist. The latter is not interested in sensationalism. He lives with those under observation, over a prolonged period. Say, for 18 months, often 4 to 5 years. He participates in their day-to-day life. He observes what they do, say and think. He arranges his material in some viable order. He analyses and explains his data. He formulates hypotheses within a viable theoretical framework.

In contrast to the survey and the experimental method, participant observation does not start with a research design. This is a flexible technique. Data collection and analysis, construction of hypotheses and report writing go hand in hand. A participant observer does not begin his work with a hypothesis. He completes his work by putting up a hypothesis.

Field of Research

The field location of participant observation has to be chosen carefully. The field is limited in extent. It must be appropriate for the purpose in hand. It must be accessible. For instance, some border areas are not open for researchers. Similarly, army men cannot be studied without permission from the competent authority. Availability of finances and knowledge of the local language are other constraints. The chosen field should be typical or otherwise appropriate for study. It should have some acceptable facility for accommodation, meals and, above all, interaction. Participant observers often study small islands, far off villages, hospitals, factories or small communities.

Even though some brave women have done participant observation, this technique is seldom open to women researchers. It is difficult for them to live alone in far off places. Till not long ago this method was used by outside scholars only. For example, Malinowski studied Trobriand islands in the South Sea. Radcliffe-Brown studied the Andaman Islands in the Indian Ocean. However, nowadays Indian scholars are also using this method. For example, Satish Sabbarwal studied a small town in Punjab, and K. Raman Unni studied hamlets in his native state Kerala. It is easier to do participant observation nearer home. It is costly to go abroad and live there over a prolonged period of time. Also it is not necessary to learn a new language when one chooses a filed near one's own place. It is easy to meet people and discuss everything with them. One can observe whenever one can spare some time from one's day-to-day chores. On the other hand, insiders suffer from preconceived notions about their own culture and society. They have grown up there. They have lived there throughout their lives. Everything is obvious for them. It is difficult for them to distance themselves from what they have been used to. It is easier for an outsider to observe exotic ways of life. They fascinate him. They attract his attention. While observing them he is consciously and unconsciously comparing in his mind the facts of observation with the state of affairs back home. Such anchorage facilitates grasp and understating. An outsider can ask naive questions without fear of ridicule. He is not expected to be well-conversant with these things, since he has not grown up there. This makes it easier for him to comprehend the matter. It is easier to observe others without any preconceptions. However, outsiders may suffer from ethnocentrism. They can make the mistake of imposing their value judgements on others Outsiders can miss certain subtle features perceptible only to insiders. In any case, there is a lot of complexity and heterogeneity in countries like India. Many people with different religions, castes, cultures, are ignorant about each other, even though they have been living side by side, but without effective contact, for generations. For example, until the advent to television, many Hindus and Muslims (especially women) in Punjab were ignorant about the domestic life in the rival community. They did not even know each other's kinship terms, until they recently happened to encounter each other on the television screen. In such a situation, even insiders are practically outsiders. Being nominally an insider does not close the doors for becoming a participant observer.

Fieldwork

In order to complete his work, the researcher need not extend his problem too far. Those days are gone when a researcher lived for years in another community in a far off island amidst deep seas in order to do in-depth and intensive study of an exotic community. These days, we select a few aspects for investigation. To start with the researcher formulates his problem. Some points are kept in mind at this juncture—the researcher's needs, his personal qualities, field of interest, available resources, suitability, and so on. What type of personal qualities are required? The researcher should be capable of establishing contact, creating rapport, and interacting with others. He should be good company. If he possesses these qualities, to begin with, he can afford to be ignorant and ask basic or naive questions Thus, he can clarify his doubts on all sorts of points.

How much rapport has to be established with the community under study? Just enough to gather the required data. Over-participation or going native hinders observation. The observer should not fall into the trap of allowing others to take undue advantage of him and make him act foolishly, jeopardising his relations with others. The aims and objectives of fieldwork have to be kept in view. Contact with the untouchables impairs interaction with the higher castes. However, the observer should not allow his contact man to decide whom he has to meet and whom he must avoid, or to observe this and bypass that. Sometimes when people watch the observer being busy apparently doing nothing but standing and watching, they are likely to think that he is an idler wasting his time and wasting the time of others as well. If they think so, they may not take him seriously when he asks them for some information. Such definitions of a situation have to be rectified in time.

Language can also become a problem here. Learning grammar does not mean that one has learnt the language. Different cultures have their own signs, symbols, and idioms. Words and actions used by them are clear only to them. The people being studied have to be understood within their own nets of pressures from their own community.

Perceptions are functionally selective. (Tulsi Das : *Jis ki rahi bhavna jaisi, prabhu moorat dekhi tin taisi*!) We observe what we want to observe. A researcher's social background, his interests, ideology, motivation, anxieties influence his findings. The observer is also a part of his field. His viewpoint can be distorted by his attitude, pleasant and bitter experiences, and even his genetic predispositions. Therefore, a researcher should be well-aware of his prejudices, ethics and compulsions. He has to learn to observe objectively.

A participant observer has to keep a balance between participation and observation in his field. Too much involvement with the subjects' definition of the situation comes in the way of a proper understanding of what is going on. A participant observer is like a lawyer. He is not very much concerned about whether his client wins or loses a case. He processes the case. He puts up effective arguments at the proper time. He has to keep proper distance from his subjects, neither more nor less. He does his job well.

Rapport

A researcher steps into his field carefully. Wrong moves in the beginning can upset his research subsequently. A letter from the head of the institution, recommendation from influential well-wishers can help him in pursuing his task. It is good to inform prominent persons, leaders, officers before entering the field as they often do not like somebody from outside to interfere in their domain and ask all sorts of questions from whomsoever they wish to. Observers can be suspected of being spies under the garb of researchers. They may also be suspected of poking their nose into the shady side of political and social affairs. In every society some areas are out of bounds for outsiders. It is necessary to obtain permission from competent authorities and power holders before entering there. It is better to approach influential persons first, either directly or through mutual well-wishers, and get their consent before proceeding with the fieldwork. Let them verify your antecedents. Answer their queries willingly. This assures them that the researcher is a decent person. A researcher's good conduct adds to the prestige of those who introduced him. Therefore, it is better to be careful. Starting one's work without caring for the influential people who matter may create difficulties later on. Clearance by a receptionist facilitates acceptance in the field. In the same way, before leaving the field, it is proper to bid farewell to all concerned.

While writing the research report, it is not common to reveal the real names of persons and places, for these may sometimes create unnecessary unpleasantness. The real names of persons and places are kept concealed by using pseudonyms. It is also important not to disclose your subjects' names and addresses indiscretely. These people may not like their privacy being infringed upon in this way.

The observer is a stranger in his field. His first day in his new setting is important. He must be polite and cheerful. He must refrain from frowning or shouting at people. Instead of antagonising others, he wins over their goodwill. He refrains from putting others to inconvenience. He greets those he comes across. He is willing to tell those who are interested as to who he is, where he has come from and what he is doing. He guards against creating apprehensions in their minds. He makes friends in the field. He tries not to antagonise anybody by talking ill of him, or to indulge in self-aggrandisement. His task is to create a *niche* for himself and prepare himself for observation. The subjects are tied to each other in networks of intertwined relations. They discuss among themselves about the newcomer. If he makes a bad impression in the beginning, it would be difficult for him to successfully complete his task. He has to establish good relations in his field. Therefore, it is incumbent upon him to keep his eyes and ears open and find out what the people say about him. If rumours are not nipped in the bud, they create difficulties later on.

Maintenance of goodwill and good relations with everybody, however insignificant, or at least being pleasant when others are present, facilitates fieldwork. One has to establish a favourable reputation in order to win over others. The observer places himself near them. He gains acquaintance with them. He inspects the social milieu. Then he can hope to gather useful information. Nobody will quickly come out with everything. The researcher thinks and feels like them. The course of social action is interpreted with empathic understanding. The researcher has to maintain a mildly friendly, open and sympathetic attitude towards the people he is observing. Appreciate. Grasp their position. Do not get converted to their confession. The researcher does not show off. He is a gentleman. He desists from creating problems for others by talking ill of them. He does not carry tales. He does not insult anybody. He meets people and discusses various aspects of his research problems with them. He is not in a hurry. He wins over some people. Approaches others through them. For this purpose, he has to be tactful. He activates his memory. Meeting others does not bore him. He keeps a pleasant and smiling face. Does not grumble. Makes use of his time. He keenly goes about collecting the required material without fuss. He does not accept anything that his subjects say without evaluating it critically. He arrives at a conclusion by keeping in mind who is telling the truth and who is lying and why. While it is important to establish good relations with others, it is equally important to be careful not to become so close to some people that it becomes difficult to distinguish between right and wrong. A participant observer must know his limits. He must not allow some subjects to monopolise his attention, lest others should be ignored.

Informers are useful for data collection. They belong to the locality. They know the people. Being natives, they know the language and the local idiom. Depending upon their state and disposition, they have to be kept satisfied with a modicum of money, gifts, or acknowledgement. It so happens that sometimes the researcher places so much reliance on his assistants that some others in the field get annoyed. Some informants try to amuse themselves by making him look foolish. Some may solicit undue gifts from him. Some may ask him to get their wards a job, or to speak to somebody on their behalf, irrespective of the merits of the case. This may invite annoyance from their rivals. A researcher has to be shrewd enough lest he should allow himself to be used by others for bringing their chestnuts out of the fire at his cost.

The researcher has to make arrangements to guard himself against crisis situations. He must know how to deal with persons and how to handle problems. Going through situations and facing problems makes the underlying structures transparent. Factionalism in the field makes it difficult to find out all the facts from various parties. Being seen in the company of the members from one faction makes it difficult to interact with their rivals and get information from them. In crisis situations, factional allegiances become visible. Dissatisfied opponents, dismissed employees, unfaithful concubines are ever ready to talk. But it is difficult to get out everything from opposing parties. Sometimes, instead of providing information, such people cleverly use the researcher as a source of information and get facts which should not have been divulged. A participant observer should not identify himself so obviously with one side that the others regard him as a spy. Thus, it would become difficult to enter into meaningful discussions with the other side. If a researcher can take on the role of an honest middleman between rival parties, he would be able to get reliable information from both the sides. Being over-friendly or familiar also makes it difficult to observe dispassionately. It is better to establish ties with a selected few to begin with, and then proceed to others through them. Some people will keep aloof from you. For winning them over, you will have to maintain a proper distance from others. It is incorrect to assume that those who keep away from you will not come to terms with you later on. Keep trying. Sooner or later they will also come round.

In order to get information from the subjects of one's research, it is useful to know why some persons are willing to oblige you, while others keep away. Why do some people respond? Because the researcher and the subject fulfil each other's needs. They would like it that the researcher gives some attention to them, and that he approaches them when he wants something. They like to talk to a visitor. Some people are lonely. When somebody comes and talks to them, they feel happy. Some are full of anger and complaints. They are always on the lookout for somebody who would listen to their tales of woe. Why do some people withhold their responses? They may be careless, sad, or suspicious. Sometimes they may have a skeleton to hide. They may be apprehensive that their secrets may be leaked out, or their privacy may be infringed upon, or the outsider might upset their apple cart.

A fieldworker is often on the horns of a dilemma. On the one hand, he is required to establish a modicum of rapport and build up friendly relations for collecting data through participant observation. On the other hand, over-rapport due to over-identification with the subjects in the field under observation leads to faulty perceptions. One has to guard oneself against malobservation and non-observation.

Data Collection

In participant observation, collection and analysis of data go on side by side. Relevant data are carefully collected from the field. Prolonged stay in the field makes it easy for the researcher to do so. Methodical participation in the social life of the people who are part of the study facilitates observation.

Participant observation is a taxing job. Access to the field, makeshift accommodation, unsatisfactory meals, distance from family and friends, danger of catching infections can be cause for a lot of discomfort. On the other hand, it provides good training. The researcher's disposition to work hard and to win friends becomes sharper. He becomes more tactful and learns how to get things done.

As already noted, in participant observation, data collection and analysis are not discrete stages. These go hand-in-hand. The researcher observes and verifies what is going on around him. The observed facts are used to derive general statements. He tests these generalisations by gathering additional data. Thus, the data and the generalisations are brought face-to-face in order to formulate acceptable hypotheses.

In order to observe, move around in the field, meet people, greet them, talk to them. Ask them about their health, welfare of their children, and other members of their family. Further, interact with them. Build up relations. Hang around and listen. Discern. Keep in mind their faces, behaviour, style. Ask them questions about what is in your own mind. Apply your mind to what they themselves have to say. Enter into dialogue with them. Clarify various points. Remember landmarks and corner-stones. You will be able to recall these memories later on when you need them. Eavesdropping can provide good information. But when it is found out, one may not be able to win over the trust and confidence of the persons concerned after that.

Keep a diary. This is like a science practical notebook. This makes it easy to record the facts of observation. Notes are made on various points before they fade out from the memory and get lost. Do not put off till tomorrow what you can record today. Make notes soon after you make the observation. If you are engrossed in something else in between, your attention will be diverted. Thus, essential details may be forgotten. But at the same time it is important to remember that entries in the diary are not to be made in the presence of others. This changes the situation. Write the diary when you are not participating or observing. Then you can concentrate fully on the task.

Standardisation of procedures for keeping the diary facilitates referring back to it. Write in permanent blue-black ink on one side of strong paper in such a way that the written material can be easily deciphered when needed. Do not use a lead pencil or a ball-point pen. These become illegible. For the time being, write only on the right side page of your notebook. Leave the left side page blank. You will need it later on at the time of classifying, abstracting and generalising the data. Protect your diary from rain, moisture, fungus, insects and inquisitive intruders. Keep it safely in a well-protected dry corner.

What is to be recorded in a diary? That depends upon the writer's theoretical orientation and methodological choices. Still, first of all make a map of your field. Mark important spots. Then take a census of the field. Write down the details in your diary. Collect material about the present and the past background. Gather relevant information from official records and published reports, wherever available. Where are their roots? How do they identify themselves in their social milieu? Verify the facts. Do not generalise on the basis of deviant cases alone. However, exceptions may prove to be the rule. Some respondents try to project their own image. They put you on the wrong track. They are amused by your discomfiture. Analyse their statements, apprehensions, hostilities and misdemeanour in the light of your theoretical background. Sit back with single-minded attention for, say, six hours, and write down what you have observed in one hour only. Put down the facts of the field on paper. Note down who said what, to whom and under what circumstances. Describe what you have heard, seen, smelt, tasted and touched. Thoughts, words, pose, symbols, are noted down. What did you ask? What did the subject say? If something appears to be significant, but you are at a loss to grasp it right now, note it down. You may be able to comprehend it later on in the light of additional information received subsequently. At the time of analysis, pages of the diary can be photo-copied. These are then cut, pasted, and arranged in various ways. Check up the veracity of different statements with each other. Extract the essential points. Look behind the adopted stances. Separate the wheat from the chaff, information from noise. Fill the gaps through extended fieldwork. Gather additional material on the same topic. Participant observers accumulate a lot of facts. In due course, these are tabulated, classified, reduced to a small space, and interpreted.

How long does a participant observer remain in his field? As long it takes to get proper insight into the matter under study. It is not advisable to spend less than eighteen months in the field. Often this activity takes 4 to 5 years. There is so much to observe. There is always so much to know. However, one has to call it a day some time and stop somewhere. Do not allow your work to become Hanuman's tail. Recall that Hanuman's tail remained intact even after the entire city of Lanka was burnt down. Many participant observers keep returning to their field again and again, whenever they get an opportunity to do so. This helps them to refine their old gencralisations, and to gain insights with respect to the ongoing changes.

Data Analysis

As mentioned earlier, data analysis is not to be postponed until data collection has already been completed, and the participant observer has left the field. These things are carried on side by side. The analysis starts when the observer is still in the field. On returning from there, facts gathered from various sources are put together. General statements are abstracted from them. Various statements are compared in order to draw conclusions.

Exceptions draw our attention towards rules and regulations. Thus, we can draw inferences about what is really general. Carefully look into what happens under various circumstances. Weigh the evidence. Make charts and tables. Classify. Organise facts. Identify the structures and flows. Compare them with the known patterns elsewhere at other times. Rectify what you have found out. There is a magical formula for all creative activity : CONCENTRATION.

Create order from chaos, clarity from confusion. Think out a framework. Fit the data into it without concealing some facts and unduly highlighting others. The framework is adjusted in order to accommodate the available data. This provides us suitable hypotheses.

Your attention please. Do not forget that our generalisations are constructed by meaningfully arranging the data. They are not armchair reflections or random thoughts on the subject matter. We construct our theories in the same way as we build a house. Arrange and rearrange the data, with an eye on the problem under investigation. Interpret them in the light of some sociological theory. Treat the data as building materials. Put together the bricks, sand, cement, stones, wood, pipes, etc., to construct a house in the light of the map prepared by the architect. Bring significant portions of the data under common names, or concepts. Arrange red threads from the concept together according to their relevant features. Tie up their ends in a novel and meaningful way. Display the concepts within a theoretical framework. Carefully connect them with logical considerations. Ensure that there is no mismatch. The quality of a researcher's training and experience sharpen his subjective judgement. He is able to set the relevant apart from the irrelevant. He knows how to put everything in its proper place. He can find unity in diversity.

Report Writing

In contrast to the survey method and the method of experiment, report writing is not the last stage in participant observation. This work goes on side by side while we are doing the fieldwork. The task involves constructing a theory with the data collected from the field. While writing a monograph, thesis or dissertation, the researcher writes down the story of various steps taken by him while beginning his research work, carrying it forward, and finishing it. The report has to suit the needs of its potential readers.

The report should be fluent. In contrast to the mainstream sociologists, social anthropologists are marked by a literary bent of mind. Each writer has his own way of writing—a distinct style and idiom. Instead of showing off, state everything clearly and to the point. Avoid big words. Do not maximise what you want to state. Describe the social environment. Show how far the field selected by you is typical of a milieu. What research tools did you use? What difficulties did you face in the field? Which data did you gather? How and why did you use various concepts, hypotheses and alternative explanations for your material? Elaborate. In the end, give a summary of the report. Draw the main inferences. Show their theoretical importance. Elaborate their implications for policy-making. Give suggestions for future researchers. Warn them about the possible pitfalls. Make a list of books and articles used by you in an alphabetical order. Wherever appropriate, present maps, charts, photographs, and tables. In other words, have something to say, and say it in the best manner you can.

Before finalising the research report, it is advisable to show it to a select group of the subjects of study. The report may have to be suitably modified as a result of the dialogue with them.

Ethics of Participant Observation

Things have to be done in a proper way. Certain norms have to be followed. Research work cannot be carried out too far without them. If a researcher indiscriminately writes down everything that he observes, this might injure the feelings of his subjects. Their names and addresses are not to be given to anybody without their explicit consent. The confidence reposed by them in the researcher has to be carefully guarded by not letting out their secret rituals, magical formulae, gadgets, and so on. Instead of reproducing names of persons and places, *pseudonyms* are used. Moreover, it is improper for a researcher to make false promises to his subjects for getting things done in the field if they co-operate with him. It is also unethical to conceal one's real identity from the subjects. If it is found out during the fieldwork, the project can be jeopardised. If it is found out later on, other researchers will suffer. Beware of unethical conduct.

Example 1: You are doing participant observation in a Hindu temple. Will you agitate if they do not allow SC/ST to go in there for worship? No, empirical research is value-free. Objectivity is different from desirability.

Example 2 : Theodor Adorno faced all-round criticism when violent rioters indulged in arson quoting his writings. He replied, "I had given a theoretical model. How did I know that some people would try to realise it with Molotov Cocktails?" What do you say?

Participant Observation and Social Surveys

Participant observation is often compared with social surveys. The survey method is the main method of sociological research. It is often used for finding out the magnitude of variables and ascertaining their mutual relationships. It is useful in selecting one out of several alternative hypotheses. Data gathered through a social survey are amenable to the application of statistical tests. As against this, the participant observation method is used by a capable researcher, who remains in the field for a prolonged period of time. Surveys are done by teams. Trained research assistants wander from pillar to post and administer an interview schedule to a representative sample of the population. Postal or telephone surveys are also possible. In such methods, the relationship between the interviewer and the interviewee is superficial and standardised. One cannot go deep and probe at great length. But the participant observer is a well-trained person who has to spend a lot of time in the field, and collect his data personally after winning over the trust and confidence of his subjects. He obtains deep insight by penetrating deep down into the minds of the people under observation. In fact, both these techniques are complementary. Participant observation is used for ascertaining the different variables in the situation, their shape, and their relative position. The variables so identified are utilised for constructing a questionnaire and conducting a survey. After ascertaining the magnitude of the variables and the exact relationships between them in this way, we can go ahead and perform experiments. These enable us to pinpoint cause and effect relationships. In this way, participant observation, surveys and experiments represent three different stages of social research. The former prepares the ground for the latter, and the latter for the last one.

Conclusions

Participant observation is an important method of social anthropological research. It is used for identifying the relevant variables and their constellations. The field for this type of research work has to be carefully selected. Establishing rapport is a key to its success. Data collection, analysis and report writing are not discrete stages. These activities go on side by side. We meaningfully arrange our data and construct hypotheses. Unethical conduct is harmful not only for an individual investigator but also for his successors. Participant observation clears the way for survey research.

REFERENCES

Beteille, Andre and T.N. Madan (eds.), *Encounter and Experience: Personal Accounts of Fieldwork*, Vikas Publishing House, Delhi, 1975.

Bogdan, Robert J. and Stephen J. Taylor, *Introduction to Qualitative Research Methods*, John Wiley & Sons, New York, 1975.

Srinivas, M.N., A.M. Shah and E.A. Ramaswamy (eds.), *The Fieldworker and His Field: Problems and Challenges in Sociological Investigation*, Oxford University Press, New Delhi, 1979.

6

Interviews and Questionnaires

INTERVIEWING

An interview is a formal meeting for gathering the required information. It is common to interview candidates for jobs. Big men grant interviews to complainants and solicitors. Social surveyors interview representative samples of the population for collecting data about society and social change. Increasing democratisation and rationalisation of social life have made it necessary to consult the persons concerned before making decisions. It is becoming necessary for policy makers to give the people a voice in making decisions by ascertaining public opinion beforehand.

Social surveyors follow standardised interview procedures. Let us try to understand what standardised interviewing is, by distinguishing it from what it is not.

(a) Soft Interviewing

Standardised interviewing is different from soft interviewing. Here the interviewer shows the direction in a vague sort of way. Thus, he listens attentively. The interviewee tells us whatever he wants to say.

Soft interviewing is often done by psychoanalysts. The doctor expresses sympathy with the patient. He speaks gently to him. He befriends the patient. He wins his trust and confidence. He gains his willing co-operation. The patient rests on a couch. He slowly relates his difficulties. He tells the healer about himself, his routine, his self-image, his apprehensions, and so on. He recalls his childhood experiences. The analyst listens to him sympathetically. He gathers the required data. He fits them into his theoretical framework. Where there are gaps, he patiently looks for additional data. He uses his theoretical repertoire to connect the symptoms with their causes. The patient is made aware of the causal connections. He is made conscious of his aspirations, apprehensions, weak and strong points. Psychoanalysts ask their patients to solve their problems by confronting, adjusting with, escaping from or otherwise coming to terms or effectively dealing with their problems.

In order to construct their theories, ethnologists observe the deeds and artifacts of preliterate cultures. They ask them a variety of questions formulated on the spot about how they perceive themselves. They carefully listen to what the latter have to say. They patiently find out how the people under observation interpret their symbols, beliefs, actions and artifacts. Ethnologists try to gain a fair idea of their social and cultural patterns with due regard to their nets of meaningful understanding.

Soft interviews are time-consuming. They are costly too. In this type of interviewing, the interviewers and interviewees have to depend too much on each other. The interviewer shows the way and then listens attentively. The interviewee himself says what he has to tell.

(b) Stress Interviewing

Standardised interviews are different from soft interviews as well as stress interviews. Here the interviewer takes up an active role. He insists upon knowing the whole truth. This method is often used by the security services for interrogation of suspects. The armed forces use it for getting intelligence from enemy agents. In order to get information from the enemy's spies, the interviewer inflicts pain on the interviewee. He insists upon knowing how everything went on. The suspect is locked up and pressurised to come out with the whole truth. He is asked question after question, without waiting for answers. His total impression, countenance, manner, words, tone of voice, language of the eyes, are observed carefully. He is asked to come out with what he has to say. The interviewer gets at his mind. This puts him under stress. He is cursed, cajoled, asked to defend himself, giving facts. The information given by him is closely examined with a view to identifying gaps and contradictions in the narration. Some questions are asked recklessly, without any purpose.

In the beginning, the interviewers ask questions about what, when, with whom, how long, etc. They frighten, bully, ridicule the suspect in their own way. They insult, abuse, belittle, provoke. When his face shows that he feels hurt, or he is telling a lie, the interviewer threatens him with dire consequences. Two interrogators may take on complementary role. One of them torments the suspect. The other poses as if he is his well-wisher. One of them applies pressure. The other one promises relief.

One of them terrorises. The other placates the suspect. The objective of such sustained interrogation is to get out the whole truth somehow or the other. Permissible degrees of physical and mental violence are used. The victim is forcibly given medicines. The aim is to bring the suspect under control somehow. The interrogating officer tries to find out with whom the suspect shares his joys, gifts and secrets. The clues are followed up. His links are traced, strict vigil is kept. For collecting clinching evidence, the suspect's hide-outs are raided. Sensitive and incriminating documents are traced out. Addresses in diaries are followed up. Suspected accomplices are nabbed and interrogated. Various statements are compared and contrasted in search of causes to solve the mystery. Two and two are added to make four. The reconstructed story is narrated before the suspect. The lacunae are removed. His statement may be recorded. His signatures are obtained thereon for further necessary action.

The investigating agencies may even adopt the form of organisation of the groups under investigation in order to be able to reach them more effectively under assumed names and roles. They may pose to be a smugglers' den, or a terrorist outfit, or human rights activities with a view to eliciting the latter's spontaneous co-operation.

It cannot be ruled out that in this type of interviewing the applied stress crosses the limit of tolerance. This may distort the personality of the interviewee as well as the interviewer. Both of them may suffer from trauma. The consequences can be grave. This can fill the subject's mind with hatred against the interviewer. In trying to contain himself, the victim may become deaf and dumb. His emotions and intellect may be blunted. He can become hyper-suspicious, sensitive, a loner forever afterwards. He may lose confidence in the legitimacy of social norms. His personality may become dehinged. Besides getting a screw loosened here and another one there, he may never again be able to demobilise his nerves and suffer from a nervous breakdown. He can become a nervous wreck for the rest of his life. He may suffer from psychosis. He may be maimed, or suffer from brain stroke. Those who have nothing to say are the worst sufferers of stress interviewing. The interviewers themselves may become rigid, curt, irritable, querulous, fanatic, eccentric, sadistic, tyrannical, and so on. The fear of retaliation by their victims can drive them mad.

Torture techniques include stress positions, sensory deprivation and sexual humiliation. These are unbearable, degrading and demoralising for the interviewer as well as the interviewee. A well-organised society is based on restitutive rather than retributive law. The use of stress is, therefore, not allowed to transgress certain limits. Transparency of procedures ensures that these limits are not crossed. The investigators are duly trained in logic and scientific methods of investigation as well as human rights. In any case, stress interviewing is not a suitable method of social research.

(c) Standardised Interviewing

In contrast to the two types of interviewing methods given above, open dialogue is not permitted in standardised interviews. The respondents are neither pampered, nor threatened. The neutral impersonal interviewer maintains a proper distance from the person being interviewed. He establishes detached formal relations with the respondents. This is done with a view to obtaining the desired information from them. He carefully listens to whatever his respondents have to say. He agrees with a light nod, irrespective of the content of the latter's statements. Strong agreement or disagreement with them is not permitted. All the respondents are asked the same questions in the same sequence and the same tone. Once an interview schedule has been duly approved, it cannot be changed midway. On-the-spot clarifications and unapproved examples are not allowed.

Standardised interviewing enables us to collect data from a representative sample of the respondents in such a way that their answers can be tabulated together. Quantification facilitates statistical applications. The data become comparable. The conclusions become precise. They have a known degree of certainty. Standardised interviews are conducted with individuals. They may be interviewed one by one or in groups.

Non-standardised interviewing yields inaccurate results. Even when they act in self-interest, people may claim that they are altruistic. They may not reveal the whole truth. They may try to impress or please the interviewer. They assess what they want to hear, and say the same. It cannot be denied that often there are gaps in what people think, say and do in various situations at different times and places. Even when they are motivated by self-interest, respondents claim that they are motivated by altruism, or a certain ideology. For instance, in a study on top managers, the respondents mentioned intelligence, hard work, initiative, higher educational qualifications from prestigious institutions as their strong points. They failed to mention their political links, wealthy family background, or available opportunities. Genuineness or otherwise of the claims made by the respondents remains to be tested. However, in a large-scale sample survey, bias on the left and right hands cancels itself. Non-standardised interviewing yields inaccurate results. In spite of this defect, surveying with standardised instruments is the most important method of empirical sociological research. A lot of empty operations of the law enforcing agencies can be avoided by understanding the ongoing trends, through routine social surveys. Individuals cannot be held responsible for each and everything.

Interviewers

(a) Qualities

A large number of respondents has to be covered in a social survey. There are so many things to be done that it is hard for a single researcher without assistants to handle everything. Surveys are done by teams. Interview schedules were filled in by a large number of interviewers. Experienced researchers are aware that different interviewers may elicit different responses from the same interviewee. Due care has to be taken to standardised the responses. Some personal qualities are often believed to promote proper role performance by interviewers—balanced, capable of establishing contacts, careful, clever, disciplined, enjoy meeting people, flexible, hardworking, intelligent, neutral, pedantic, obedient, skillful, straight-forward, systematic, tactful, tolerant, and other similar qualities. Undesirable qualities include—inferiority complex, irritability, nervousness, partiality, prejudice, self-praise, shyness, strong views and so on. The interviewer's dress, gestures, manners, style, tactics, tone do affect his interaction with the interviewees. His age, caste, class, community, cultural attainments, gender, religion, skin colour can promote or hinder his ability to interact with others. If a high-caste interviewer considers it beneath his dignity to meet low-caste respondents, he will not be able to perform his task effectively. Status inconsistency between interviewers and respondents in terms of age, class, gender, etc., can distort communication. Middle class, upper caste female interviewers find it hard to get proper replies from lower class, lower caste rural male interviewees. It is helpful to match the relevant characteristics of the interviewers and interviewees. An interviewer should be like those whom he interviews. Sons of the soil are needed for this job, subject to the condition that they also possess the required skills and values, and enjoy doing their duty with heart and soul.

On the other hand, there is no doubt about it that inspite of widespread unemployment, ideal interviewers are seldom available. Some good qualities for one survey may become undesirable attributes for another investigation. Special studies will have to be carried out by interviewers with compatible qualities. But such jobs are rare and should not be permanent. After some time, interviewer fatigue sets in and makes the performance of routine tasks boring. In actual practice, we have to recruit all sorts of interviewers—retired teachers, housewives, fresh graduates, etc., on an ad hoc basis. Often, they are not paid anything for their work. They are either friends and well-wishers of the researcher, members of voluntary organisations, or students who want to oblige their teachers or fulfil the conditions laid down for clearing their examinations.

(b) Recruitment

The politics of scarcity is rampant in countries with a shortage of organisational talent and skill for swift command and control. Jobs are not available for everybody. These are grabbed by those with proper connections at the proper place and at the proper time. The productivity of the research team suffers because of their presence. Soft work culture hinders the effectiveness of research teams. They cannot submit a worthwhile research report to the sponsors in time. Therefore, we have to be very careful at the time of recruitment. Once they have joined duty, their jobs are protected by legislation and the local power groups. It becomes impossible to get rid of them.

It is useful to associate local talent with the work of doing social surveys. Those who were born or brought up in the field area of the research project or reside there are, therefore, well-conversant with the area, possess insight into the culture, lifestyle, motives and needs of the region. They know how to get things done. However, they may have their own vested interests in the locality. They nurse their friendships and animosities there. If the interviewers are interested more in the outcome and less in the reliability and validity of their findings, a partisan survey is the result. This gives distorted results.

It is necessary for the successful completion of an assignment that the supervisors of the project should have a say in recruiting the right man for the job. For example, a traditional woman who needs escort for visiting the field is not suitable for this purpose.

Allow the interviewers flexibility in doing their job. Let them do things at their own pace. It is far better to pay them at piece rates rather than fixed salaries. While calculating piece rates, take into account the time needed for going to the field, identifying and locating the respondents, establishing rapport with them, and interviewing them, as well as office work. Include the transportation costs in the piece rates. Pay one and a half to three times the normal rates for covering far off places and interviewing difficult respondents. Do not make advance payments which are not likely to be recovered.

While on the one hand employees with secure jobs tend to shirk work, on the other hand, ad hoc employees are inadequately committed to their work. They are on the lookout for a regular job, and leave as soon they get one. It is imperative that we provide for dropouts at the beginning. Have a long waiting list. Recruit and train more hands than required. Those who want to build up a team ought to recognise such realities beforehand.

(c) Training

We have to train the interviewers for asking standardised questions, and recording the answers clearly and legibly. In the beginning, lectures, reading material and clarifications are useful. Provide the interviewers the opportunity to interact with one another. Let them conduct some dummy interviews under the supervision of experienced interviewers. Then ask them to interact with one another. Point out their mistakes, in a friendly manner. Tell them in detail what they actually have to do, the aims and objectives of the research project, and its significance in the broader perspective. The trainers also pass on the research folklore to the trainees. They encourage them to feel committed to their work. Too much mobility hinders the successful completion of the project. Keep an eye on good workers. Try to have them absorbed on a permanent basis wherever feasible.

It may be pointed out that such training is useful for beginners. Later on experience becomes more important. Those who do not fit in will either drop out, or will be dropped out.

(d) Rapport

Interviewers from universities and private research institutions have to persuade the interviewees to cooperate with them. They cannot be compelled to do so. Refusal to cooperate with the census authorities in a country like India and Pakistan is a legally punishable offence. The interviewers have the right to get information from their respondents. The former do not have to seek a favour from the latter. As against this, ordinary researchers have to establish rapport with their respondents in order to win over their trust and confidence. How does one go about it?

Contact the locally important persons such as officials, leaders, and other relevant people. Reveal your identity. Show them the letter from the director of the survey centre to which you belong. Explain to them the nature and scope of your study. Secure their consent before starting your work. Make it clear to them that you are not from a taxation office or an intelligence bureau.

Start from the apex of the social hierarchy. Gradually move down. Send the interviewees advance information about your visit. This may often be done by post. The introductory letter should state the broad objectives of the research project, institutional affiliation, sponsor, and above all the approximate date and time for the proposed interview. Meet the interviewees at their convenience—Their residence or workplace, tea stalls, common places, street corners, etc. You may have to make repeated visits in order to locate the interviewees and for questioning.

There is no standard procedure for establishing rapport. Set at rest their mistrust. Win them over. If they ask you, clarify how somebody's name was included in the sample, while someone else's was excluded. You may have to explain to them the sampling procedure in order to bring them round, lest they should adversely influence others, you may have to conduct fake interviews with them. Keep a few extra blank forms with you for this purpose. When required, assure the respondents that the data will be presented in such a way that the identity of the individual respondents will not be revealed. If some of them have no confidence in the promised confidentiality, they will be reticent. Avoid writing names, addresses, or other identification marks on the interview schedules. Some interviewees will ask for a copy of the research report. Do not make false promises that you have no means of fulfilling. Try to send them something appropriate in due course. Be happy to meet the respondents. Create a congenial atmosphere. Be willing to note down what they want to say. Control yourself. Do not ridicule them or talk unnecessarily. Do not compete with your respondents for a higher status in their field. Do not make the task of future researchers difficult by making false promises to the respondents if they answer your questions. Concentrate on gathering your data from the field. After finishing your work, thank them.

The most important point is that the relationship between the interviewers and the interviewees has to be standardised.

Interviewees

There are many reasons why the respondents are not always willing to be interviewed. It is possible that they are suspicious about the interviewers' intentions. They might be visualising him as some sort of inspector, whose report may somehow harm their interests. Some people are so busy in their own affairs that they do not have the time to attend to strangers. Some respondents may be worried about the infringement of their privacy and misuse of data. Mutual mistrust and non-cooperation are marked characteristics of some social milieus. Some keep away because of their alienation, distress, etc. Some are tired of visiting salesmen in the garb of researchers.

Why do respondents cooperate with the interviewer? There are a number of reasons for that. They may associate the study with census operations. People are used to the decennial census. They feel it is their duty to provide the required information. Some respondents may also cooperate out of courtesy or curiosity or fear. Some of them take pity on the interviewer and want to do him a favour. Some people feel lonely. They are glad to receive visitors who want to listen to them and help them out of their boredom. The credibility and prestige of a reputed sponsor or researcher is also helpful. If previous surveys have been followed up by somebody with improvements—loans, sanitation facilities, provisions, etc.—then some people cooperate in the vague hope of a repeat performance An interviewer can also appeal to a respondent's altruism, feelings, or wisdom. Try to win over their trust and confidence without promising them more than you can deliver. Some firms send free gifts like calendars, ball-point pens, diaries, soaps, etc., for the respondents. In some countries, it is common to make payments to respondents for this purpose.

Interview Situation

There are innumerable reasons for the interviewees wanting to conceal from others, and even from themselves, their shortcomings. For instance, income. Respondents hide their income from illegal sources, or the income which they have concealed from the tax authorities. Irregular income from gifts, inheritance, even agriculture, cannot always be recalled or translated in terms of money. Other respondents boast about their being better off and having a higher income than they actually earn, with a view to impressing others. A standardised interview situation is not appropriate for the purpose of collecting reliable data on income.

The interviewer is at the mercy of the respondents. The latter may be careless. They may not like to get involved in an unnecessary controversy. They may put off the interviewer. They may give a quick reply without grasping the matter, and go away. They may reply in terms of what should be rather than what is. Instead of applying their own minds, they may reiterate the official statements published in newspapers and appearing on the television. Not only the researcher, even the interviewees may mould their statements in terms of what they believe the sponsor wants to hear. This results in *sponsorship bias*. The answers often differ according to whether the research project has been sponsored by the World Bank, Bureau of Public Enterprises, or the Tata House. The important point to remember is that the precision of the analysis is affected by the quality of data obtained from the respondents.

Table 1
Why do they get interviewed?

Unwillingness	*Willingness*
Alienation	Altruism
Lack of time	Curiosity
Privacy	Habit
Mistrust	Loneliness
Tired of salesmen	Prestige
	Cash

(a) Presence of Others

The responses obtained by interviewers are affected not only by their own social background, personality characteristics, hopes and apprehensions, but also by the interview situation. The situation includes season, (harvesting, examinations), place (home, office, *dhaba*, street corner), time (weekend, holiday), state of mind, presence of others, and so on. The interviewees may respond in one way at their place of work, and in another way at home. It is difficult to talk to students at the time of their examination, farmers at harvest time, Muslims during Roza fasts in the month of Ramzan, and accountants at the close of the financial year.

Interviewers find it cumbersome to move about in rural areas during the hot and humid rainy days, especially when the pathways are flooded.

Again, avoid the presence of a third person at the time of the interview. The interviewee has to desist from annoying the respondent, or unnecessarily pleasing him by going out of the way. Such behaviour impairs impersonality and endangers validity. However, very often one cannot do anything about the presence of a third person, but to tolerate him. He cannot always be requested to leave. Such situations cannot be avoided. In some cultures, only intrigues are carried on behind a curtain, or inside closed doors. Ordinarily, such people are expected to act as silent listeners, or as addressees, or catalytic agents of communication. The presence of little children or other members of the family (spouse, mother-in-law), friends and neighbours can change the situation as well as the nature of response, depending on the problem being studied. School children are likely to give one answer in the presence of their teachers, and another when the teacher is not around. Often, we can do nothing about the presence of others at the time of the interview. It is embarrassing to ask for privacy, in countries like India.

When a third person is present at the time of interviewing the respondents, this becomes a source of bias. The interviewees may become reticent, or play to the gallery. Some of them may discretely keep quiet on some points, or act subserviently, for fear of annoying the higher-ups. Others may respond aggressively, in order to brag before those below or to cow them down. A third person might also intrude with what he thinks is the right answer to a question. Even when such persons do not intervene directly, they exercise indirect influence. The effects are more pronounced in some items than in others, and in case of some social segments than others.

In order to deal with this problem, the interviewers have to politely and tactfully check third party intervention. After getting interviewed, the interviewees may exchange their views with others. Thus, those who are being interviewed later on have the opportunity to meditate over what they have to say. This impairs standardisation. Therefore, those who are interviewed have to be requested not to tell others what questions were asked. This hardly works. Some of them do not act upon this advice. This way, standardised interviewing is helpful in taking care of such variations, especially in smoothening them out, because the interviewers move elsewhere soon. It is, therefore, imperative that we do not prolong our work in a locality.

(b) Interviewing per se

Give 25 per cent more copies of the interview schedules to the interviewers than the number of respondents allotted to them. Some of them may be spoilt or lost. Give them the list of names and addresses of the persons to be interviewed. Tell them how to find out replacements, in case the original persons are not available. Allot work to the interviewers within a limited area, lest they should be put to inconvenience in moving from one place to another. This will also save the project some money on account of travelling allowance. Instruct them to meet the people when they are available. In underdeveloped countries, maps are seldom available. Few are adept at handling them. One has to seek the help of the local residents like shopkeepers, postmen, watchmen, etc., for this purpose. Participant observers prepare their own maps. Surveyors have to make use of maps prepared by others, because they deal with wider areas.

Often, the heads of households have to be asked questions. In India, it is usually the oldest male member of the family. For this purpose, a household is defined as related persons sharing the same roof and taking their meals from a common kitchen. If this is not done, the interviewees have to fulfil certain specified criteria, like being inmates of a college hostel, newly married couples in a locality, etc., depending upon the need of the topic under study.

(c) Asking Questions

Before asking questions, the interviewer should have a grasp of the problem himself. Wandering here and there from the prescribed sequence is not permissible. The questions are to be read before the interviewees, not spoken. These are to be asked in a relaxed tone, without any tension. On-the-spot formulations are not allowed in case of interview schedules. The interviewers are expected to patiently ask their respondents each question. They are not expected to be in a hurry to be done with it.

The interviewer has to maintain a lightly sympathical stance through expression, gestures, feelings. Neither intense sympathy nor antipathy are permissible. He should be instructed neither to be callous nor zealous. He should not prompt the answers to the respondents. The interviewee must say what he wants to say and not what the interviewer wants him to say. Do not suggest any answers. Write down what the interviewee has to say. The interviewer should not be impatient while asking questions and getting answers. He is not expected to get overawed by a respondent's high status, or take pity on a poor interviewee.

(d) Getting Answers

Indicate light agreement with whatever the interviewer has to say. Say 'yes', 'fair enough', 'okay', etc. Go on noting down the responses as they are given. When appropriate, ask what, who, where, when, how, which, whom, etc. Apply your mind. For instance, if a respondent says that he is a government servant, this is not his occupation. Probe and find out a narrower category like office superintendent, plumber, policeman, tehsildar, etc., whichever is applicable to him. Be careful to maintain rapport.

(e) Perception

Perception is functionally selective. It may distort the replies obtained by an interviewer according to his vision and prejudices. He selects that from his respondent's reply which he believes is relevant. His wishful thinking and apprehensions and training do influence such a selection. He may ignore important aspects, defining them as irrelevant. His attitude, ambitions, experiences, ideas can reduce reliability. He can unwittingly suggest certain answers as proper. Lack of interest, deficient training, and inattentiveness can bias the answers.

(f) Probing

Request, purposeful listening, asking for more are useful for eliciting responses. In order to get a complete reply, the questioner has to clarify the exact response. This would ensure that the answer is to the point and relevant. Even simple facts like age and education can be off the mark.

How do we look at the replies carefully? Ask questions. Listen. Wait attentively in expectation. Give reasonable time for response. Find out what exactly he wants to say. Encourage shy persons to speak out. If necessary request them to speak clearly and a bit loudly. Repeat your question without changing the wording, maintaining a standard tone. Say 'pardon' or 'excuse me' if necessary. Note down the answer. Ask supplementary questions. Request him, if necessary, to repeat. Unless it is a word association test, give him time to think and refine his reply. If somebody gets irritated, give him time to compose himself. Wait with a light smile. Do not go on talking unnecessarily. Probing brings out clear answers. Overdoing is counterproductive.

(g) Recording

There are elaborate recording procedures for participant observation. This task is simple in case of surveys. The interviewer should make use of a hard board with a clamp, like the one used by school children at the time of their examinations. Listen attentively. Let the respondent say what he wants to say before you fill in the relevant response category. Record his reply to an open-ended statement in his own words. Do not summarise it in your language. However, long statements are difficult to code later on. If the respondent speaks fast, go on reading what you write down. He will soon keep pace with you. Try not to lag behind the speaker.

Unless you are using a recording device or know shorthand, it may be necessary to use abbreviations. However, do not use abbreviations which you cannot decipher later on. Do not leave some columns blank. Note down clearly whether it is a case of 'not applicable', 'no response', or 'don't know'. Go through the entire form after filling it. Make the illegible legible. Fill in missing data. Look for inconsistencies. Reconcile, where necessary. If some columns are to be filled in on the basis of an interviewer's own observations, perform this task too after careful inspection.

Use of recording devices is not without problems. They are costly and cumbersome. They make noise, interrupt, break down, and require a lot of time for transcribing. They make the respondent apprehensive. Do not use them without the respondent's permission.

(h) Cheating

Sometimes it so happens that instead of taking the trouble of going to the field and asking the right people, an interviewer sits at home or elsewhere. He himself fills in some or all the columns in the interview schedule in fictitious dialogues with the respondents, from imagination. Sometimes he asks a few questions on the social background of the respondents on phone, or otherwise, and fabricates the answers on attitudes himself. He may project his own attitudes on to the respondents. He may fill in the blanks on the basis of what he thinks is typical of such persons. It is possible to guess in a vague sort of way the attitude and behaviour of others in various social situations, on the basis of their key characteristics. However, there would have been no need for taking all the trouble of doing a survey with a representative sample of the population, if it could be safely assumed that the right responses are already known to wise men. If such practices are not checked in time, they can jeopardise the reliability and validity of the entire survey. The poor quality of the collected data yields erroneous results. This may lead to wrong policy choices by decision makers for whom the survey has been conducted. A researcher has to carefully guard his study against cheating. In order to avoid this, the interviewers have to be recruited on the basis of merit, and not merely on the basis of somebody's recommendation. Proper recruitment has to be followed up with proper training. One can also appeal to their fear of God, or their honour. Effective sanctions have to be applied. Reply paid post-cards can be sent to the interviewers to get feedback from them. Some of those who are accessible by telephone can be approached in order to check up the veracity of what the interviewers have done. We can get a part (say 2 per cent) of the interviews conducted twice by different interviewers, using *interpenetrating samples*. The research supervisor has to keep his eyes and ears open. Occasional spot inspections are useful. Defaulters have to be effectively dealt with. Let us not forget that nobody can be punished without providing him adequate opportunity to explain why action should not be taken against him for dereliction of duty. In India, it is almost impossible to hire and fire employees in a summary sort of way. Job security is guaranteed. Moreover, the researcher should not expect too much from the interviewers. He must organise his own work properly. Take care of their convenience. Do not allot them elements from the sample in far-flung areas without giving them extra incentives. If they are heavily loaded with a lot of unnecessary work, they may find an outlet for themselves by cheating. Avoid overwork as well as undue hurry. Soft work culture prevalent in a setting causes *goal displacement*. It hinders the effectiveness of a research team.

Apart from some interviewers, some interviewees may also indulge in cheating as a matter of habit or to befool others. Even some researchers have been found guilty of using fictitious data. These things cannot carry any discipline or its practitioners too far.

Do not expect too much from lotus eaters. Research work is bound to remain underdeveloped in those settings where everybody wants everybody else to be honest and efficient. Management of survey teams is problematic. The junior level staff is often inadequately motivated. The senior level staff do not have direct contact with the interviewees. This makes their analysis bookish and unrealistic.

(i) Finish

While on the one hand it is not advisable to abruptly leave the respondent, on the other hand it is not proper to keep sitting with him unnecessarily.

Social life is intolerable and impossible without good manners. Before leaving the respondent thank him for his cooperation. We must learn to say 'please' before getting something, and 'thank you' after getting it.

(i) Data Processing and Analysis

The data collected with the questionnaires and similar tools are duly coded, processed and analysed. These steps are being dealt with in another chapter of this book. The purpose is to submit a report to the sponsors. This would help them to decide among varying alternative policies. The findings may be widely circulated through press notes, articles, books, etc. Afterwards, the data may be deposited in a data bank, for eventual secondary analysis.

Thus, to conclude, Democratisation has made it necessary to give people a voice in making policies that affect their fate. Public opinion research is becoming common. Data for social surveys are collected with questionnaires and similar tools. While constructing such an instrument, a researcher has to take due precautions for properly wording his questions and putting them in an orderly sequence. He uses standard procedures for interviewing the respondents. His questions have to be precise, unambiguous, directed, and free of any bias. They have to be placed in a proper frame of reference. The researcher has to take sufficient care in recruiting and training to establish rapport with a representative sample of members of a universe, and to get the required data from them. Data are processed and analysed in such a way that the given hypothesis can be adequately tested for formulating theories. In this way, social surveys are used to build up a body of the required knowledge.

Survey is team work. This is too much for individuals. In western countries, research entrepreneurs are setting up many more business firms for carrying on sponsored programmes for marketing research, public opinion polls and electoral research on behalf of the political parties. Even individual scholars have started getting their data sets prepared by such commercial undertakings. This makes them free to devote their attention to designing their studies, preparing their tools, and writing the research reports.

QUESTIONNAIRE

Recent advancements in the methods of data processing and analysis have facilitated the task of drawing precise conclusions from survey data. However, techniques of wording questions for interview schedules and interviewing the respondents have lagged behind statistical advancement. This reduces the reliability and validity of the conclusions drawn from survey data. It is, therefore, imperative that we exercise proper care while constructing our questionnaires, and interviewing our respondents. A researcher has to acquire the necessary skills before launching a survey.

Types of Questionnaires

Psychologists often make use of readymade question inventories prepared by subject-matter specialists. Sociologists prepare their own questionnaires for generating the required data. Thus, the questions can be creatively adjusted to the local situation. This removes one source of bias, since instruments of research do influence the outcome. What is a questionnaire? How is it constructed? Questionnaires and interview schedules are forms. They are somewhat different from each other. They contain questions to which we need answers from the persons concerned.

A questionnaire is distributed by post, through internet, or even personally. The respondent fills up the questionnaire himself, just like an application form for getting a bank loan or a passport. Like crossword puzzles, questionnaires may be printed in newspapers or magazines. The readers are asked to fill up and return the same. Some of them are given prizes through lottery, etc. On the other hand, an interview schedule is personally filled in by an interviewer while actually interviewing the respondent concerned in a face-to-face situation. Here the questions are more adequately formulated than in an interview guide. The latter includes some partially formulated questions or even points on which information is required. In contrast to a questionnaire, an interview guide provides flexibility in wording and sequencing various questions. A face-to-face interview also permits greater probing. In which field of research do we use questionnaires? Demoscopy, electoral research, public opinion research, psephology, social surveys and sociology.

Use of questionnaires is advantageous in a number of ways. It saves manpower, time and money on data collection. Establishment costs on account of salaries or piecerate wages are lower. Travelling allowance for data collection tends to be high if interviewers are employed. The respondents are free to fill in a questionnaire with well thought-out answers whenever they can spare some time for the purpose. As they are expected to fill in the information themselves, without any assistance from anybody else, this method eliminates eventual distortion on account of the influence of the interviewer. The respondents are free to write what they want. Therefore, anonymity is guaranteed. There is no doubt about it that the questionnaire method suffers from a number of disadvantages. Questionnaires have to be very carefully worded. They should not be ambiguous, because the interviewer is not there to give clarifications. For the same reason, the response rate is low. An interviewer is not there to establish rapport with the respondent. Most addressees do not care to send a reply. A questionnaire cannot be filled in by an illiterate person. The respondents may not necessarily follow the standardised sequence while filling in their replies, because there is nobody to check them. Since they can write the answers whenever they can find the time, their answers are not always spontaneous. Some persons hastily scribble in illegible handwriting, or give irrelevant answers, or leave some items blank. Some of them may even pass on their questionnaires to a subordinate in the office, or another member of their family to fill in the replies on their behalf. The rate of response is low. Thus, the sample becomes unrepresentative. If somebody is interested in the outcome of an opinion poll (say, on the relative popularity of film actors), he may get hold of a large bundle of the questionnaires, fill in the entire lot all by himself, and then pass them on for counting of votes. Thus, something like booth capturing or *Jhumritallaya* effect (commercialisation of fake polls) is possible.

A number of steps can be taken to increase the rate of proper response. It is higher if the questions are of interest to the respondents. Write an appropriate covering letter. Add a letter of recommendation from some opinion leader. Personalised hand-written or single typed separate letters evoke a better response than printed or cyclostyled circulars. Instead of business reply cards, envelopes with stamped or handwritten addresses are more effective. When despatching a questionnaire do not forget to enclose a copy of instructions on how to fill in the questionnaire. Remind the addressee to go through the questionnaire and ensure that all the items have been duly answered. Request him to return the questionnaire without delay to a given address. Do not forget to thank him for his co-operation. To increase the rate of response, the questionnaire is sent in twice. The recipients are requested to ignore the second copy of the questionnaire in case they have already filled in and returned the first one. A third copy can also be posted if necessary. As a matter of fact, a questionnaire is less useful than an interview schedule. Since the interviewer is present while filling in the interview schedule, he can establish close rapport and persuade the respondent to answer the questions seriously. Questionnaires can be safely used when the response rate does not matter. This is so when the population is homogeneous. In case the respondents are willing to co-operate, the questions can even be asked on telephone.

Interviewing on telephone is becoming common in Europe and North America. In that part of the world, nine-tenths of the households possess their own telephones. This method cannot be used in countries where most people do not have telephones, or where the telephones are out of order most of the time, or the lines are always engaged. In any country, some segments of the population do not own telephones. Younger people with lower income and education, and dwellers in rural areas, are less likely to have a telephone. Some owners do not like their names being entered in telephone directories. Moreover, the interviewer and interviewee can only hear, not see, each other. They cannot be very sure about who they are. In addition, they cannot be shown figures, cards, or scales. Many respondents hang up the receiver before completing a task. All these limit the reliability and validity of telephone surveys. In spite of the disadvantage of teleinterviewing, more and more surveys are being done by this method.

In computer-assisted telephone interviewing, the apparatuses can be connected with tape recorders. The data received from the interviewees can even be directly processed and printed out, without the intervention of trained manpower.

In group interviewing, many respondents are interviewed at the same time. However, these group interviews are different from those carried out by admission committees and recruitment boards where a small group of respondents is given a topic for discussion. The cleverest ones can be singled out and selected. In our group interviewing, copies of a questionnaire are distributed in a school class, office branch, or similar groups. The matter and the procedure are explained to them. They fill in the questionnaires themselves. This saves a lot of time and money.

The form of a question governs the nature of the answer to be given. Which means the answer depends upon the question. Questions are not asked in the vague hope that somehow something will emerge from them.

These are designed to elicit exact information about well-thought out underlying variables.

A questionnaire is made up of items. Each item is a stimulus. It is designed to get information from the respondent on a point. An item may be direct or indirect or both. A direct item is analysed straightaway for its direct content. An indirect item is used for a purpose which is clear to a trained analyst. The research techniques, TAT, word association test, all fall under this category. Some items can be analysed for their direct as well as indirect content. For example, Who is the local MLA? The answers to such a question can be used for measuring political awareness as well as political interest.

Table 2

Comparison of questionnaires and interview schedules

Questionnaire	***Interview Schedule***
Flexibility wanting.	Flexible.
Response rate low.	Response rate high.
Standardisation doubtful.	Standardised.
Item sequence in disorder.	Item sequencing in order.
Well-thought out replies.	Spontaneous replies.
Some items left unanswered.	Full response.
Money saved.	More expensive.
Time saved.	More time-consuming.
Anonymity guaranteed.	Anonymity partial.
Wider accessibility.	Some respondents left out.

An item is constructed around a variable. If an item is unstructured (open), some space is left vacant in front of it for writing the answer. The open-ended items are often made use of in exploratory studies. The researcher puts the answers together later on. He brings them under common names. In case an item is structured (closed), then the possible response categories are written in front of the item or under it. These are well-thought out before-hand. The respondents are asked to choose one of them. This is done by putting a mark or a cross on it, or even better, by encircling it. Examples of structured items are given below :

Example 1. To which caste category in this city do you think you belong?

(a) Upper (b) Middle (c) Lower

Example 2. If there are elections to the Lok Sabha next Sunday, for which political party would you vote?
BJP/ BSP/ Cong/ CPI(M)/ Any other (specify)

Example 3. Would you say that you are very proud, quite proud, or not at all proud, of your country?
(a) Very proud (b) Quite proud (c) Not at all proud

Different response categories are written in an alphabetical, or logical, order. It is not advisable to ask the respondents, to code the answers themselves. This becomes a source of error. An example of an open-ended item is given below :

Example 4. Please ask yourself : Who am I? Then list twenty words or phrases, which best describe who you are.

Unstructured (open) items provide spontaneous information. But their coding is open to ambiguity. This happens especially when the interviewer is not theoretically clear about what is to be done with the replies. Thus, he goes on recording long statements without knowing what is appropriate and what is not. It is difficult to bring together open-ended replies under viable explanatory categories. Closed items are easier to knit together with explanatory frames. At the same time, open items are too demanding for lower class uneducated respondents. On the other hand, upper class educated respondents find structured categories inadequate to express exactly what they want to say. In this case, closed items violate facts by trying to compress different types of shades into small pigeonholes. The respondents may even find them strange and funny. Closed-ended items keep out superfluous information. Open-ended items have a broad reach. These can be coded according to need.

The number and wording of answer categories for closed-ended items can distort responses. For instance, the following two categorisations yield qualitatively different data. There can be various interpretations.

Example 5. To which social class, in this region, do you think, you belong?
(i) Upper/Middle/Lower
(ii) Upper/Middle/Working/Lower

Possible response categories can be constructed through deep insight, before hand. Closed-ended items can be easily coded. Open-ended replies have to be inductively brought together under common concepts, with an eye on the hypothesis. While constructing closed-ended questions, we have to ensure that response categories are mutually exclusive. They should not overlap with each other. Moreover, the categories should be collectively exhaustive. All possible responses should fit into them.

The construction of questionnaires requires a lot of skill. But as the saying goes, practice makes a man perfect. Even then, keep a few points in mind. The collected data are to be analysed with a view to constructing theories. Before preparing a research design, we have to anticipate the relations between facts, on the basis of our previous knowledge. These are used to formulate an appropriate hypothesis. Based on this we formulate operational definitions of concepts in the hypothesis. These enable us to measure the concepts and test the hypothesis. Operational definitions are used to prepare items for the questionnaire. A questionnaire may be divided into blocks. Each block contains items on a specific aspect of the topic under study. These are carefully arranged in a sequence. It is clear that data collection is different from a hunting expedition. We have to proceed systematically, leaving almost no scope for chance.

Formulating Questions

We will get the right answers only if we ask the right questions. Questions worded dissimilarly elicit different responses. Standardisation improves reliability and validity. We must take care that everybody understands the questions in one and the same manner. We can get a uniform outcome only by asking many persons the same questions in the same sequence and the same way.

As already mentioned, the art of drafting questions needs skill and practice. The following points should be kept in mind in order to avoid errors:

(a) Precision

The questions should be within the mental reach of the respondents who have to give the answers. For this purpose, the questions should be brief and to the point. Do not tax the patience of the respondents. Do not ask involved and slippery questions. Take the local idiom into account. Otherwise, the questions will not be understood by some of the respondents. Avoid words which have a different or an offensive meaning in a neighbouring language of a local dialect. Apply your mind. Refrain from accumulating superfluous facts. Ask exactly what you want to know.

Some choices are open to interpretation. For example, instead of :

(a) Very often (b) Often (c) Sometimes
(d) Rarely (e) Never

Quantify the response and formulate the answer as follows :

(a) Everyday (b) 2 to 6 times a week
(c) About once a week (d) About once a month
(e) Never

Small changes in the wordings of the questions can change the meaning. "A stone hitting the window glass" is not the same question as, "a window glass hitting the stone". Similarly, "Do you know mother Teresa?" is inadequately precise. Therefore, depending upon the purpose of the survey, either ask, "Have you known Mother Teresa personally?" or ask, "Have you ever heard of Mother Teresa?" Again, do not be vague. Group the nuances and the distinctive shades of various words, and choose appropriate ones. For example, the term 'beauty' can be beautifully vague. Make it more precise by adding specifications like perfect figure, smooth skin, smiling face, elegant dress, graceful walk, smart manners, sensible talk, and so on.

We have to clearly specify exactly what it is that we want to know. For instance, age. Do we want them to tell us according to the English calender how old they were on their last birthday? Do you want them to tell us in the Indian way in which year of life they are now? Infact, the Japanese add one more year to the actual age in order to account for the time a child is in the mother's womb. Many persons cannot recollect their birth date or their age. They may only be able to relate their age to certain events at the time of their birth, say, partition. Again, in order to get jobs, they may overstate their age. In order to be able to appear in competitive examinations, and not to retire from service soon, they may understate their age. In order to appear consistent they tend to distort their responses. Therefore, one who asks a question has to be precise.

Where the interviewees do not understand the researcher's language (say, English), prepare precise or functionally equivalent translations in the local language (say Tamil or Telugu). On-the-spot translations by the interviewers are not permissible. These impair standardisation. In order to verify the reliability of the translation, retranslate the same and compare it with the original. If there is no gap in communication, the translation is correct. Be careful that even if the words are not similar, their meaning should be equivalent. Imprecise questions will elicit off-the-mark answers.

Precision can be improved with figures. Take the example of the following item on time consciousness:

What would you say, how fast does time pass? Could you tell me with the help of this figure? (Figure 1). Here 1 mean that time almost stands still, and 7 means that it passes very quickly. Which number between 1 and 7 is typical of the times we live in?

(b) Unequivocality

Equivocation means that different things have the same name. Equivocal or amorphous words or phrases, ambiguous grammatical constructions and involved questions cannot be understood by respondents. They fail to grasp them correctly. Do not ask such questions. Many respondents are not capable of properly narrating their experience. Therefore, at the time of preparing operational definitions of concepts, the researcher has to use such words as can be understood by all the respondents in the same way. The questions should not be ambiguous. These should not be interpretable in more than one way. None of the words used in the questions should be ambiguous. These should not be interpretable in more than one way.

All the words used in the questions should have one and the same meaning for all the respondents. Sometimes there are gaps between an object, its conventional definition, and its meaning in the mind of an individual. This creates problems for preparing questions and for interpreting the answers to such questions. For instance, in Hindi and Punjabi, 'sarkar' means government or ruler. But in various contexts, a person may speak of a piece of land, a policeman, bull, his own wife, or even himself, as 'sarkar'. In the same way, in different contexts 'achha' may mean anything and everything. It may mean good or bad or surprising or 'I will see you', or 'I will teach you a lesson', and much else.

Figure 1
Time consciousness

Source: Noelle-Neumaan, E. : *Macht Arbeit Krank? Macht Arbeit Gluecklich?* Piper, Munich, 1984.

Let us take another example:

Example 6. Should the police cats get justice?

(a) Yes (b) No

Those who favour as well as those who oppose the police cats can say 'yes' to this question. They may define 'justice' in their own way. Consequently, the interpretation of the responses will be erroneous. Similarly, choice of alternative words may call forth diverse perceptions. A terrorist can be a militant for one person and freedom fighter for another. Phrases like 'foreign hand' or 'international conspiracy' or even simple words like 'all', 'any', 'below', 'confidence', 'common', 'few', 'government', 'some', 'young' can be understood in different ways by various respondents. They call forth different responses. In the following question, the use of the word 'forbid' instead of 'allow' can elicit negative instead of positive responses:

Example 7. Do you think that the government should forbid (or allow) the local women to marry foreigners?

(a) Yes

(b) No

Of course, a change in the interviewer's tone can lead to the same effect. Standardisation takes care of that. A researcher has to read out his questions in a standardised tone.

In spite of their apparent similarity, some words and phrases have two or more meanings. The meaning gets altered in various contexts. Many words have different connotations in various languages. In a multi-lingual field, the interview schedule may have to be translated into a number of languages. When this is so, instead of trying to find out a beautiful or a faithful literal translation, we have to look for functional equivalence of the concepts underlying the required items. Translations have to be checked up with retranslations by others. The problem is so complicated that when several languages are involved, sometimes we are asked to forget about the equivalence of items in a questionnaire. Instead thereof, we are expected to get universal statements by comparing the generalisations from various settings across time and space.

(c) Double Barrel

This is in fact a two-in-one question. Two questions are disguised as one. Such items have to be excluded. These are replaced with others. For instance :

1. Are you in favour of building the Tehri dam and raising agricultural productivity?
   (a) Yes (b) No
2. Break up the above question into two parts :
   (i) Are you in favour of building the Tehri dam, or not?
   (a) Yes (b) No
   (ii) Are you in favour of raising agricultural productivity, or not?
   (a) Yes (b) No

This would give the respondent an opportunity to say 'Yes' on one point and 'No' on the other. The double barrel puts the interviewee in a dilemma. He may be against building a dam over the river, and in favour of raising agricultural productivity, or even vice versa. Thus, he is at a loss to know what to say and what not to say.

(d) Bias

Bias means going off the mark due to one preconception or another. Even when there is no deliberate attempt at falsification, the interviewee tends to answer questions in terms of his own preconceptions. This is not the purpose of our research work. Therefore, we have to avoid being biased. Beware of biased words with emotional tilts, moral judgements, and predispositions. For instance, corruption, secularism, terrorism, and so on. Such words can distort the responses one way or another. Similarly, do not use words which are evaluated as good by one section of the respondents and bad by others. Use value-free vocabulary. For instance, instead of 'theft' use the definition of theft, i.e., taking away something that belongs to others, without their permission or knowledge. A biased question can give one-sided tilt to the responses. For example :

In your opinion, should the government allow or forbid the cultivation of bt. brinjal?

(a) Allow (b) Forbid

Before asking indiscrete questions, first create a proper atmosphere for eliciting replies. This can be done by saying that it is something common. As everybody is doing it, there is nothing secretive about it. Exclude those items where some category in the structured alternative creates some problem.

(e) Jargon

Avoid using stereotype phrases or ornamental tags. Jargon and cliches provide loopholes for escape routes. These create confusion. Therefore, do not use big words. Beware of rhetorical language. Do not mix up images. Use correct idioms. Do not expect everybody to be conversant with technical details. Abstract, scientific and technical concepts may create perplexity and uncertainty. For instance :

(i) Should deficit financing be given up?
(a) Yes (b) No

(ii) Are you in favour of demonetization, or not?
(a) Yes (b) No

(f) Acquiescence

This means the tendency to go on saying 'yes' all the time, no matter what the question. The acquiescence effect creates problems in getting true responses. Some people do not want to spoil their impression by admitting their ignorance about something. Some people have not learnt to say 'no'. They may say 'yes' out of ignorance, courtesy, deference towards higher castes and classes, or out of fear of offending others. Freedom may be defined as the capacity to say 'no' sometimes. However, some people never feel free. This has become their habit. So, they round off their answers, go on agreeing with the interviewer all the time, or tell him what they think he wants to hear. Let us take, for example, the following question :

Are you in favour of or against holding elections in states where there is a lot of political violence? Should elections be held there only when they have given up violence?

(a) Yes (b) No

Agreement or disagreement with such a question may mean anything. Moreover, in some cultures being tactful is valued more than truth or honesty. Therefore, the impact of the answer on the interviewee is valued more than the truth or falsity of the answer. Out of courtesy or respect the respondent may say what he thinks the interviewer wants to hear. Asylum-seekers in search of greener pastures exaggerate their tales of woe. Some respondents may overstate their status, achievements, and attitudes. Thus, the acquiescence effect may arise from a number of sources. What can we do about it?

(a) Write the response categories in a simple and straightforward way. Avoid unidirectional wording. Vary the direction of the items in such a manner that agreement and disagreement do not refer to the same direction all the time. Build something in the item itself to discourage the tendency to go on saying 'yes' all the time. Change in the polarity of the item reverses the acquiescence effect. Therefore, formulate half the items positively and the remaining ones negatively. Thus, agreement would mean disagreement, while disagreement would mean agreement with the item. Mix up these questions. However, double negation can be misleading. For example:

Are you in favour of, or against, the agitation of the opposition against the globalisation policy of the government?

(a) Yes (b) No

One more way of countering the acquiescence effect is to vary the Yes/No answer categories with Agree/Disagree, Favourable/Unfavourable, etc., with a view to discouraging routine ritualised answers. Moreover, instead of putting all the items together in one lot, spread them in various parts of the interview schedule. Reverse sequencing of items can also be useful for this purpose.

(b) Counter-balancing of an item eliminates confounding. Therefore, not only an argument in favour of something, but also an argument against it, should be built into an item on a controversial issue.

Should restrictions on free trade between India and Pakistan be removed or made more strict?

(a) Removed (b) Made strict

If an argument can persuade, a counter-argument can dissuade. The method of asking a question can also turn tables. We will come to that later on.

(c) Follow up an open-ended item with : Why? Alternatively, use a scale in this case for measuring the intensity of the response. When we seek such a clarification, the respondent's mind opens up. He may even try to defend himself by trying to remain consistent. This refines his answer. It also provides us insight for interpreting the main item.

Example 8. Would you like your son to become a school teacher? Why?

(a) Yes (b) No

Example 9. Do you approve or disapprove of a married woman earning money in business or industry even if she has a husband capable of supporting her? Why?

(a) Approve (b) Disapprove

(g) Frame of Reference

Precision of analysis depends upon the quality of data obtained from the respondents. For example, the responses about the organisational size are moulded by whatever comes to the mind of the respondent at that time—his own department, the local factory, or the entire undertaking with branches all over the country. Therefore, the frame of reference has to be clearly specified in the question being asked.

General questions elicit more 'Yes' responses than specific questions. For ensuring clarity, the frame of reference has to be built into the question, or controlled. For example :

Example 10. How much is your house in Delhi worth?

The answer will depend upon whether the questioner is perceived as a tax assessor or a prospective in-law, or a property dealer. Different frames of reference bring out different replies.

Example 11. How would they rank your family (in your village)?

(a) High (b) Middle (c) Low

For controlling the frame of reference, ask the next question:

Why?

Answers obtained in different contexts, place, time, cannot be uncritically cumulated together. Cumulation and replication are not permissible without controlling the frame of reference.

(h) Suggestion

Construct your questions in such a manner that the respondents do not feel constrained to give their replies in a particular direction only.

(a) In a leading question, the questioner is interested in somehow getting a certain type of answer only. The item is couched in such terms that the respondent feels tempted to answer one way instead of another. Therefore, in the interest of objectivity, do not ask a leading or a loaded question. Such a question is not innocent. Do not put words in the respondent's mouth. Provide him a fair chance to give an appropriate reply. For instance:

Example 12. Have you stopped beating your mother-in-law?

(a) Yes (b) No

In case the interviewee answers positively, this may mean that she has been beating the mother-in-law earlier. If she answers negatively, this may mean that she does so even now. Both these interpretations may not be true. In other words, this is a suggestive question. There is a trap. It may yield a false answer. Do not ask such questions.

Similarly, 'too often', 'too few' 'much too much' are leading response categories. These are biased in favour of a positive response.

(b) Questions can be made suggestive by threatening, or flattering the respondents, or throwing around suggestive responses. These can also be induced by adding such phrases before-hand as "Everybody knows that..." and "There is no doubt about it that...". Such tricks tilt the responses in the suggested direction, creating bias. Such perceptions call forth distortions.

(c) Either leave an item open, or close it. Partial structuring compels the respondents to choose one of the given alternatives. It discourages them to think of something else. For example :

Marital status : (a) Married (b) Unmarried

Further probing might reveal that divorced or separated respondents may have haphazardly chosen either of the two categories given above. Again, overstructuring is also to be avoided. For example :

Example 13. To which social class in this country, do you think, you belong?

(a) Upper (b) Middle (c) Working (d) Lower

In this case, many respondents find it hard to express their subjective identification with any class. The category 'working class' overlaps with others. Like partial structuring, overstructuring distorts the responses.

(d) When all the items have the same format, the respondents go on ticking one way or another without applying their mind. In order to get rid of the response set, introduce variety by mixing structured and unstructured as well as positive and negative items.

(e) Personalisation tilts the question. For example :

Example 14. (in your opinion) Should the smuggling of narcotic drugs from abroad for the addicts of this country be allowed or banned?

(a) Allowed (b) Banned

Privatisation of questions elicits responses about personal opinion rather than public opinion.

The point is that it is well and proper to provide adequate opportunity to the interviewees to come out with what they have to say. It is unfair to pass on suggestive hints. We are interested in ascertaining the public opinion. We are not interested in putting our words in their mouths.

(i) Inclusion or Exclusion

Inclusion or exclusion of alternative categories can divert the responses in different directions. For instance, the inclusion of 'Don't know' as a response category increases the proportion of such cases. However, in case it is excluded, some respondents will be forced to choose one of the alternatives, which approximates their true response. Arbitrary response categories like 'a great deal' vs 'some fun' can lead to the same result. As already pointed out, it would be better to seek clarification immediately by asking : Why? or to introduce a scale for measuring the intensity of the same response.

We have to be careful with our words while formulating our questions. Different words have different meanings. They elicit different answers.

Sequencing Items

All the items in a questionnaire are placed in such a sequence that the whole questionnaire becomes a unit in itself. Items on each aspect of the topic under study may be kept under separate, numbered, blocks. For example, in a survey of progressive farmers, items on their personality characteristics, social background, adoption of technological innovations, and felt needs, can be placed under separate blocks. Within the blocks, the items may be placed after each other in a logical order. In case of historical questions, move chronologically. If this is not done, the respondents will have to jump suddenly from one item to another. This causes them unnecessary inconvenience. Therefore, the items have to be placed in a logical order, with a view facilitating response. While shifting from one topic to another, to transitional phrases for connecting the two together.

A preceding item builds up the atmosphere for a succeeding one. The former response may leave a bias effect on the latter. This may well happen among others, because the respondents do not want to appear inconsistent. Therefore, a researcher has to take care of the sequence. Thus, in a study of factory workers, questions on indiscipline at the place of work should not be asked just after questions on performance appraisal. If this is done, there will be under-reporting. Similarly, after "What are the most important problems facing this country?" do not ask for 'confidence in leaders'. To start with, do not ask sensitive questions. Ask innocent questions at first, lest the interviewees should get scared of being interviewed, and refuse to go ahead with the interview. In the beginning, the interviewees are hesitant. Items at the fag end are answered carelessly. Unpleasant or difficult questions are asked at the end of a sequence, not just at the start.

In a *question battery*, mutually interrelated questions are placed one after another in such a manner that the reply to one question facilitates the reply to the next question. The various items can be analysed together. Let us take up the example of a question battery :

1. Do you smoke? Yes/No
2. Do you get tense easily? Yes/No
3. Are you suffering from diabetes? Yes/No
4. Do you have cholesterol problem? Yes/No
5. Are you happy without any wish? Yes/No

Let us take up one more example of a question battery :

Everybody has dreams, and thinks of doing something extra special. Have you ever dreamt of doing any of the things in this list?

I have often imagined ...

1. Winning lottery Yes/No/Uncertain
2. Taking a trip around the world Yes/No/Uncertain
3. Working for bringing peace in the world Yes/No/Uncertain
4. Saving somebody's life Yes/No/Uncertain
5. Working towards putting through important improvements for others at work Yes/No/Uncertain
6. Making important discoveries for mankind. Yes/No/Uncertain
7. Being a voluntary worker for development projects in a poor country Yes/No/Uncertain
8. Actively working for environmental protection Yes/No/Uncertain
9. Working for those on the margins of society Yes/No/Uncertain
10. Leading a group of freedom fighters Yes/No/Uncertain

In a *question funnel*, first we ask questions on the general aspects of a problem. Gradually, we move on to specific items. This makes the questioning smooth. In a reverse funnel, we start from particular points and gradually go on broadening the focus of our attention. This facilitates recall by the respondents.

Filter questions are used to keep out respondents who are not required to answer the succeeding questions. For instance :

1. Have you ever received an award for gallantry? If yes, answer the following question... Yes/No

In this example, if the researcher is interested only in those answering positively or negatively, then the later questions are called *branches*. Such questions are relevant only for some of the respondents and not applicable to all.

The movement from one question to the next should be smooth. Various blocks are connected together with interesting questions, like, What did you see in Shimla?

One defect with question batteries is that they tend to bring in the same answers in a superficial manner. Often, it is advisable to spread the battery to various parts of the questionnaire. Some items should be negatively formulated.

The most important questions are asked neither at the very beginning nor at the fag end. They stand in between. The start, the middle and the end have to be interconnected with each other in a clear and logical order. This has to be done in such a way that there is a smooth transition from one question to the next. Thus, the respondents are not placed under stress. At the end, give your respondent sufficient opportunity to say something else if he wants to say so. You should give him such an opportunity even if you do not need the answer for the analysis in hand.

Get the questionnaire translated into the local languages. Do not use bookish language for this purpose. This facilitates communication with all sorts of interviewees. Linguistic variation distorts equivalence of data, comparability of statistical measures, and validity of conclusions.

How long can a questionnaire be? This depends upon the topic under study. It also depends upon the mentality of the respondents and the skill of the researcher. Restrict yourself to as few questions as possible. Do not ask the same questions again and again. Do not ask unnecessary questions. Ask a question only if you need the data on an underlying variable.

Pretesting means filling in, say, one dozen interview schedules with the assistance of persons belonging to the groups under study. This is done before conducting a full-scale study. This serves a number of purposes. It enables us to improve the wording of our questions, with a view to improving their understanding. We check up whether the scales are suitable. We improve the sequence and the flow of questions. We become aware of the practical difficulties, and take care of them in time. Omission and commission are identified. The interviewer's instructions are refined.

Pretesting does not mean carrying on a full-scale investigation. A pretest is different from a pilot study. The latter is a small-scale rehearsal or simulation of all the steps. This helps us to check up whether we have made proper arrangements for systematically doing a large-scale survey with a representative sample from the universe. Pilot studies are exploratory in nature. These my be done with open-ended structured categories of a full-scale survey.

Printing

While getting the interview schedule printed, the convenience of the interviewers should not be forgotten. Leave a sufficient margin. Provide enough space for writing down the answers. If large spaces are left vacant, the interviewers would tend to write down long statements. This makes coding tedious. In practice, the interviewers tend to somehow fill in all the vacant space. If the space is small, they write in small-sized letters and use many abbreviations. Coders have difficulty in deciphering them later on. While coding, the first response is more reliable. Avoid printing mistakes. On the front page of the interview schedule, use the right hand corner at the top for entering the serial number. In the top left hand corner, indicate in bold letters that the matter is confidential. Numbering the blocks and items facilitates data processing at a later stage. Instructions regarding filter questions, branches, etc., should be clearly provided. Printing should be legible. Do not split an item into two different pages. Proper printing facilitates coding. Use good quality paper. It is not correct to waste money on expensive quality paper. On the other hand, if the interview schedule has been printed on blotting paper, it becomes difficult to write smoothly on it. Better write with a fountain pen, using permanent blue-black ink. Avoid using a pencil or a ball point pen. Provide complete instructions for asking questions, coding and punching. Do not give so many instructions for interviewers that they do not feel inclined to go through the entire matter before starting their task, and follow the instructions in letter and spirit. If the punching operators are going to punch the data directly from the interview schedule, put down the duly numbered coding cells, with the computer card and the column numbers in convenient corners arranged in a systematic order. Pre-coding facilitates data processing. Do not ask the respondents to code the data, or even a part thereof. This becomes a source of error. Let them concentrate on answering the questions. Do the coding yourself later on. If there are large masses of data, meticulous coders are mobilised for the task. Checks on coding are very necessary.

Conclusions

Use of careless, flimsy, ridiculous, shabby questions creates a bad impression on the respondents. This makes it difficult to complete the task well. It is not permissible to alter the wording of the questions and their sequence during the course of the field work, except in case of an interview guide.

Well begun is half done. Once a questionnaire or an interview schedule has been printed, it has to be administered to the respondents.

A fool can ask **so** many questions in one minute, **as** a wise person cannot answer all his/her life. In practice the questions asked can be answered in, say, half and hour. A questionnaire should not be too long. Otherwise, it would bring down the rate of response.

References

Bradburn, Norman N. and Seymour Sudman, *Polls and Surveys: Understanding What They Tell Us*, Jossey-Bass, San Francisco, California, 1988.

Cannel, C.F. and R. Kahn, "Interviewing", in G. Linzey and E. Aron (eds.), *The Handbook of Social Psychology*, 2nd ed., Vol. II, Amerind Publishing Co., New Delhi, 1975, pp. 526-95.

de Vaus, David A., *Surveys in Social Research*, UCL Press, 1991.

Hoinville, Geralt et al., *Survey Research Practice*, Heinemann Educational Books, London, 1984.

Mayntz R. et al., *Introduction to Empirical Sociology*, Penguin, Harmondsworth, 1976.

Rossi, Peter S., James D. Wright and Andy B. Anderson (eds.), *Handbook of Social Research*, Academic Press, New York, 1983.

Singh, Jaspal, *Methodology and Techniques of Social Research*, Kanishka, New Delhi, 2001.

7

Measurement and Scaling for Social Research

Mount Everest in Nepal is 8,848 metre high. The deepest point in the ocean is 10,990 metre down below. River Nile in Egypt is 6,695 km long. The sun is away from the earth, 14,94,76,000 km., on an average. Everything cannot be measured. What we know is limited. What we do not know is infinite. Measurement precisely expresses what we know, without speculation, just exactly.

A rational-legal society is systematically organised. It gives measure for measure. Accountability, with reasonable calculation, counting, are its characteristic features. Transformation of qualitative matter into quantitative readings facilitates their processing, on the way to analysis. Numbers carry forward the essential attributes. That enables us to give some sense to the matter under observation. Thereby we can exactly express the underlying structures and processes, and extend the available explanations. Application of reliable and valid statistical operations makes it possible for us to draw precise conclusions, and to work out their implications.

As a matter of fact, there is much more in quality than quantity can bring out. Measurement means standardised transformation of some aspects of quality into quantity according to rules. It systematically throws away redundant information that we do not need for the time being. This makes it easy for us to focus our attention on the underlying variables in a theoretical framework. Thus, we can give some sense to the facts being observed. Quantitative manipulation of data alongwith their qualitative analysis is a unity. Both these operations go hand in hand. Measurement and scaling serve as means for achieving the goal of exactly expressing the matter under observation. Classification is a sort of measurement.

Classification

Systematically placing objects together on the basis of their similarities and differences is called classification. Mutually exclusive and collectively exhaustive categories are brought out by arranging them into classes or distributing into groups. Classification is done for a given purpose at some point of time, according to flexible rules. It brings out gaps and missing links. This opens up new lines of enquiry.

Example 1 : Freud classified human beings into two types—sadists and masochists. The former feel happy by inflicting pain on others. The latter derive pleasure by imposing punishment on themselves. (Ahmed Faraz : *Nafrat hi sahi, dil dukhane ke liye aa*!) A sadist gives tension. A masochist takes tension. Sadists and masochists fall in two different classes.

Figure 1

Classification of ethics (morality, right and wrong behaviour) in western philosophy into three types

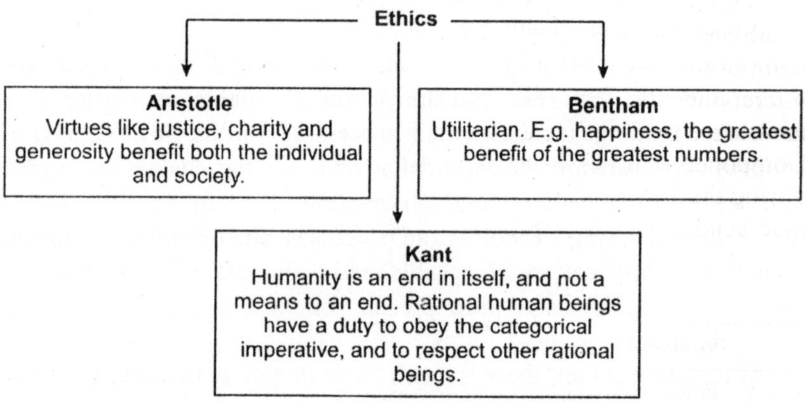

Measurement

Measurement shows a greater degree of flexibility and precision. This involves assignment of quantities (or numbers) to qualities, according to rules. Numbers possess calculability. These can be skillfully analysed. Measurement exactly brings out relevant information eliminating redundance. This can be done with indicators, indices and scales.

In this presentation, we are dealing with various procedures for constructing and applying different types of measuring instruments. This can be done with indicators, indices and scales.

Indicators

An indicator points out with a moving finger. It provides empirical referents for a concept. Indicators possess differentiating features. These are visible symptoms, not their underlying causes. An indicator provides for the knowing power an opportunity to understand the facts under observation. It is valid if there is no lack of fit between the indicator and the concept signified by it.

Example 2 : For Durkheim, the legal system (retributive or restitutive) is an indicator of the type of social solidarity (mechanical/organic).

Example 3 : Different from traditions as well as emotions, rationality is, for Max Weber, an indicator of the capitalistic path of development.

Index

An index is a set of indicators. Figure 2 shows some indicators that can be combined to construct an index of quality of life. Figure 3 puts forth a composite learning index used by UNESCO (Canada). It consists of four interconnected and interdependent pillars, 17 indicators and 37 measures. These have been methodically combined to yield a single score. Components of this index have been recognised as goals of education during the 21st century. A high score signifies that conditions of learning that build up cultural progress are available. Again, a science citation

Figure 2
Quality of life

	Variable
1.	Freedom from hunger and disease.
2.	Availability of affordable housing.
3.	Freedom of speech.
4.	Equality of educational opportunity.
5.	Getting married to a person of one's own choice.
6.	Freedom of travel at home and abroad.
7.	Inexpensive justice without delay.

index (SCI) is built up by taking foot notes and references of over a thousand scientific journals into account. This facilitates professional communication as well as competition for advancement.

While combining indicators into an index, we have to take care that their meaning is clear and to the point. The former should be significantly related to the latter.

Scale

A scale is different from the indicators and an index. In case of an index, the indicators are intuitively selected. Then these are put together into an index. A scale follows a formal procedure for deciding whether an element belongs to it or not. It is more meaningful than an index. This yields precise information, and brings it down to a continuum.

Figure 3

Learning to know, to do, to be, to live together

Inspired by the Four Pillars of Learning developed for UNESCO by Jacques Delors.

Pillars of Learning	Composite Learning Index
Learning to Know	Literacy, numeracy, general knowledge, and critical thinking
Learning to Do	Technical, hands-on skills that are closely tied to occupational success
Learning to Live Together	Civic engagement, respect and concern for others and social and inter-personal skills
Learning to Be	Development of the mind, body and spirit through personal discovery, creativity and achieving a healthy balance in life

A scale is a standard tool. It accurately measures the position of various points on a continuum. It represents concrete objects with abstract numbers. Abstract differs from concrete in the same way as the sound of music differs from the instrument that produces it.

Table 1
Grading system in some schools

Grade	*Elaboration*	*Grade points*
E	Excellent	5
A	Very good	4
B	Good	3
C	Satisfactory	2
D	Unsatisfactory	1
F	Fail	0

For instance, the grading system of evaluation given in Table 1 Grade point average behind certificates, diplomas and degrees given after examination at the culmination of a course of studies certifies the content and quality of education imbibed by the students.

We can say that while measurement is the process of estimating the magnitude of objects, indicators, indices and scales are measuring instruments.

Measurement is neglective fiction. The same object can be measured in many different ways. All the readings can be reliable and valid from different points of view.

Socio-economic Status

Europeans like to use the term 'class'. For analytical purposes, Max Weber divided this concept into economic class, political power and social prestige. Class implies class consciousness and class conflict. For ideological reasons (functioning should be more important than political power and social status), Americans prefer to use an alternative concept—SES (socio-economic status). This is an elusive term. There are serious substantive as well as methodological difficulties in the way of systematic analysis of this term. Sociologists have measured this concept in terms of income, status, style of living, community participation, reputation and a variety of other ways. Some of these cannot be measured and/or compared across space and time. For instance, how would you measure agricultural income? Nevertheless, these are characterised by a large degree of association. In a multicultural and multi-epochal society such as that of India, diversities in terms of religion, language, caste, kinship and similar other cleavages are also important. Moreover, it is passing through a period of rapid social change. Therefore, such an association between different components of the class concept or SES are unlikely. If analysis is done, it is possible only by using a composite index consisting of several variables. Each of these is to be evaluated separately before being given proper weightage. Then these are put together to yield an index of overall class position. In the first place, the number of variables considered relevant for the construction of such an index would be questionable. Some of these would be hardly amenable to rating or ranking. The grading as well as the weightage would be arbitrary. Adding up scores on different items on a scale would give erroneous results. Above all, such a scale would be unstable. Therefore, even at the cost of ignoring some unexplained residual variables, we have to remain satisfied with a single indicator, or subjective class identification.

Figure 4
Socio-economic status

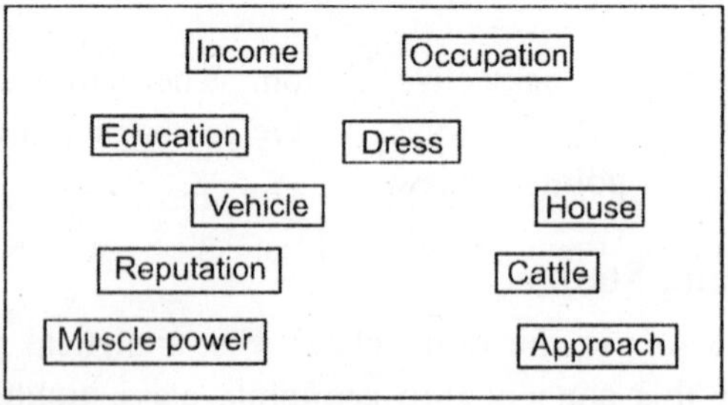

Prestige Grading of Occupations

In an urban industrial context, we can ascertain class background in terms of prestige grading of occupations. Such a procedure is not free of limitations. But it is simple. A complex procedure need not be more valid. Validity of the results can be verified in terms of social mobility of a set of respondents. Of course, this is a subjective procedure. Occupations are higher or lower with respect to one's situation and consciousness. For an old woman in a far-off village, a *patwari* maintaining land records may mean more than the deputy commissioner of the district. Nevertheless, the advantage of such a procedure lies in providing us a comprehensive view, in disregard of whatever variables may underlie such scaling. In any case, there are no hard and fast criteria for objectivity. Basically, it boils down to inter-subjectivity.

For grading, a list of occupations is prepared in alphabetical order. It is administered to, say, 30 judges. They are persons in the know of the subject-matter. They are requested to rank the items in the list in terms of, say, Likert Scale (a five-point scale). The scale represents a hierarchy, with one point for each occupation with the minimum prestige. Five points are given to an occupation with the maximum prestige. The scores are based on their arithmetic means. These are further divided into broad categories, say 2 to 5. This yields an indicator of prestige grading of occupations. This can be put to use for measuring class affiliation and social mobility.

Subjective Class Identification

We can collect data for this purpose on the self-rating of a representative sample of the universe under study or their rating of their own family. In the traditional Indian situation, family rather than individual is a unit of society. Apart from their being informative in their own right, the objective and the subjective procedures are not equivalent. However, they do provide adequate opportunity for verifying the validity of the results in the earlier procedure, viz., prestige grading of occupations. This may be done with such questions as : To which class in this city (country) do you think you (does your family) belong? The answers may be obtained in terms of, say, a three-point scale. The results can then be compared with data collected by other means.

Scale Construction

Inferences and implications are conclusions. Inferences are statements that logically follow from other statements. Implications are necessary relations of inferences.

What is beauty? Sanskrit scholars have defined beauty in terms of novelty. Guilford analysed beauty in terms of love, design, delicacy, luxury and outdoor entertainment. Some women all over the world are beautiful. How can we measure beauty? By constructing a scale for this purpose, applying it, and then drawing conclusions therefrom.

Scale

A scale is a standardised instrument for precisely finding out the position of abstract qualities of concrete objects in quantitative form. It is a series of proportionately ascending and descending steps. Scaling involves the procedures for constructing such graduated instrument.

Numbers possess certain qualities. These include : (1) identity (2 is neither 3 nor 4). (2) Rank order (2 is less than 3 and more than 1). (3) Additivity (2+2=4). Qualitative data do not possess such characteristics. Nevertheless, while interpreting them we have to see to it that the statistically significant values are theoretically important. The gaps between the two have to be carefully scrutinised, lest we should have to hear that some people know a lot of sociology without understanding what society is.

While constructing a scale, we must clearly define what it is that is going to be measured. We think out operational procedures so that the measurements can be done. We break up the problem under study into its components, and these into variables. If a variable is not available, or cannot be measured, we look around for a functional equivalent that will serve the purpose. Then we proceed to construct appropriate items around these variables. These are included in the scale. An item is like an unpeeled banana. A variable is the fruit inside. For example, Figure 5 shows the components of alienation.

Besides being within empirical grasp, variables for constructing scales ought to occupy strategic points in a theoretical framework. We begin with several variables. Multivariate analysis is used to bring them down to a few reliable ones that fit in. For instance, Figure 6 puts up certain variables for constructing a scale on workvalues. Answers to items constructed around these variables may be obtained on a five-point scale. These should be of use for empirical verifications in the context of Max Webers' theory of the protestant ethic and the spirit of capitalism.

Figure 5
Components of alienation

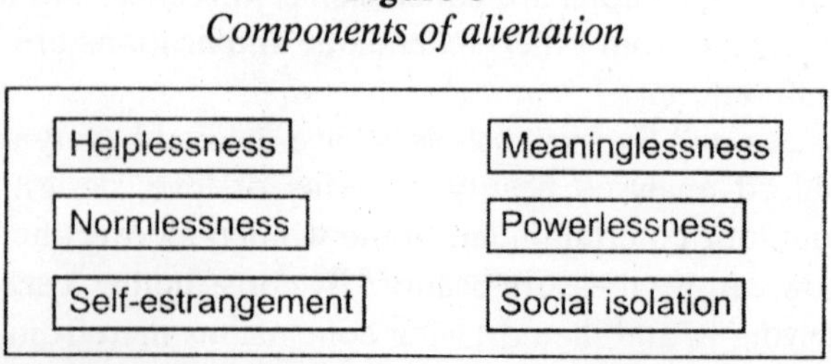

Table 2
Some variables for constructing a scale on work values

S.No.	Variables	S.No.	Variables
1.	Achievement	15.	Precision
2.	Attendance	16.	Pride in quality of work
3.	Commitment	17.	Punctuality
4.	Cooperation	18.	Quick reactions
5.	Creativity	19.	Recognition
6.	Dedication	20.	Responsibility
7.	Dependability	21.	Risk-taking
8.	Discipline	22.	Savings
9.	Flexibility	23.	Tact
10.	Fitness	24.	Team work
11.	Hard work	25.	Thoroughness
12.	Honesty	26.	Trust
13.	Job security	27.	Truthfulness
14.	Positive attitude	28.	Willing obedience

Qualities of Scales

A scale should possess the following qualities : (1) reliability, (2) validity, (3) sensitivity, and (4) unidimensionality. Let us take these one by one for consideration.

1. Reliability

This means that the scale gives out consistent results. The outcome remains unchanged from one measurement to another. Repeated measurements yield the same results. These are exact and dependable. Reliability can be ascertained with the following methods :

(a) Test-retest : A scale is applied on similar respondents under similar conditions, again and again. Readings at different places and times are compared. Averages, percentages or correlations reveal the realiability of the scale.

However, the residual effect of testing may change the attitude. Respondents become alert, making later readings atypical. Instrumental decay after some time distorts the measurements. Retest can not always confirm the reliability of a test.

(b) Split halves : This tests internal stability of the scale. It is divided into two parts (say odds and evens). The two halves are tested separately. Their correlation is interpreted.

(c) Multiple forms : Two alternative forms of the scale are prepared. Correlation between the two shows reliability of the scale.

2. Validity

Reliability is synonymous with consistency of measurement. Reliability and validity are two related but separate concepts. A reliable scale need not necessarily be valid. However, unless it is reliable, it cannot be valid. Reliability is a necessary, but not a sufficient condition for validity.

Validity measures what a scale purports to measure. It shows how far the collected data are compatible with the characteristics of the people being measured. Some mutually overlapping and far from being collectively exhaustive methods are given below :

(a) Face validity : This means that it appears to be valid. Nothing seems to be wrong with it. This is a matter of its social acceptability. However, this involves subjectivity. Face validity is questionable.

(b) Expert validity : Experts with practical experience and insight into the matter are of the considered opinion that the scale is valid. Informed opinion of a multiplicity of judges means intersubjectivity. If we go deep into the matter, objectivity boils down to intersubjectivity.

(c) Known groups : The scale being tested is applied on a selected few persons. We are somehow sure that they are like that. For example, a scale for measuring extremism is applied on to those in jail on account of terrorist activities. The outcome reveals the validity or invalidity of the scale being tested.

(d) Predictive validity : We foresee the coming events. On the basis of an available scale, they cast their shadows before, in the form of scores on scales. The scale captures the meaning of what is being measured. In that case, we can safely put it to use in future.

(e) Construct validity : We put up a hypothesis. It is used to construct a scale. We apply the hypothesis to the measurements. If the hypothesis is rejected then there is something wrong, either with the hypothesis or with the scale, perhaps both. If a t-test shows that there are no significant differences between the instrument and the hypothesis, we speak of construct validity.

(f) Criterion validity : It is founded on the relationship between the scale score on the one hand, and some external guidelines or standards on the other. For example, when the criterion is effective in estimating an outcome.

(g) Content validity : Items on a scale are representative of everything relevant to the scale. Content validity is ascertained in terms of how far a scale captures the meaning of the various aspects of what is being measured. This is a matter of careful selection of items from the universe.

(h) Concurrent validity : Two scales measuring the same underlying concept are used at more or less the same time. A fair degree of correlation between the two shows the validity of the scale being used for this purpose. For instance, radicalism is correlated with voting behaviour. The results are valid if there are no significant differences between the two sets of measurements.

3. Sensitivity

This means that the scale is accurately adjusted. A scale should be adequately affected to serve the purpose in hand. A less sensitive scale need not take note of minor differences. Construction of an unduly oversensitive scale is a waste of time. For instance, scale for weighing gold has to be more sensitive than one for weighing vegetables. Again, cloth merchants measure the materials with yards. Thieves do so with the immediately available wooden staffs. Fluctuation in readings creates problems for the reputation of the tailors as well as the looks of those who wear the dress. A sensitive scale helps us to give and take measure for measure.

4. Unidimensionality

This means that only one attribute or aspect is being addressed. Hitherto existing scales have been looking for unidimensionality. The point, however, is that social facts possess several dimensions.

These days, researchers well-versed in electronic data processing and social statistics are putting forward some interesting multidimensional scales. Multivariate techniques are being applied for constructing them. Such a scale visualises information from more than one dimension. It optimises goodness of fit to the supporting theoretical models. However, models like skeletons, do not tell us the whole story.

Their arbitrary application yields insufficient results. Such scales are not only unwieldy, but also shaky. Much of the time, it is scaling for the sake of scaling.

Let us wrap up our discussion on qualities of scales. A combination of these four types of qualities is expected from a scale : reliability, validity, sensitivity and, unidimensionality.

Levels of Scaling

Scales can be arranged into a staircase with four stairs : Nominal, ordinal, interval and ratio. These correspond to four rising levels or phases of measurement. They yield additional qualities as we go ahead.

Nominal Scales

Words are replaced by numbers. These are discrete categories. Numbers are arbitrarily assigned to them, like labels for identification and differentiation. As a matter of fact, the numbers in this case are not quantities. These are alternative forms of naming. These can be switched around. Nominal scales are simple tools of measurement. The objects under investigation are classified on the basis of whether they possess or do not possess certain peculiarities. For example, gender (male/female); voting behaviour (Akali/BJP/BSP/CPI(M)/Congress/others); ownership (owner cultivator/landless tenant); and so on. Nominal data are marked by equality. These cannot be arranged in a meaningful order. These cannot be placed higher or lower with respect to each other. For instance, only a fanatic would place Christians, Hindus, Jews, Muslims and Sikhs at higher or lower pedestals with respect to one another.

The nominal scales have to possess certain qualities. These are :

(a) The categories are classes. These are related to each other along the same dimension. All persons within a category are alike. For example, ownership of cattle, community recognition, and political participation.
(b) The categories should be distinct, mutually exclusive. Thus, relations are relations, while professions are professions.
(c) Various categories should be ordered in such a way that these are collectively exhaustive. Taken together, these should take care of all the data. In case some interstitial spaces are somehow left out, we create a special category for the outliers.

The relationship between the categories is symmetrical (a=b, b=a). Mathematical operations (+, –, ×, ÷) are not applicable to nominal scales. We can calculate their mode (average) and calculate their coefficient of contingency.

Ordinal Scales

In addition to the qualities possessed by nominal scales, ordinal scales show transitivity (when a=b, and b=c, then a=c). Unlike nominal scales, the numbers are interchangeable. They possess asymmetrical (2>1) order or succession. Hence, each class always stands between the same two neighbours. The items can be ranked higher or lower with respect to each other along certain dimensions. Ordinal numbers point out the relative placement in order of importance. But they do not reveal the exact distance. While they say that one category is higher than the other, they do not tell us how much. Ranks are applicable only within a given set of categories. The given ranks are not relevant outside that set. Ranks cannot be added up. Mathematical operations (+, –, ×, ÷) are not applicable to ordinal scales. Unlike nominal variables, ordinal variables can be compared with one another.

Figure 6

Ordinal scale for environmental problems of the 21st century

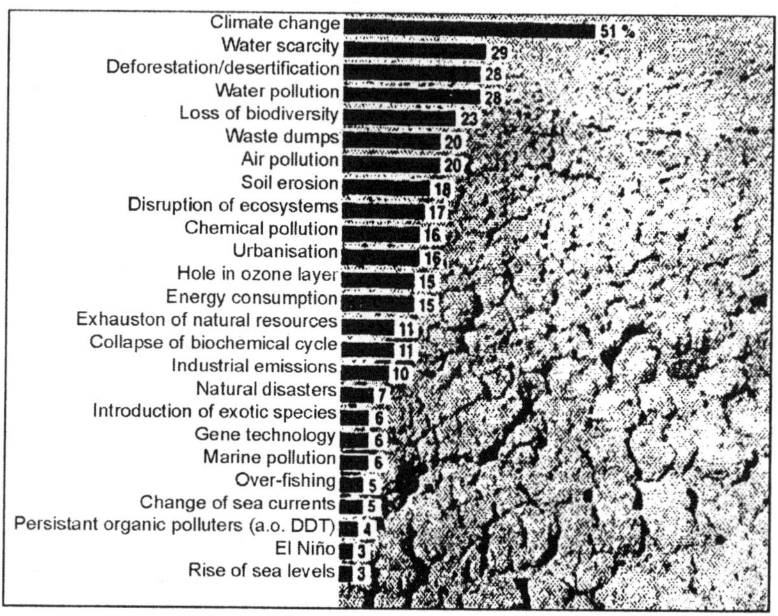

Source: The Tribune, Chandigarh.

Ordinal variables do not reveal the exact distance between ranks. Ordinal data cannot be ordered according to their intensity as high or low. Statistical tests which are applicable to nominal scales are also applicable to ordinal data, e.g., marks, grades, preferences.

Figure 6 shows an ordinal scale for the most important environmental problems of the 21st century. These have been put together on the basis of the opinions of 2,000 experts and scientists of the United Nations Environmental Programme (UNEP), in the year 2000.

Interval Scales

In case of such a scale, not only the ranks, but also the distance between the items is known. However, these need not necessarily be equidistant. In case of such a scale, the exact distance between adjacent ranks is known. It may be negative, or even zero. In this respect, there is no difference between interval scales and the next higher form of scaling, viz., the ratio scale. The distance between two categories is exactly the same. Let us take up an example (see Figure 7). The intelligence quotient (1Q) between 110 and 120 is greater than that between 100 and 110. In addition, to that, there is no zero point in this scale, or it is arbitrary. Once more, we cannot assert that a person whose IQ is 120 is one and a half times as intelligent as another person whose IQ is 80. Mathematical operations (only + and –) are applicable to interval scales.

Figure 7
Interval scale for intelligence quotient (IQ)

90 → 100 → 110 → 120 → 130

Ratio Scales

In addition to all the properties of an interval scale, it possesses a conceptually meaningful zero point. This cannot be negative.

Table 3
Ranking of interpersonal relations between boys and girls in a university in India (1978)

Types of relationship	*Rank*
Hesitating to talk to the opposite sex	1
Exchanging class notes	2
Taking tea together in canteen	3
Going to cinema together	4
Falling in love/infatuation	5

Figure 8
Ratio scale

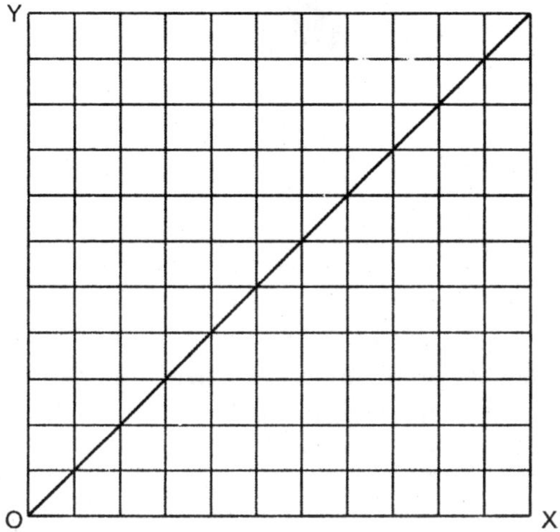

Zero exists at a point where a scale possesses no quality this way or that. For example, nobody has zero intelligence. However, something can have zero weight. Nobody can be as tall as six feet above the ground and six feet below.

In other words, a ratio scale possesses four qualities : (1) identity, (2) tansitivity, (3) being metric and (4) having an absolute zero point. Mathematical operations (× and ÷) are applicable to it. For instance, centimetre (0-100) and gram (0-100). Ratio scales are hardly ever used in sociology. Its subject matter is of complex nature. Mathematicians and economists always use ratio scales (see Figure 8). The rates of growth used here are constant.

As we proceed from nominal to ordinal to interval to ratio scales, the degree of certainty of the outcome gradually goes up. Thus, the four types of scales given above are in a hierarchy, in an ascending order. Each succeeding level possesses the characteristics of the preceding level. The strength of measurement goes on increasing as we move over from the lowest to the highest level of scaling.

Statistical Tests for Scales

Inadvertent misapplication of statistical techniques becomes a source of error. The underlying assumptions must be kept in mind. Otherwise, the conclusions would be erroneous.

Table 4
Properties of different levels of scales

Level	*Direction, intensity*	*Rank order*	*Distance*	*Absolute zero*
Nominal	✔			
Ordinal	✔	✔		
Interval	✔	✔	✔	
Ratio	✔	✔	✔	✔

Before applying specific statistical measurement, it has to be ensured that the give conditions have been fulfilled, e.g., Pearson's product moment coefficient of correlation is not applicable to anything less than ratio scales. Do not unconditionally impose factor analysis where t-test would do. Continuous or polytomous variables may have to be dichotomised in order to ensure that the proposed statistical tests are applicable to them.

Item Analysis

Item analysis is a tool for selecting the best items that work well. In case of paper-setting for examinations, the items are moderated for being tough or lenient. This helps the paper-setter to decide which items are to be included in the question paper, and which ones are not fit for this purpose. Thus, the required percentage of candidates is allowed to get through at different stages of a competitive examination. This is done with a view to shortening the list with view to filling the available number of job vacancies. Similarly, the number of successful candidates in competitive admission tests can be cut according to the number of the available seats. Simple statistical measures are available for this purpose.

In case of scale construction for attitude measurement, the items are checked up for being meaningful, balanced and comprehensive. For this purpose, we correlate single items with the total score for the scale. This gives internal consistency. In addition to that, we calculate dispersion. In order to ensure a modicum of homogeneity, items with weak dispersion and outliers are excluded. Those that do not fit in at the proper place are reformulated or discarded.

Table 5
Application of statistical tests at different levels of scaling

Level of scaling	*Example*	*Math'l operations*	*Average, zero*	*Significance*	*Correlation*
Nominal	Gender	Counting	Mode	Chi-square	Coefficient of contingency
Ordinal	SES	<=>	Median		ANOVA
Interval	1Q	+ –	Mean	t-test, F-test	Spearman's rank correlation
Ratio	Income (Rs/month)	x ÷	Geometric, harmonic mean		Product moment cooefficient of correlation

Staple Scale

Let us take up some well-known scales for consideration. There are scales and scales. Each one of them possesses unique qualities. These can be put to use in different situations.

Staple means main, prime, principle product, etc., for day-to-day ordinary usage. Punjabis prefer wheat *chapatis*. Rice *bhat* is the staple diet of Bengal. Staple scale is a unipolar, frequently used analytical tool for measuring the intensity of perceptions. The respondents are shown a card with ten boxes. Boxes have numbers, graphic rating scales have, say, minimum 1 to maximum 10, without a zero and without a verbal label. The respondents are asked to give some marks from this card to something under analysis. The object may be, say, Barrack Obama, Nano car, a village school or Bharatnatyam dance performance by Yamini

Figure 9
Well-known scales/techniques for measurement

- Staple scale
- Likert scale
- F-scale
- Thurstone scale
- Guttman scale
- Bogardus scale
- Semantic differential scale
- Psychometry
- Multidimensional scale
- Sociometry

Krishnamoorthy. The total score for the object will be the median for all the respondents. We can compare the median scores for two or more samples of the population. This provides us data on the direction and intensity of the object under consideration. Additional data on background and personality, etc., of the respondents can be collected for extended analysis.

Figure 10
Staple scale for measuring attitudes

	or
10	+5
9	+4
8	+3
7	+2
6	+1
5	–1
4	–2
3	–3
2	–4
1	–5

A staple scale is not very demanding. It is easy to construct and administer. It yields straightforward results. We do not have to use a complicated scale when a simple procedure gives satisfactory results.

Thurstone Scale

Here we will confine our attention to Louis L. Thurstone's (1887-1954) method of paired comparisons. Selection of relevant statements to construct a scale, and assignment of scale values to them before administering them to respondents are important steps in this method. These statements are administered to knowledgeable persons, with a view to working out the scores before using them to gather data from a field. The subject-matter specialists are asked to agree or disagree with the statements placed before them. Let us look at various steps of this procedure.

(a) Collecting statements : In order to put up a scale on, say, birth control, we gather a number of relevant statements, say 100. These express all sorts of opinions on the concept under consideration.

Selection is done on the basis of the ability to discriminate between different types of reactions. Some of these items are positive, while others are negative. These can be collected from newspapers, observation in the field, or already existing studies. The items should be brief and to the point. Each of them should contain an opinion.

(b) Assigning scores to statements : The collected statements are placed before subject-matter specialists, say 30 of them. They should be like the rest of the population under study. They are asked to place these statements on an eleven-point scale, ranging between positive and negative extremes. The specialists are not expected to give their own opinion in this regard. They rate how much favourable or unfavourable the expression is towards the object under examination. We figure out average scores assigned by the specialists to the statements. Their dispersion is also noted down. This tells us their degree of clarity and lack of ambiguity. Widely fluctuating statements, those about which there is difference of opinion among the specialists (dispersion is high) are removed. We select a few statements out of the rest in such a way that they lie at more or less equal distance from each other. They should have a broad spread from one end of the chain of attitude to the other. These statements, say, 20, form our Thurstone scale. We disturb their disorder by arranging them anew. This is done in some logical or numerical or random order. They stretch from low intensity at one end to high intensity at the other. A small amount of mixing up serves to avoid response set. The scores are not revealed to the respondents. This checks their possible tendency to tilt the replies in one direction or another.

(c) Calculating total scores for individuals : During the course of a survey, these statements are administered to a representative sample of population in the universe. Large size samples need not necessarily be representative samples. It is the method of selection that matters. A survey is as good as its sample. Those under study are asked to agree or disagree with the statements. The averages (medians) of the accepted (not rejected) statements add up to yield summated ratings. This shows the total score of the scale. This indicates the attitude of our respondents towards the object under investigation. In the present case, this is birth control. Group scores are averages of the total individual scores.

Figure 11
Eleven-point scale for judges in Thurstone scale

+5	+4	+3	+2	+1	0	–1	–2	–3	–4	–5

Table 6
Thurstone scale for attitude towards birth control

	Item	*Score*
1.	The practice of birth control is equivalent to murder.	0.0
2.	Birth control should be absolutely prohibited.	0.9
3.	Birth control is racial suicide.	1.1
4.	Birth control reduces marital relationship to a level of sex.	1.7
5.	Decency forbids the use of birth control.	2.3
6.	The practice of birth control evades man's duty to propagate his race.	2.8
7.	The practice of birth control may be injurious physically, mentally and morally.	3.3
8.	Birth control is morally wrong in spite of possible benefits.	3.6
9.	The slight benefit of birth control hardly justifies it.	4.5
10.	Birth control has both advantages and disadvantages.	5.4
11.	People should be free to do anything about birth control.	5.8
12.	Birth control has nothing to do with morality.	6.6
13.	Birth control is necessary for women who must help earn a living.	7.4
14.	Birth control is a legitimate health measure.	7.6
15.	Birth control increases the happiness of married life.	8.0
16.	Birth control information should be available to everybody.	8.3
17.	Uncontrolled reproduction leads to overpopulation, unrest and war.	9.2
18.	Birth control is the only solution to many of our social problems.	9.6
19.	Only fools can oppose birth control.	9.8
20.	We simply must have birth control.	10.5

Thus, those who want to construct a scale start with several items. Their effectiveness is statistically ascertained with the assistance of experts and comes down to a few statements. Then their scores are calculated. These are put in order for use in measurements.

Table 6 shows a Thurstone scale for attitude towards birth control. Down below there is a scale prepared by Shukla *et al.* on attitude towards science and technology. Its validity, realiability and culture-fairness remain unknown for want of details of statistical treatment.

The Shukla scale is at least a collection of useful items for scaling purposes.

1. Science and technology make our lives heathier, easier and more comfortable.
2. Science changes our lives fast.
3. We depend too much on science.
4. New technology makes our lives interesting.
5. Modern science and technology will create better opportunities for the next generation.
6. The quality of science education in Indian schools is satisfactory.
7. Scientists should be allowed to do research on animals.
8. People should live a simple life without much technology.
9. Technological development creates an artificial and inhuman life.
10. Technological development will eventually destroy the earth.
11. Computers and factory automation will eliminate more jobs than create.

(d) Interpretation : During the course of a survey on family planning, one may use a Thurstone scale. Analysis of data on the basis of evidence and logical reasoning may reveal that a variety of reasons stated in favour of son-preference constrain the success of this programme. These include apprehension of being left alone without needed support in old age. The daughters will go away. An old mother with daughters who was a queen in young age, has to perform household chores. She may have to fetch water from outside in her old age. This implies that if you want them to restrict their family size, or give up practices like son preference, somehow give them a standard of living worth protecting and a modicum of social security.

(e) Limitations of Thurstone Scale : Thurstone scale has made valuable contributions for the measurement scales. However, this method suffers from a number of defects. Gaps between subject-matter specialists and the respondents reduce the validity of the scale. Moreover, this technique is time-consuming. Table 7 compares and contrasts the Thurstone and the Likert scales.

Likert Scale

Renesis Likert (1903-81) scale takes the following steps one by one :

(a) Collecting statements : First of all we generate, say, 50 statements on the matter under consideration. We have somehow the intuitive understanding that these are suitable for measuring the object, say, citizens' attitude towards nuclear energy. The items need not be directly related to what is being measured. The statement should be subtly interrelated, even if the relationship is not clear at the start. About a half of them should be favourably inclined, and the remaining ones unfavourably. Some of these statements are to be positively formulated, others negatively. We administer them directly to the respondents without the intervention of subject-matter specialists. The respondents are asked to rank these statements on a five-point scale, duly verbalised to bring out the direction as well as intensity of reactions.

(b) Assigning numbers : The answers from the respondents are given numbers (say, 1 to 5). The numbers should be applied in the correct direction (positive or negative meaning of the statement). Thus, if an item is negative, i.e., strong agreement means strong disagreement, then the items are given reverse scores. This brings all the statements in the same direction. While assigning numbers we proceed on the basis of the assumption that the chain of responses (agreement/disagreement) is divided into five equal intervals. This assumption is not true. However, it is justified to start with several items. Statistically calculate their effectiveness. Remove items that do not work, e.g., outliers. In practice, inaccuracies on the left cancel out those on the right.

(c) Moving towards unidimensionality : Statistically calculate their effectiveness. Evaluate all the statements. Correlate the scores on each statement with the total scores on all the statements. This enables us to find out which ones are related to one another and the object under study. This enables us to eliminate the statements that are not unidimensional. Item analysis for Likert scale is done by selecting statements with high discriminating power, i.e., those on the two extremes. Thus, 25 per cent statements have the highest scores, and 25 per cent have the lowest scores.

Table 7

Likert scale (by Stouffer) for soldiers' reactions towards dangers of battle

Statement	*Often*	*Sometimes*	*Once*	*Never*
1. Urinating in pants.				
2. Loosening control over the bowels.				
3. Vomiting.				
4. Feeling weakness or feeling faint.				
5. Feeling stiffness.				
6. Feeling slip in the stomach.				
7. Shaking or trembling all over.				
8. Sinking feeling of the stomach.				
9. Violent pounding of the heart.				

Item analysis can also be done by plotting an item trace-line between a subject score on an item and his total score on all the items. Non-linear items are those with a zero slope. These are rejected. Linear items with a slope between 1 and 4 are retained.

In order to find out internal consistency, we apply the t-test. This helps us to exclude unstable items and objects. Factor analysis would reveal that a common factor accounts for the relationship between items.

(d) Calculating total scores : The scores of all the respondents on all the selected items are added upto yield a summated rating. Each item is given equal weightage in the total score. While giving, say, five marks to 'strongly agree' and one mark to 'strongly disagree', it is assumed that the former is five times as large as the latter. It is also assumed that the points in between are equidistant from each other. As a matter of fact, these assumptions are not true. Cutting points between the response categories have a hazy distinction. Nevertheless, in practice occurrences left and right cancel each other out. The model works well. An individual's score is obtained by adding up his scores on the selected items. This represents his attitude towards the object under study. The items are pooled up. These are interpreted together, not one by one. This is done after obtaining their coefficients of correlation, or applying other suitable statistics. For example, t-test is applied in order to ascertain significant difference of means between the high and the low groups.

Table 8
Likert scale for job satisfaction

Dimensions	*Highly dissatisfied*	*Dissatisfied*	*In between*	*Satisfied*	*Highly satisfied*
1. Income					
2. Job content					
3. Conditions of work					
4. Social environment					
5. Distance between place of work and place of residence					

(e) Interpretation: This means grasping from outside and understanding from within. The result is translated into familiar terms. It is different from speculation. It is explained with a view to bringing home a point. For example, during the course of a survey on perception of life satisfaction, one may prepare a Likert scale. This scale may include satisfaction on health, economic independence, family size, religiosity, liking for neighbours, frequency of social contacts as well as quality of social interaction. Multivariate analysis would reveal that such and such variables are so much significant for making them satisfied. This would also signify that residuals have been left unexplained upto a given extent. In this way, the empirical data are knitted into a theoretical framework.

(f) Criticism : The Likert scale is often claimed to be an interval scale. It is dealt with as such. It is assumed that the response categories are divided into equal intervals. For statistical purposes, it is safer to look at it as an ordinal scale.

Nevertheless, Likert's is a robust scale.

Comparison of Thurstone and Likert Scales

Research studies have shown high degree of correlation (.99) between Thurstone and Likert scales. Their findings converge.

Table 9
Comparison of Thurstone and Likert scales

	Thurstone scale		*Likert scale*
1.	Method of equal appearing intervals.	1.	Method of summated ratings.
2.	Item analysis not used.	2.	Applies t-test and or correlations for item analysis.
3.	Clearly related items.	3.	Items and scores empirically consistent.
4.	Two degrees of response.	4.	Five degrees of response.
5.	Pseudo-precision.	5.	Equally weighted statements.
6.	Subjectivity of judges involved.	6.	Items and scores empirically consistent.
7.	Unwieldy.	7.	Convenient.

F-scale

The F(ascism) scale was constructed by Adorno et al. (1903-69) for measuring the attitude of individuals towards their predisposition to authoritarianism. Its items have been knitted around a variety of carefully selected variables. The same are shown hereunder:

1. Obedience and respect for authority are the most important virtues children should learn.
2. A person who has bad manners, habits and breeding can hardly expect to get along with decent people.
3. If people would talk less and do more, everybody would be better off.
4. The businessman and the manufacturer are socially much more important than the artist and the professor.
5. Science has its place. But there are many more important things that can be understood by human mind.
6. Every person should have complete faith in some supernatural power, whose decisions he obtains without question.

7. Young people somewhat get rebellious ideas, but as they grow up, they ought to get over them and settle down.
8. What this country needs more than laws and political progress, is a few courageous, tircless, devoted leaders in whom the people can put their faith.
9. No sane, normal decent person could think of his being a close friend or relative.
10. Nobody ever learnt anything really important, except through suffering.
11. What the youth needs most is strict discipline, rugged determination, and the will to work and fight for family and country.
12. An insult to our honour should always be punished.
13. Sex crimes, such as rape and attack on children deserve more than mere imprisonment. Such criminals should be publicity whipped and worse.
14. There is hardly anything lower than a person who does not feel a great love, gratitude and respect for his parents.
15. Most of our social problems would be solved if we could somehow get rid of the immortal, crooked and feebly-minded people.
16. Homosexuals are hardly better than criminals, and ought to be severely punished.
17. When a person has a problem or a worry it is best for him not to think about it, but to keep busy with more cheerful things.
18. Nowadays, more and more people are prying into matters that should remain personal and private.
19. Some people are born with an urge to jump from high places.
20. People can be divided into two distinct classes : the weak and the strong.
21. Some day it will probably be shown that astrology can explain a lot of things.
22. Wars and social troubles may some day be ended by an earthquake or flood that will destroy the whole world.
23. No weakness or difficulty can hold us back if we have enough will for power.
24. It is best to use some pre-war authorities in Germany to keep order and prevent change (you will have to pretend that it is pre-1946 when you answer this question).
25. Most people do not realise how much our lives are constrained by plots hatched in secret places.

26. Human nature being what it is, there will always be war and conflict.
27. Familiarity breeds contempt.
28. Nowadays when so many kinds of people move around and mix together so much, a person has to protect himself, especially carefully catching infection or disease from them.
29. The wild sex life of the old Greeks and Romans was tame, compared to some of the goings on in this country, even in places where people might least expect.
30. The true American way of life is disappearing so fast that force may be necessary to prevent it.

The answer category for all items is the same :

Strongly disagree	Mostly disagree	Somewhat disagree
Strongly agree	Mostly agree	Somewhat agree

At the time of administering the scale to a representative sample of population in the universe under study, the scores are NOT to be revealed to them.

(a) Interpretation : The famous F-scale is used in the context of a social survey with a representative sample of the population under study. We may come out with such conclusions as : The authoritarian personality develops in an authoritarian family under the strict bringing up of a dominant father. Individuals get used to following the orders of the higher-ups without asking questions. They become rigid moralists as well as sullen and insecure cyncis. They lack self-confidence and have flat emotions. They think in terms of stereotypes. Their deep-rooted prejudices make them prone to discriminating against marginalised groups.

Table 10

Evaluation of results for F-scale

Score	*Interpretation*
<2	Overliberal
2-3	Liberal
3-4.5	Disciplined and tolerant
4.5-5.5	Fascistoid
5.5>	Fascist

Such a way of thinking gives rise to an authoritarian state. Demagogues, backed by political and economic vested interests sway the masses.

The authoritarian mentality in a society can be liberalised with flexible socialisation and compensatory education.

(b) Criticism : Often there are gaps between thinking, feeling and acting. Even if we switch on our head before we operate our mouth, verbal expressions need not possess implementational implications. F-scale may yield misleading results. What Adorno's F-scale measures is not exactly authoritarian personality, but something like that.

Guttman Scale

Louis L. Guttman (1916-87) put forth a hierarchy in the matter under consideration. Items are ordered by the degree of difficulty of the underlying latent attributes. An individual's score on a scale is the rank of the highest item in the hierarchy that it endorses.

This scale is known as scalogram analysis, or cumulative scaling. The items for the scale are chosen in such a way that they are short in size. They possess good discriminating power. They are highly structured. They are unidimensional. This means that they use a single trait and are homogenous. The reactions are in a single direction, or monotonous. Being cumulative means that the various items composing the scale can be ordered in a single series or continuum of intensity with varying grades. The items are so arranged that those who answer a given item positively will also answer the preceding one in the same manner. A respondent would agree with all the items upto a certain limit, and reject

Table 11

Items for a Guttman scale on political participation

	Item	*Response*
1.	Turning out to cast one's vote in general elections.	Yes/No
2.	Following the election campaign on TV.	Yes/No
3.	Attending a political meeting during an election campaign.	Yes/No
4.	Campaigning for the candidate of a political party in an election campaign.	Yes/No
5.	Giving subscription to a political party.	Yes/No

all the subsequent items. The escalation can be concealed by mixing up various items.

For example, the five items in Table 11 form an acceptable Guttman scale. A respondent who possesses the first characteristic also possesses the subsequent four characteristics. In case a respondent here or there does not fit into the response pattern, this is an error. Errors are not permitted to cross a threshold of acceptability. The detailed procedure for constructing a Guttman scale is given hereunder :

(a) Selecting statements : Collect a large number of statements with good discriminating power on various points on, say, political participation. Arrange them according to their favourable/unfavourable attitudes. One intuitively reduces these statements to at least ten in number, with homogeneous content. Application of item analysis is not necessary.

(b) Gathering data : Administer these statements to a representative sample of the universe under study. Ask the respondents to express their agreement or disagreement with them one by one.

(c) Calculating scores : For this purpose, give 1 mark to those who agree. Give zero mark to those who disagree. Add up the scores of all the respondents. Those who answer the given question positively will have higher scores than those who give negative answers. Remove items with larger as well as smaller scales. Calculate the averages of all the items. The response pattern can be reproduced if we know the total score on the scale.

(d) Examine reproducibility : Arrange the items as well as the individuals in an order. Examine the structure of responses. Closely observe and intuitively assess the pattern of responses for each respondent. Select appropriate patterns. The latent structure of the data can be unfolded with scalogram analysis. See that there is an unambiguous error-free unidimensional pattern. In case a particular item

Figure12

Cumulative steps for Guttman scaling for womens' cosmetics

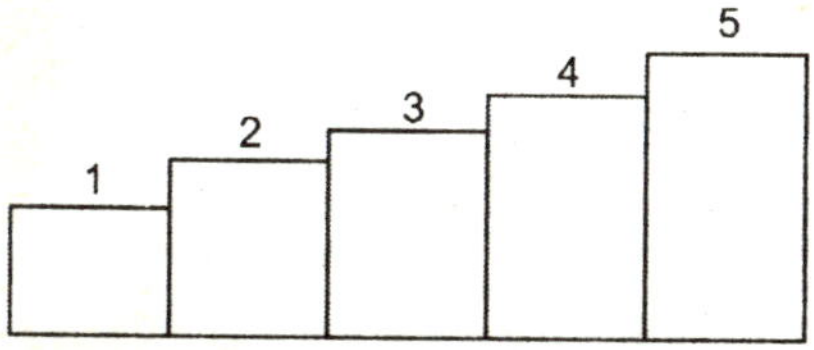

where : 1. Toothpaste, 2. Face powder, 3. Face cream, 4. Lipstick, 5. Perfume.

does not fit in, this would be an error. This indicates deviance from a perfect hierarchy. The hierarchy is seldom perfect. So we calculate the coefficient of reproducibility (Rep.) as follows:

$$\text{Rep.} = 1 - \frac{\text{No. of errors}}{\text{No. of items} \times \text{No. of respondents}}$$

Rep. is also known as C.R. Value. In case a scale with ten items has been given to 100 respondents, the number of responses would be 10 × 100=1000. The score of reproducibility of 0.9 would be 100 errors for all the responses and respondents. Thus, 10 per cent errors are permissible. This is a satisfactory result. Table 12 clears the pattern in case of 5 responses for 5 respondents.

Cull out the items that detract from reproducibility and unidimensionality. These are either unreasonable, or invalid, or outliers. Change the items. Suitably modify the scale in such a way that it suits all responses.

(e) Arranging statements : Arrange the statements in such a manner that those who express agreement with the earlier statements also do so for the latter statements. List the items before and after each other in such a way that the pattern comes out well. Show cutting points between different levels, where there is a category shift. A few errors would have to be tolerated. There should be more non-errors than errors. If and when necessary, Rep. can be increased by changing one or more of the statements.

Table 12

Cornell-Guttman technique for scalogram response pattern

Respondent	*Items*					
	1	*2*	*3*	*4*	*5*	*Total*
1.	+	+	+	+	+	5
2.		+	+	+	+	4
3.			+	+	+	3
4.				+	+	2
5.					+	1

(f) Criteria : 1. As pointed out earlier, Rep. or degree of deviation of the data from its model must be at least 0.9.

2. Errors should be random.

3. The number of non-errors should be larger than the number of errors. Meaningless responses should be eliminated.

4. The number of items should be large. At least ten items are to be used. Remove items that do not work.

(g) Interpretation : Alongwith data on the scale, we may collect additional data on social background, motivation and expectations of those in a sample of the universe under investigation. This enables us to come out with such statements as : Political participation is a function of SES. Politics is elite competition. Prejudice and discrimination against those who are looked down upon as outsiders is widespread.

(h) Advantages of Guttman scaling : It is simple and inexpensive. It generates ordinal data from nominal data. The Guttman scale is a joint scale. It ranks the items as well as the respondents. It guarantees unidimensionality.

(i) Criticism : This scale is unstable, and gets altered over space and time. The order is difficult to achieve.

Bogardus Scale

In a way, human beings are like porcupines. In a cold wintery night, they go into a burrow. They feel warm by coming near each other. If they come too near, and do not maintain their borders by keeping proper distance, their spines prick one another. So they neither come too near, nor keep away, but remain in-between. Keeping proper distance from one another is a principle of good manners. Without good manners, human life is intolerable and even impossible.

Bogardus (1882-1973) constructed a scale for measuring social distance between different groups. Like Guttman scale, the procedure used by him is called scalogram analysis. Guttman has precedence over Bogardus.

In case of the Bogardus scale, the respondents are administered a set of items with varying degrees of closeness. Thereby they are asked to indicate which types of contacts of varying degrees of closeness they would like to maintain with one another. Their attitudes are measured in terms of the distance indicated by them. The respondents are asked to agree or disagree with each item. The items are inter-connected in such a way that if a person agrees with, e.g., the fourth item, he is likely to agree with the preceding three items. Some amount of jumping here and there can not be avoided. However, it is ignored. The total score of all those individuals who respond positively would be high. Similarly, the total score of the individuals who respond negatively would be low. A score of 1 for a group means that there is least social distance. In the same way, a score of 7 would mean that the groups are far apart. While insiders are included in the core, outsiders are excluded therefrom. They are relegated to the periphery. There is prejudice and discrimination against outsiders.

This scale can also be reversed. In this way, the affected persons' perception of their being near or far from one another can be found out. The categories in Table 14 may then be formulated as given in Table 15.

The results are reduced to a single score on this scale. It is used for measuring attitudes towards different types of social groups. Readings with social distance are compared with factors that influence such decisions.

(a) Instructions : Please place a check (ü) mark to indicate the degree to which you would be willing to admit members of each of the ethnic categories mentioned below. Make sure that your reactions are to each category as a whole, not to its best or worst members you may have come across.

Table 13
Members of ethnic categories

Category	*1*	*2*	*3*	*4*	*5*	*6*	*7*
Christian							
Hindu							
Muslim							
Parsi							
Pathan							
Scheduled caste							
Scheduled tribe							
Sikh							

Data from Bogardus scales can be interpreted to yield such conclusions as : A large majority of the respondents are marked by unfavourable attitude towards outsiders. They would not like to mix up with those who do not belong to them to a lesser or greater extent. Their attitude towards some ethnic groups is worse than others. Additional data may reveal that social distance is a function of social background and cross-cultural experience.

Table 14
Bogardus social distance scale (modified)

	Item	*Response*
1.	Reading in the same school.	Yes/No
2.	Getting your daughter married to them.	Yes/No
3.	Performing the last rites in the same cremation ground/crematorium.	Yes/No
4.	Sharing your place of worship.	Yes/No
5.	Going to the same heaven/hell.	Yes/No
6.	Eating in the same vessels.	Yes/No
7.	Practising untouchability.	Yes/No

Table 15
Reverse Bogardus social distance scale

	Item	*Response*
1.	Would they mind reading in the same school?	Yes/No
2.	Would they get polluted by touching you?	Yes/No
3.	Would they mind eating in the same vessels?	Yes/No
4.	Would they mind your visiting their place of worship?	Yes/No
5.	Would they mind getting their daughter married in your family?	Yes/No
6.	Would they mind performing last rites in the same cremation ground/graveyard?	Yes/No
7.	Would they mind going to the same heave/hell?	Yes/No

(b) Criticism : The Bogardus scale rests on uncontrolled procedures. The choice of indicators is not methodical. It is just a set of items from the least to the most extreme in order of acceptability. The scale is somewhat arbitrary. Verbal statements cannot always be taken at their face value. Often, these serve to conceal prejudices rather then revealing attitudes. Cross-cultural validity of the Bogardus social distance scale remains to be tested.

Multidimensional Scaling

Lazarsfeld stood on Guttman's shoulders and looked beyond. He developed his latent structure analysis. Guttman assured unidimensionality. This served as a stepping stone for Coombs to construct his multidimensional scale. Mokken used Guttman's insights to construct a multidimensional scale from an item pool that is sensitive to many dimensions. Instability does pose a problem in all these cases.

The earlier scales are built on the assumption of unidimensionality. Such a supposition is hardly ever met by the actually existing reality. Real life is intricate. Therefore, attempts are being made to construct multidimensional scales. This enables us to look at several directions of an object under study. Widespread availability of facilities for electronic data processing have made it easy to perform the task of taking up enormous amounts of data into consideration. Table 16 gives the example of a multidimensional scale.

Table 16

Compulsive buying behaviour scale by Elizabeth Edward

	Item
1.	I feel driven to shop and spend, even when I do not have the time or the money.
2.	I get little or no pleasure from shopping. (R)
3.	I hate to go shopping. (R)
4.	I shop only out of necessity. (R)
5.	I go on buying binges.
6.	I feel 'high' when I go on a buying spree.
7.	I buy things even when I do not need anything.
8.	I go on a buying binge when I feel upset, disappointed, depressed or angry.
9.	I buy things even though I cannot afford them.
10.	I worry about my spending habits, but still I go out shopping and spending money.
11.	I feel guilty or ashamed after I go on a buying binge.
12.	I buy things I won't use or won't need.
13.	I sometimes feel compelled to go shopping.

(R) = Reverse.

Multidimensional scaling is a general data analysis technique. It displays the structure of data as a geometric picture. This helps in the discovery of their underlying structure.

Widespread availability of computers has replaced cumbersome manual calculations with speedy electronic processing of large masses of data. Appropriate softwares for the purpose are now available in plenty. Nowadays, ins and outs of large masses of data can be probed from many directions. Multidimensional scaling makes it easy to analyse the given social facts without distorting the reality under consideration.

The thirteen items in the table above are composed of five factors:

Factor 1 : Tendency to spend
Factor 2 : Compulsion/drive to spend
Factor 3 : Feeling joy about shopping or spending
Factor 4 : Dysfunctional spending
Factor 5 : Post-purchase guilt

Consumerism takes care of overproduction in a modern industrial society. However, it may create problems for some individuals. Often they are driven by the quest for acquiring material goods as also by overselling by advertisers and other forces in the market. Their failure to control their own impulse puts them under debt. This paves the way to financial, occupational and interpersonal damage.

In order to measure the direction and intensity of such damage, Edwards did a survey on self-admitted victims of consumerism. She constructed a scale of compulsive buying behaviour. Later on, she reduced her original 29 items on five underlying factos into 13 items in order to construct her scale on compulsive buying behaviour. It provides a continuum of lower to higher for measuring consumerism. She statistically checked up the reliability and validity of her scale.

She came to the conclusion that their itch to go on doing so may be attributed to low self-esteem.

(a) Criticism : Just as a skeleton tells us more than a single rib, a multidimensional scale gives us more information than a unidimensional scale. However, there are more things in the human body than a skeleton. No scale can measure each and everything.

Table 17 gives us another example of a multidirectional scale. The table reproduces its duly analysed factor structure.

The issue under consideration has become a controversy in the developed countries. Companies like Monsanto are keenly interested in denying the charges framed by environmentalists, like unnatural multiplication of cells becoming a cause of cancer.

Pope and his colleagues conducted a survey with a view to developing an instrument for measuring the predisposition of consumers towards genetically modified foods and crops (bt brinjal). Study of the available literature in the field brought out a large number of variables. They applied computer programmes to reduce these to 16 variables along five dimensions.

The scale possesses reliability as well as validity. Cross-cultural validation remains to be done. The five factors are as follows :

Table 17
Rotated factor matrix and item reliability for a multidimensional scale by Pope et al.

	I	*II*	*III*	*IV*	*V*
The use of genetic modification in food is dangerous	.926	—*	—	—	—
There will be negative long-term environmental effects of the use of genetically modified crops	.879	—	—	—	—
Eating genetically modified food is risky	.871	.126	–.142	.112	—
Genetic modification of plants can harm the environment	.833	—	.242	.142	—
I am well informed about biotechnology	.112	.870	—	–.121	—
I consider myself knowledgeable about genetics and biotechnology	.266	.790	—	—	—
I lack knowledge about genetically modified food	.219	–.710	—	–.137	.135
I am personally informed about the use of genetic modification in food production	–.694	—	–.316	—	
I trust newspapers as a source of providing advice about food	—	—	.813	—	.110
I trust television news and current affairs as a source of information providing advice about food	—	–.107	–.785	–.168	—
I do not trust the information concerning biotechnology provided by mass media sources	.165	—	.638	.198	—

...Cont'd

...Cont'd

It is important to trust those responsible for regulating the risks of genetic modification in food production	—	–.356	.555	–.246	.116
I think that genetically modified foods should be clearly labelled as such	.112	–.155	—	.839	—
Genetically modified foods should be labelled so that consumers can decide whether or not to buy them	—	—	.248	.764	—
I trust the government as a source of information providing advice about food	–.137	–.134	–.241	–.149	.844
I trust a doctor as a source of information providing advice about food	—	—	.162	.397	.776

* loading < 0.10

This shows a clear five-factor solution, with no item loading significantly on more than one factor. The factors were described as: Factor I—Dangers of genetic modification (four items), Factor II—Knowledge about genetic modification issues (four items), Factor III—Trust in media information sources (four items), Factor IV—Labelling of food products (two items), and Factor V—Trust in food information sources (two items).

Osgood's Semantic Differential Technique

This is Charles Osgood's (1916-91) general technique for looking into connotations (intentions, attributes, depth) of abstract concepts. Its objective is to find out the dimensions underlying attitudes. Thus, if a person's mentality is like 'that' in Lahore, he is also likely to behave in more or less the same way in Bangalore. This is just as Natha Singh and Prem Singh are one and the same thing.

Semantic differential technique lies on the common borders between many disciplines – Linguistics, philosophy, psychology, sociology and so on. Its roots can be traced to the old debate between nominalists and realists. The former are of the opinion that while genuine things exist in reality, their abstracts (universal) are mere words, just figments of imagination. For nominalists, universals have an independent existence of their own, perhaps in the world of ideas. General terms stand for real object.

Semantic differential is a bipolar concept. It compares and contrasts polarity, e.g., rural-urban, traditional-rational, status-contract, militant-industrial, war-peace an so on. Attribute pairs possess multidimensional features. They measure how a given object is perceived in a universe. How they understand the meanings of a term under examination. For this purpose, the respondents indicate their reactions to a single concept (say Bharatnatyam) by marking their position on a seven-point bipolar line. The two ends of the pole are defined by adjectives. Addition of some adverbial quantifiers (seldom, often, always, etc.) brings in intensity of measurement. These stimuli have to be selected carefully. They lie along the same continuum. Intuitive judgements, previous studies, statistical tests, etc., are relied upon for choosing the stimulus. Inadequate application of mind while choosing the terms can tilt the findings one way or another. There is a battery of scales.

Stimuli on the left are matched with those on the right. For example, in case of Table 18, the average ratings on both the poles are compared with each other. These can vary between +21 and –21. These are factor analysed. The factor analysis simplifies the set of data. After doing that, we go ahead to prepare their conceptual profile, with a view to interpreting the same.

Table 18

Bipolar profile for semantic differential scales for nuclear energy

	Extreme	*Quite*	*Sightly*	*Neutral*	*Slightly*	*Quite*	*Extreme*	
	+3	*+2*	*+1*	*0*	*–1*	*–2*	*–3*	
1. Active								Passive
2. Constructive								Destructive
3. Good								Bad
4. Positive								Negative
5. Right								Wrong
6. Safe								Unsafe
7. Wise								Foolish

This technique measures the direction of responses as well as their intensity. We can sum up the results. Extended analysis can be done with additional statistical examination.

Studies in different cultural milieus at different times have shown that the adjectives and adverbs under enquiry can be reduced to three underlying dimensions : E, i.e., evaluation (good or bad), P, i.e., patency (powerful or powerless), and A, i.e., activity (motion). This EPA structure links words with attitudes. It also helps us to clarify the relationship between attitude and behaviour.

The point is that the semantic differential scale provides a single generalised attitude space. A further advantage is that it is independent of the specific object under consideration. Each and every type of attitude remains reduced to these three dimensions. Thus, we can safely agree that scholars who get the insight that the latent structure of the alluring Bharatnatyam, the luxurious hotel Taj Mahal as well as the magnificent mausoleum Taj Mahal, is one and the same. Similarly, operations of the tiny atomic structures are akin to the seemingly disparate patterns in the infinite universe. This is a breakthrough indeed!

Let us put up hypothetical analysis of a hypothetical situation. Table 19 shows a made up test (with a view to bringing home a point) on attitude towards SC/ST. The data pertain to two comparable groups. The attitude of both the groups towards SC/ST is unfavourable. However, group I perceived them as strong and active.

Table 19

EPA, comparison of two groups

EPA	*Direction*	
	Group I	***Group II***
Evaluation	Unfavourable	Unfavourable
Potency	Strong	Weak
Activity	Active	Passive

Group II perceived them as weak and passive. Being anxious to avoid conflict, group I is inclined towards avoiding them. On the other hand, group II is disposed in favour of exploiting them, with a view to deriving benefits.

The validity of the semantic differential test has been established again and again. It yields predictable results. The technique has been found to be very useful. Subsequently, many scholars have come out with several innovative versions of this technique.

(a) Interpretation : It brings out such conclusions (inference + implication) as : The latent structure of stereotypes is the same everywhere. Stereotypes lead to prejudiced attitudes as well as discriminatory behaviour. Prejudice discredits other people. Discrimination oppresses them.

(b) Advantages : It is a reliable test for measuring all sorts of attitudes, and their latent structures.

Figure 13

Semantic differential space (EPA)

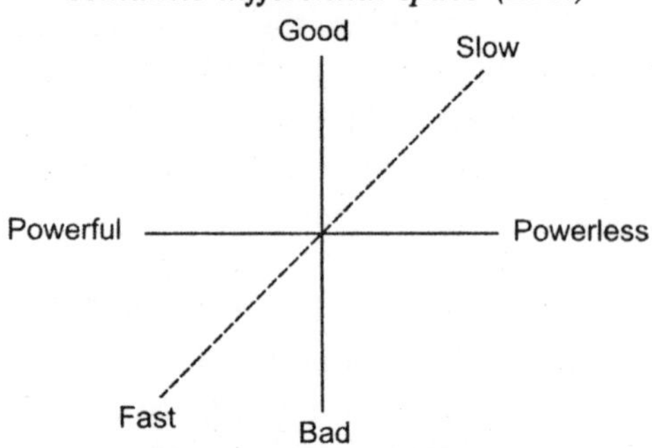

Interests of the sponsors and subjectivity of the researcher can tilt the findings one way or another. Respondents are also inclined to saying what they believe the investigators want to hear.

They tend to take socially desirable positions. Gaps between what actually is and what ought to be distort the findings. The semantic differential test is an effective tool of social inquiry.

Sociometry

In order to understand what sociometry is, let us distinguish it from what it is not. Sociometry is not anthropometry, econometry, psychometry, and similar other disciplines.

Anthropometry deals with measurement of different parts of the human body in terms of weight, height, head shape, finger prints, blood type, and so on. Colour of the skin, eyes and hair, shape of the nose, etc., are taken note of. The results have been used in comparative studies of different races. For example, Hitler's Germany followed the ideology of racial superiority. Anthropometric measurements were made use of at the time of recruitment, promotion, etc., of military officers. Their qualifications included pure Aryan racial features. These included a round head, blonde hair, and blue eyes. These days, its branch called **ergonomics** finds use in machine design as well as dress design, and time and motion studies, etc. Ergonomists make use of body measurements of operators for designing machines for use by them. Relying upon time and motion studies, they do not quickly get tired, and give higher output. Garment and footwear manufacturers design dresses according to standard body sizes in the regions where their products are to be marketed. Measurements perform multiple tasks. Nowadays, anthropometricians extract data from three dimensions of the human body. Variations are correlated across different territorial and climate zones.

(a) Econometry applies mathematical and statistical tools like matrix algebra, linear equations, regression and so on. This is done with a view to giving empirical content to economic theory. For example, econometricians make use of their models based on regression analysis of the available data, in order to estimate that this much input is going to produce that much output. Thus, which aspects of the economy and society would benefit from construction of a particular hydroelectric dam? How much support price for wheat is likely to result in higher production+votes for a political party? How much sugar can be exported from the country during the next financial year? What would be the ecological cost of economic development?

(b) The term **psychometry** is a synonym in use for research methods in psychology. Application of statistical techniques to mental processes is its main concern. Emphasis is placed on designing and administration of standard psychological tests. It also makes use of projective and other tools of research.

Projective Techniques

Besides other techniques of psychometry, psychologists also make use of projective techniques. Such techniques are suitable for exploring extensively in the unconscious mind. Projection is a defence mechanism. It involves expulsion of unpleasant feelings from one's mind. This frees the individual from anxiety and tension. While reacting in such a manner, an individual becomes suspicious. He makes a mountain of a mole hill. He blames others for what he himself secretly wants to do. For instance, he may try to get rid of his own guilt feelings for being jealous, and wishing to damage others by accusing them of being green-eyed monsters. He attributes his own fears and illusions to others, without being aware of what he is doing. Projective tests enable us to understand and explain the latent attributes and personality characteristics that cannot be observed otherwise. Such tests place the subject in a situation. Then he is asked to react to an ambiguous stimulus. Perception being functionally selective, he reacts in his own way. Thus, he unwillingly provides vital clues for a trained analyst to the structure and dynamics of his personality. Aspirations, expectations, difficulties and much else. Many projective tests are available for use.

These screw deep down into the unconscious mind, such techniques can bring out what the individuals are wont to conceal not only from others, but also from themselves. Recognition of realities places us in a position to apply corrections and come to terms with problems.

Rorshach Test

The Rorshach ink blot test is a projective technique where the subject is presented ready made suggestive ink blots. This test was first constructed by Hermann Rorshach (1884–1922). Several versions thereof are in use these days. These help analysts to diagnose personality characteristics—neurosis, psychosis, brain damage and so on. These tests are constructed by methodically throwing large ink blots on sheets of paper. The sheet is then folded to provide symmetry. Then it is imposed on a paper plate. The blot is standardised for repeated use. When it is shown to a subject, he interprets the ambiguous ink blots in his own way. He perceives the unclear situation according to the structure of his personality. His reactions throw light on this structure. The test-giver interprets the responses according to the standardised procedure prescribed by the test-maker for this purpose.

By the way, poets have used clouds, smoke coming out of a factory's chimney, or for that matter thick hair of a beloved, for getting similar results.

The Rorshach test consists of a series of ten standardised plates. Their shape and colour are carefully designed to vary the stimulus presented before the subjects. The investigator is not permitted to deviate from the prescribed ritual. Before administering the test, the tester establishes rapport with his subject. One third person is allowed to be present at that time. The plates are not just placed before the subject. These are handed over to him one by one in fixed order. The plates are not to be viewed from a distance of more than an arm's length. The subject is free to turn the plates around as he likes it. The tester asks the subject to respond spontaneously to each ink blot. He asks him, "What could this be?...Where?....Why?" There is no fixed time for exposure. The subject takes his own time. At least one response is compulsory. No reply is suggested. All answers are correct. The number of responses, reaction time, pauses, refusals, are recorded in a preplanned inventory. This provides for the location of the blot perceived by the subject (whole, details). The inventory also provides for the quality of the response (form, movement, colour, texture). It also contains columns for recording what the subject sees : Human beings (clowns, ghosts), animals (bat, bear, butterfly, caterpillar, crab, rabbit), objects (popular or original). Characters, emotions, themes, motives are methodically noted down. A point to be noted down here is that what the investigator records is different from what the subject says. What is perceived by the former is a cue for the latter. This indicates something other than itself to the investigator. Quick and accurate scoring requires a lot of practical training, indeed drill. The drill-master trains and disciplines the reflexes. The scored categories are interpreted, assigned meanings, according to the standardised scoring key provided by the test-maker. While responding to ambiguous or unstructured stimuli, those being tested inadvertently reveal various dimensions of their personality—Their apprehensions, unpleasant memories, conflict, source of stress, mental disease, and so on. They come out with what they cannot and will not speak out. This enables the investigator to draw meaningful inferences. He understands the matter. He classifies the personality. One advantage of this test is that it can be administered to even illiterate persons. Moreover, its standardised evaluation facilitates comparison.

The glamour of this technique cannot be denied. However, its reliability and validity can not be asserted. Various investigators come out with different interpretations.

TAT

Like other projective tests, in thematic apperception test, the subject voluntarily provides us a peep into his unconscious mind. That is directly inaccessible to the conscious mind, even though it affects human behaviour and emotions. The subject is presented a stimulating diagram depicting a situation. He is asked to make up and narrate a story, using his imagination. He describes what he sees in the diagram (see Figure 14). A time limit may be prescribed.

Alternatively, the subject is asked to make up a story based on leads provided to a specific starting point like : 'It is hard to say that ...'

The responses are interpreted to yield relevant conclusions for personnel selection, marriage counselling, clinical practice or basic research. TAT is a good diagnostic tool.

Unlike the Rorshach test, TAT is concerned with the substance rather than the style of the matter. Here the quality of the responses is more important than their quantity. The subject reveals his inner needs like that for achievement, power or affiliation. The investigator may make it out intuitively, or use a standardised scaling key for this purpose. A subject identifies himself with his subject. Then he projects his own needs on his subject, by either asserting or denying the same. Nevertheless, the scoring key for TAT is not reliable. Its validity is questionable. Moreover, previous coaching does affect the results.

Figure 14

Thematic apperception test (TAT)

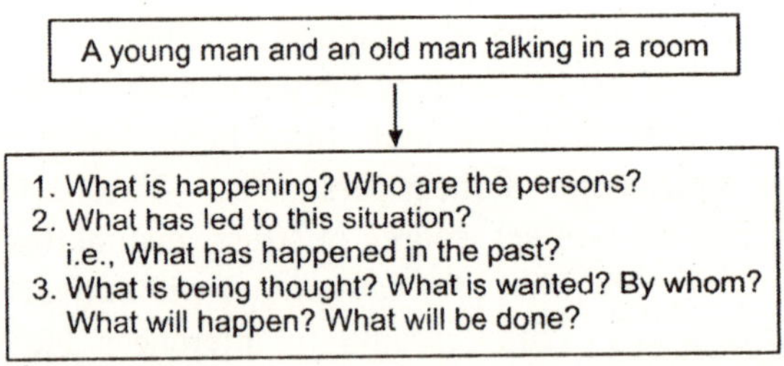

Word Association Test

The subjects are asked to associate a given word with a similar other word. While doing so, he is not given an opportunity to think twice. He is expected to spontaneously respond to the stimulus. He comes out with something that comes to his mind there and then. While doing so, he more or less constantly tries to avoid uttering a word that he wants to avoid. The analyst finds out what weighs on his mind, using different indicators, reaction time being one of them. This may be some hope or wish or apprehension, or a defence mechanism, etc. Free associations enable him to comprehend the neurotic trend. The subject may be made to recognise the existing realities and opportunities, so that he can come to terms with them. However, this test is useful not only for therapeutic but also for analytical purposes.

Who am I?

The applicants are asked to answer this question in, say, 250 words. They are expected to say something about themselves. They may provide information about their social background, motivation, expectations, aspirations, and so on. Their replies are content-analysed to find out their derived characteristics, like linguistic ability, task-orientation, positive attitude and so on.

Like a face-to-face interview, this test helps us to form first impressions. We may then go deep into the matter from various points of view.

Example 4 : If an applicant uses more verbs than adjectives we can say that he is task-oriented. He prefers functions over status. By making him aware of his tilt, and providing appropriate inducements, sensitivity training can encourage him to raise output at his place of work.

Graphologists reveal personality characteristics using handwritten answers to the question posed above.

Validity and reliability of projective tests is based on inside evidence, together with the subjective judgement of the researcher. Paired comparison, Stephenson's Q technique, etc., may be used for this purpose. As a matter of fact, the projective techniques possess limited validity. Their reliability is also low. Acquaintance with such tests through training (e.g., by coaching academies) can tilt the results.

Moreover, the projective tests are reflective just for the given purpose, not only for the observer but also for the subject concerned. They do not yield standard results. Mistrust and stereotypes do affect their results. Cultural and linguistic differences within and between cultures make it difficult to devise ecologically fair measures. Projective tests demand a lot of skill and high quality subjective judgement on the part of experienced researchers. Such tests mean different things to different people at different times. Nevertheless, they are aids to making the meaning clear by providing hints, indicators, and symptoms. Nevertheless, they do provide useful hints for diagnostic and therapeutic purposes. These can be made use of for constructing hypotheses, which remain to be tested. These can be verified by supplementing them with other methods. That yields theories and even laws. Like psychoanalysis, projective tests serve as therapeutic as well as pedagogical techniques. Broadly speaking, the subjects anthropometry, econometry, psychometry, and sociometry, deal with the same subject-matter. However their focus of attention, theories, and methods, differ from one another.

Moreno's Sociometry

The term 'sociometry' rhymes well with anthropometry, econometry, and psychometry. However, Jacob Moreno (1899-1974) restricted the term sociometry to the measurement of mutual preferences and informal social relations. There are more things in society than can be studied with Moreno's sociometry alone. In any case, the work of this creative and innovative sociologist needs due attention. Sociometric data on favourable/unfavourable reactions are gathered under certain conditions involving interaction. Meeting together gives rise to opinions, choices, networks, etc. e.g., being seen together, visiting each other, playing or dancing together. Data can be gathered by observing what they do, directly asking the actors concerned what they think about it, and noting down what other people say. Their reactions differ in different situations, e.g., dialogue, team work, entertainment, etc.

(a) Observation : This involves watching carefully and noting down what goes on in the field or in the laboratory. Patterns of acting together, scratching each other's back, coming to rescue at the time of need, etc., are recorded, using an observation unevenly. What the people do is objective. What they say they do is subjective. Subjectivity means that we are ready for the moment. Objectivity means that the moment is ready for us.

(b) Verbal expressions : Those being studied are asked direct questions about their beliefs, performance, interaction patterns, friendship, and so on. The respondents are asked with whom they would like to act within different situations, e.g., trade union leaders like to go to courts of law together with a legally competent colleague, and go to jail together with a jolly good fellow. Positive, negative and neutral responses are recorded on a given scale. The scores obtained are analysed in a number of alternative ways.

Indicators can be used for finding out the direction (favourable/unfavourable) and intensity (to what extent?) of the given choices. Each response category can be accompanied by: Why? This question brings out the reasons for the choice made by the respondents.

Data analysis : Sociometric data can be analysed in a number of ways. The following methods are often made use of for this purpose.

(a) Sociomatrix : A matrix is made up of rows and columns. Objects (individuals or groups) are placed in the same order both ways. Each

Table 20
Sociomatrix

Chooser/Chosen	1	2	3	4	5	6	7	Total
1.	+	+	+	+	+	+	+	7
2.		+	+	+	+	+	+	6
3.			+	+	+	+	+	5
4.				+	+	+	+	4
5.					+	+	+	3
6.						+	+	2
7.							+	1
Total	1	2	3	4	5	6	7	

matrix shows relationship between objects. In order to clearly bring out meaningful patterns, the objects are properly arranged, with a view to analysing the patterns. Besides using various indices, sociograms can be constructed for extended analysis.

(b) Indices : Various authors have constructed several indices for measuring sociometric patterns. Sample results indicate that the person who is a star is frequently chosen by others. An isolated person remains aloof and stands apart. A rejectee is disliked by others. An expansive person selects many others, who forget to mention his name. In a elique, there is a large number of mutual preferences within the small group. Some indices are shown in Table 21.

Table 21
Sociometric indices

Index	*Details*
Social status index	Sum of acceptances – Sum of rejections
Integration	No. of positive choices in a group
Ratio of attractions	$\frac{\text{No. of attractions}}{\text{No. of attractions and repulsions}} \times 100$
Ratio of repulsions	$\frac{\text{No. of repulsions}}{\text{No. of attractions and repulsions}} \times 100$
Ratio of interest	$\frac{\text{Used choices}}{\text{Available choices}} \times 100$

(c) Sociogram : Data inputs from sociomatrices help us to construct sociograms. A sociogram presents a glamorous picture of interpersonal relations in a group. The nodes represent individuals or groups. The lines represent connecting links. It clearly brings out the network.

The links and nodes in Figure 15 bring out various configurations. Now that facilities for electronic data processing are widely available, we can prepare sociograms with large amounts of data. In earlier days, the data for this purpose were restricted to 25 to 30 respondents.

Interpretation : A sociometric index may bring out such conclusions as—the sociometric choices reveal group cohesion. Cliques in organisations weaken the overall group-integration, and bring down organisational effectiveness. Cliques can be broken up by transferring some members from one department to others.

(d) Target diagram : Each quartile of subjects is placed in a number of circles around a centre. See Figure 15. Different cleavages of subjects (rich/poor, rural/urban) are placed in separate sectors. Within these circles and sectors, men may be placed with pointed (say, triangular or square), and women with rounded signs (say, circles). Those who receive the largest number of choices are placed in the innermost circle. Those with the smallest number of choices are put in the outermost circle. Thus, the data fall in visible contours. These are easily differentiated for analytic purposes.

Interpretation : Sociomatrix, sociometric indices, sociograms and target diagrams visibly facilitate analysis. Apart from that, we can construct tables and apply statistics. We may construct target diagrams with data about personality characteristics (age, gender, attitude, trustworthiness, etc.) on one side and a sociometric scale on the other. Thus, we can find out correlates of sociometric status. For example, we might draw such statements as : Homogenous work groups are marked by greater cooperation. Group solidarity raises productivity. In other words, sociometric configurations (obtained by dint of spontaneous informal preferences) raise productivity and profitability. The point is that the sociometric configurations can be cross-tabulated with individual behaviours, interpersonal relations, and so on.

Apart from being a technique of empirical social research, sociometry can be used for pedagogical (teaching) as well as therapeutic (curative) purposes. In sociodrama, the patients are asked to play

Figure 15
Structure of sociograms

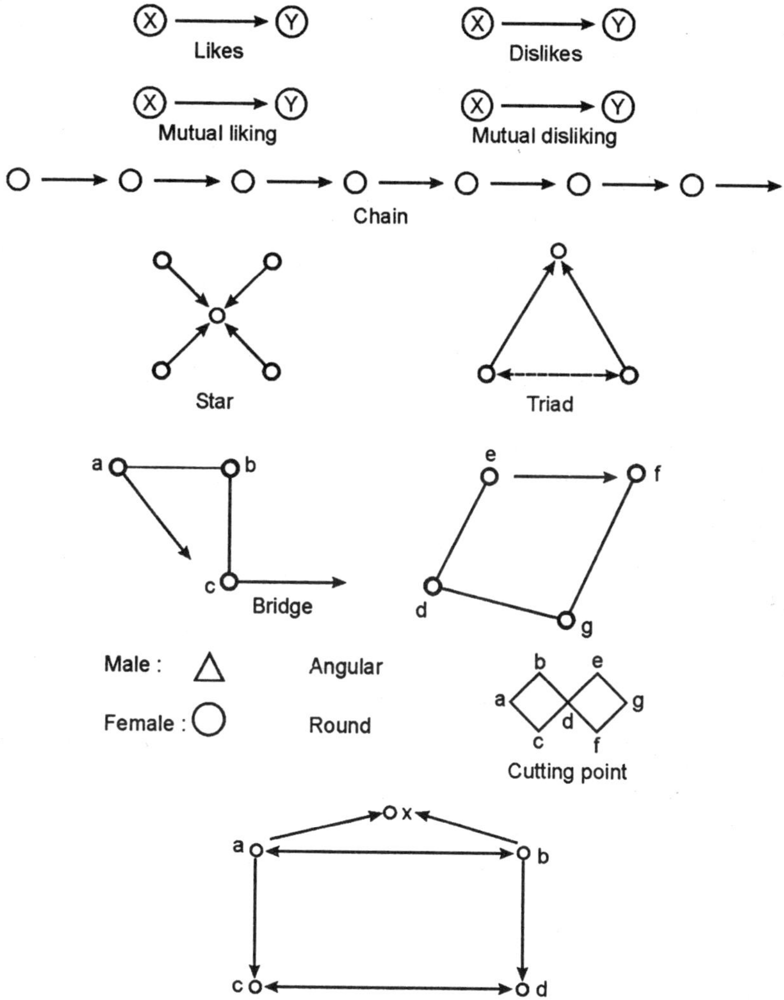

anti-existential roles. For example, a daughter-in-law plays the role of her mother-in-law. The former pretends to walk in the latter's footsteps. She mimics her. The fun of it makes her internalise and understand the old woman's problems. Such role-taking and role-play cure her of the effects of her trauma.

Advantages : Sociometric diagrams make it easy to interpret the data and summarise the relationships.

(b) An otherwise drab and dry project report becomes remarkably presentable with glamourous diagrams.

Limitations : The ignorant, the illiterate and the oppressed among the masses are afraid of saying what they think others would not like to hear. This distorts their responses. In this way, the reliability and validity of sociometric data becomes questionable.

Sociometry overemphasises informal relations, ignoring the formal aspects of social life. On the one hand, networks with affection and mutual trust are indispensable for living together. On the other hand, centralised, duly coordinated, formal-legal structures are indispensable for organisational effectiveness. However, sociometry lays too much emphasis on voluntary and spontaneous action. Nevertheless, every technique cannot do everything. Sociometry alone is far from being enough for understanding and explaining the social structures and processes. It is a useful tool of research. But it cannot do everything.

Conclusions : Choice of a Scale

During the last eight decades, intellectual craftsmen have worked hard to bring out a bonanza of scales. There are scales and scales and scales. Different methods, different outcomes. Instruments of research do affect the results. To use a scale, or not to use it, that is the question. Choice of one among many depends, above all, upon the objectives of the task before us. Correspondingly appropriate strategy and tactics are adopted. The basic purpose is to look around for regularly recurring patterns of human behaviour.

Figure 16
Target diagram

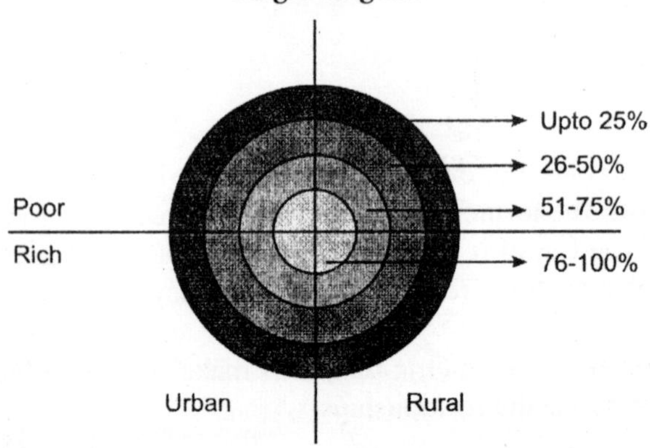

A staple scale is more than enough in many cases. Unnecessary complication of simplifications creates confusion. We do not go in for a complex scale where a simple scale will serve the purpose.

Scaling is done at an advanced stage of development of the social sciences. First of all, we apply our mind to the pros and cons of the problem before us. We grasp it from a distance and understand it from within.

My wife's gold bangles are 40 years old. During the course of time, their weight has gone down by seven gms. Similarly, the meaning of concepts gets transformed due to a number of reasons—impact of circumstances, role of mass media, etc. After some time, it is neither the same concept, nor the same scale. Structures change because there is functional load on them. People change over time. On the one hand, time is a great healer, on the other hand, it accentuates angularities.

The scale we construct ourselves, or select for our use, should be suitable as well as inexpensive in terms of time, effort and money. Empirical data are useless until and unless these have something to do with a theoretical framework.

Last but not the least, one or two readings are not enough. Unlike reading a novel, prolonged interaction and deep concentration are required. Like skills in music, or/and yoga, scale construction is a matter of learning by doing. What to speak of intellectual craftsmanship, even drug addiction is learnt under the supervision and guidance of an experienced *guru*. Practice make a man perfect.

A scale does not remain the same forever afterwards. Due to a number of reasons, it undergoes some amount of change. Following the same direction all the time, the respondents acquire a response set. Moreover, connotations of concepts get changed over time. See Table 22. It reveals change in stereotypes of Russians by Americans after World War II. Advancements in electronic data processing have changed the nature and scope of measurement and scaling. Enormous amounts of data can now be processed with speed and efficiency. This has shifted emphasis from data processing to data analysis. Problems encountered while drawing reasonable conclusions have brought out the lacunae in data gathering. Now we realise the importance of GIGO in all stages of research : Garbage in, garbage out; gold in, gold out.

Empirical data are gathered with a view to connecting them into a theoretical framework. Measurement exactly reveals a part of the story. It does perform useful functions for social research. This enables us to draw precise conclusions. With increasing globalisation and rationalisation of social life, we are moving from arbitrariness to accountability. There is greater insistence on criteria for choice among alternatives. Demand for exact measurement and scaling is increasing. A big market has emerged for valid and reliable scales in interstitial spaces between old and new disciplines. A scale is as good as the choice of the items included therein. Scale construction has already become an industry. A marketing manager can surf far and wide over the internet. There is a potentially lucrative market for research entrepreneurs in this field.

Table 22

American heterostereotypes (autostereotypes) of Russians (Hofstetter)

	Characteristics	*1942*	*1948*
1.	Hard working	61	49
2.	Brave	48	28
3.	Progressive	24	15
4.	Realistic	18	13
5.	Intelligent	16	12
6.	Cruel	9	50
7.	Conceited	3	28

Table 23

What the various techniques do

	Technique	*Function*
1.	Case study	Anecdotal evidence (indicative, inconclusive)
2.	Participant observation	Identification and configuration of variables
3.	Social surveys	Magnitude of variables and their interrelationships
4.	Experiments	Cause-effect relationships
5.	Sampling	Representativeness
6.	Scaling	Precision

Before we wrap up, let us refer back to the introductory remarks. Measurements precisely reveal various dimensions of a matter under consideration. But they conceal more than they reveal. Of course there is much more in matter and mind than a scale can tell. Neglect of the basic assumptions underlying scale construction results in scaling with a smile. Scaling with a smile is no scaling. It yields predictions with a smile. We select our scales through our own choice of action for which we alone are responsible.

References

Adorno, Theodor W. et al., *The Authoritarian Personality*, Harper & Row, New York, 1950.

Blalock, H.M. et al., *Methodology of Social Research*, McGraw Hill, New York, 1968.

Bogardus, Emory S., *Social Distance*, Antioch Press, Los Angeles, 1959.

Diekmann, *Emprische Sozioalforchung*, Rowohlt, Hamburg, 2004.

Edwards, Allen L., *Techniques of Attitude Scale Construction*, Appleton-Century Crofts, New York, 1957.

Edwards, Anne Elizabeth, 'Development of a New Scale for Measuring Compulsive Buying Behaviour', *Financial Counselling and Planning*, 4, 67-84, 1993.

Gregory, Robert J., *Psychological Testing*, Pearson Education, New Delhi, 2006.

Guildford, J.P., *Psychometic Methods*, Tata McGraw-Hill, Bombay, 1954.

Guttman, Louis L., *Measurement and Prediction*, Vol. IV, John Wiley & Sons, New York, 1950.

Lazarsfeld, Paul F. and Morris Rosenberg (eds.), *The Language of Social Research*, Free Press, Glencoe Ill, 1955.

Lindzey, G. et al., *The Handbook of Social Psychology*, Vol. II, Amerind Publishing Co., 1975.

Maronell, Gary M., *Scaling*, Aldine Publishing Co., Chicago, 1974.

Mayntz, R. et al., *Introduction to Empirical Sociology*, Penguin, Harmondsworth, 1976.

Miller, Delbert, *Handbook of Research Design and Social Measurement*, McKay, New York, 1970.

Moreno, Jacob L. (ed.), *The Sociometry Reader*, Free Press of Glencoe (Ill.), New York, 1960.

Mukerjee, R.K., *Social Indicators*, Macmillan, Delhi, 1975.

Osgood, Charles E. et al., *The Measurement of Meaning*, University of Illinois Press, Urbana, 1957.

Pope, Nigel K.Li, Kelvin E. Voges, Mark R. Brown and Ed. Forest, 'Consumer Attitude Towards Genetically Modified Foods and Crops', Proceedings of ANZMA Conferences, J. Wiley, Wellington, New Zealand, 2004.

Raijman, Rebecca et al., 'Labor Migration in the Public Eye', *ZA* Information (Cologne), No. 47, Nov., 2000, pp. 6-28.

Scheuch, Erwin K., 'Skalierungsverfahren in der sozialforschung', in René Koenig (ed.), *Handbuch der Socialforschung*, Vol. II, Ferdinand Enke Verlag, Stuttgart, 1967, pp. 348-384, 735-739.

Shukla, Rajesh et al., *India's Science Report*, National Council of Applied Economic Research, New Delhi, 2005.

Singh, Harnek, *Role and Commitment of Agricultural Workers*, Vohra Publishers & Distributors, Allahabad, 1992.

Singh, Jaspal, *Methodology & Techniques of Social Research*, Kanishka, New Delhi, 2001.

Stevens, S.S. (ed.), *Handbook of Experimental Psychology*, John Wiley, New York, 1951.

Stouffer, Samuel S. et al., *Measurement and Prediction : The American Soldier*, Vol. IV, Wiley, New York, 1950.

Summers, Gene F. (ed.), *Attitude Measurement*, Rand McNally, Chicago, 1970.

Thurstone, Louis L., *Measurement of Values*, Chicago University Press, Chicago, 1965.

Torgerson, Lewis L., *Theory and Method of Scaling*, John Wiley & Sons, New York, 1958.

8

Sampling

With increasing democratisation of social life, public opinion research, or demoscopy is becoming more and more popular. Similarly, electoral research, or psephology, is also gaining acceptance. Polls and surveys are being done on a variety of topics. In order to get policies implemented, it has become necessary to consult those affected by these policies. Due to the fast rate of social change and a wide gulf between what the people think, feel, say and do, public opinion is always in a flux. Decision-makers need information on the dynamics of public opinion. Hence, the need for its measurement from time to time.

It is costly and impractical to interview each and every person again and again. Therefore, it becomes necessary to take a representative sample of the population methodically with a view to rapidly ascertaining what we want to know. Policy-makers and planners have to feed a lot of data to their computers. Such data are often collected through sampling. Several procedures are available for this purpose. In fact this task cannot be successfully completed without the assistance of a highly trained expert in social statistics. In order to discuss with him his exact needs and to get his advice on the details of sampling procedures, a sociologist has to acquaint himself with the broad sampling procedures. Uninformed deliberations can lead to wrong decisions. Therefore, in order to carry on demoscopic research, it is necessary to grasp the sampling procedures.

What is sampling? It is based on the study of probability and stochastic processes. Probability means the likelihood of something happening. Probable conclusions have a lower degree of certainty. Samples are only approximations. A sample is taken by selecting a sub-set from a universe in the hope that the findings based on the sample are also true for the universe under study. Let us take an example. For instance, a drop of water gives clues to the chemical composition of the sea. Again, if a housewife wants to know whether grains of rice in a pot are well-cooked or not, she takes a ladle and mixes the rice in the pot. Then she takes out a sample of two or three grains for inspection to find out whether the rice in the entire pot is cooked or not. A sample of the population of anything is drawn in the same way. We take a small part of a large whole and study the former and arrive at conclusions about the whole.

All individuals, events, groups or wholes under investigation are known as the universe. For instance, all the cattle in a village. All the house-owners of Chandigarh. All the hotels in Delhi. All the steel mills in Bihar. These are the universe of their respective population. A sample is a specific portion of a universe. It is selected in such a manner that it can represent the universe from where it is drawn. If a sample is not representative of its universe, the conclusions drawn from it are not valid and are hence not applicable to the given universe. A representative sample presents a precise picture of the universe. In practice, a sample is not taken from a universe. It is taken from a population. Population consists of all the units in a sampling frame. For instance, all the cattle in a village, as per the list maintained by the village *Patwari*. All the house owners of Chandigarh, according to records maintained in the local estate office. All the hotels in Delhi, listed in a tourist directory. All the steel mills in Bihar, according to a list obtained from the public relations officer of the Steel Authority of India. In actual practice, often there are gaps between a given universe and its population.

A sample is an estimate. All samples drawn properly from a universe yield similar results. Why do we take a sample? There are a number of reasons for this. It is less expensive. A few research assistants can quickly complete the work with a sample. It is difficult and often not practical to interview everybody. So if there is no harm in taking a sample, why take an entire universe for study?

Does a sample really represent a universe? Yes, if it has been scientifically selected. Just as the housewife in the example given above decides on the basis of a few grains that the rice is cooked well before serving, in the same way if a sample is taken scientifically, then the findings drawn from it are valid and reliable. A survey is as good as its sample.

Samples often become controversial. At the same time, how can we ascertain the whole by studying only a part thereof? In order to verify the conclusions in a study it may become necessary to study the entire population. We may have to compare the sample data with the census data. Moreover, often the sample data do not tell us anything about the mutual relationship between variables. Of course, some types of sampling (like dense sample, saturated sample, and snowball sample) take care of such relations also. Other advantages of sampling are that it reduces our work. We can focus our attention on fewer units. Therefore, it yields more accurate estimates. Very often sampling gives us better results than a census.

Types of Sampling

Sampling can be done in a number of ways:

(a) Judgement sampling : This is also known as non-probability sampling. The chance of an element falling in the sample cannot be calculated. The decision about the merit of a sample is based upon the intuitive judgement or common sense of the person who takes the sample. Thus, we cannot legitimately generalise on the basis of such a sample. The sampling error cannot be calculated in such cases. It can, therefore, lead to wrong conclusions. But due to pressure of time, there is no way out. One cannot claim any accuracy for the results here. Judgement samples are not appropriate for scientific research. Their validity rests upon the prestige of the sample taker. Such samples have a number of partially overlapping types :

1. Incidental sampling : Anybody who is available and appears to be typical of a universe is included in the sample. For example, a questionnaire is published in a newspaper. Newspaper readers are requested to fill it, indicating the popularity of film actors and return it. Anybody who desires can fill in the questionnaire and mail it to the newspaper. Radio listeners or television viewers are encouraged to write letters giving their opinions about various programmes, etc. The received entries are tabulated and analysed.

2. Straw poll : An example of this is an officer travelling in a jeep and discussing the matter under study with, say, 10 persons. They are picked up on the way, given a lift and dropped at a point convenient to them. Passers-by are asked questions on what they think about something. In this way, the officer draws a conclusion with respect to the direction in which public opinion is moving.

3. Sampling according to the principle of concentration : Here the sample taker visits a place where many people of the same type are available. The findings are extrapolated to draw conclusions of all the people of the same type. For example, trade union members at Chheharta or Phagwara may be interviewed. Based on this, conclusions may be drawn about trade union members in Punjab. Or a few Parsis in Navsari may be interviewed. The results may be extrapolated to the Parsis in India.

4. Purposive sampling : This takes into consideration the features of a region and the qualities of its inhabitants (say, caste, education, occupation). The investigator takes a cross-section of the respondents. He studies, say, their attitude towards a particular brand of television set. The results are applied to the entire region.

(b) Probability sampling : This is based on the probability that the sample is representative of a larger universe. The sampling error can be duly calculated in such cases. Some amount of randomness underlies all types of probability samples.

1. Random sample : This is not a coincidental or a haphazard sample. Elements are not arbitrarily included in or excluded from the sample. The choice of elements is independent. This means that the choice of one element has no effect on the choice of other elements. The probability of their inclusion or exclusion from the sample is unconditional. Each and every element in the population has an equal and non-zero probability of inclusion in the sample. Such a chance is greater than zero and often less than 1. Moreover, all possible samples from a universe have equal probability of being selected. The researcher does not carry out a man hunt for some special people with certain qualities. A sampling frame is prepared. It consists of all the elements in the universe. Whosoever falls in the sample according to the prescribed procedure is included. Everybody else is excluded. This enables us to prepare an exact estimate of the entire population. In a *simple random sample* (SRS), the probability of inclusion of all the elements in the sample is not only equal, it is also greater than zero. The exact sampling error can be calculated. An SRS of an SRS is also an SRS.

Such samples can be selected in a number of ways. In the lottery method, we first find out the names of all the elements. Then we write down the names of these elements on equal sized chits. These chits are put into a container or a basket. They are mixed up thoroughly. Then somebody is asked to draw out the required number of chits, one by one. After taking out a chit, the name of the element is recorded and the chit is replaced in the carton. If it comes again, it is ignored. If the chit is taken out *without replacement*, the initial probability of selection would be unequal. If the universe is large, both the procedures yield practically the same result. But if the universe is small, the selected sample would be short of being representative. Apart from the lottery method, ready-made lists of random numbers, generated by statisticians, are also available. Computers can also be used for generating random numbers.

If a random sample is taken from an unbiased list, we call it a *systematic sample*. In such a sample, the cases are selected at given intervals. For instance, we take a list of 1,070 hostellers in a college. With a sampling interval of 100/10, or a sampling fraction (desired sample size—total population) of 1/10, we select every tenth element from the list. To start with, somebody is asked to select the first number, say, 3. Then unit numbers 13, 23, 33, 43, 53, ... 1063 (107 in all) form our sample. In case the list of elements is arranged in a biased manner, our sample would be biased.

In fact, even though systematic samples are not really simple random samples for all practical purposes, they are treated as such. However, in case there is some built-in bias or periodicity in the list (e.g., an outdated telephone directory or roll-call register), the sample will be non-random. Some elements which should be there will not be there, while some elements which should not be there due to a variety of reasons will be there. Therefore, it has to be ensured before hand that the lists have not been arranged in some predetermined order. Systematic samples are useful, because they are easy to use.

2. *Stratified sample :* When we use the above procedures, marginal cases may be left out or certain key variables may not be adequately represented. Therefore, we take a stratified sample instead of a random sample. Strata are mutually exclusive and collectively exhaustive meaningful layers or sub-groups within a universe. In this type of sampling, we reduce the sampling error, and increase the precision of our sample by making use of our previous knowledge about the composition of the universe. The heterogeneous population is divided into various homogeneous layers comprising it. Stratification factors like type of village, number of children, caste, etc., are specified. Random samples are taken within the strata.

If the same sampling fraction is used in all the strata, then it is a *proportionately stratified sample*. If different sampling fractions are used it is a *disproportionately stratified sample*. Then the sample size is in direct proportion to the size of each stratum. This procedure is adopted when some strata are larger than others, or when it is costly to gather data from some of the strata, or when some marginal groups are to be represented.

Precision can infact be increased by taking a smaller fraction from some strata. Smaller fractions can be made equal to larger fractions by giving them due weightage. A large-sized sample with a smaller weight is balanced by a small-sized sample with a larger weight.

Multiple stratification means that two or more stratification factors are applied simultaneously. This is more or less like quota sampling, except that it has greater objectivity.

Post-facto stratification means that first of all we select a simple random sample. Then we collect our data. While analysing the data we divide them into strata on the basis of known proportions within each stratum. This increases accuracy by giving due weightage to minority elements in the population. In this way, the capacity of a stratified sample can be combined with the simplicity of a random sample.

Implicit stratification means that the sampling frame is prepared stratumwise. Different strata are placed one after another. Then a systematic sample is selected from the list so prepared.

Optimum stratification means that sampling within the strata is done in order to reduce the sampling error in the total sample.

Double sampling means that we take a large sample in order to find out the relative size of different layers in the population. Then a smaller sample is selected within each stratum. In stratification with equal allocation, the same sample size is taken from each stratum.

3. *Cluster sample :* In this type of sampling, all the units of a cluster or group are included in the sample. The cluster can be a territory, where the respondents live in close proximity, or even an organisation. It can be a natural or an artificial whole, with units or elements within it. For instance, instead of randomly selecting 2,000 houses in a city with a population of one lakh, we select four clusters of houses with a total of 2,006 houses. This brings down costs and facilitates data collection: Random sub-samples can also be taken within a cluster.

Like stratification, clustering also improves the sampling design. In stratified sampling, samples are taken within all strata. However, in cluster sampling, all the elements in the cluster are included in the sample. Whereas strata are homogeneous, clusters are highly heterogeneous. Thus, they can represent an entire universe. As all units are included in the sample, we can collect data about relationships between various units. Clustering costs less. It facilitates data collection.

Area sampling is a variant of cluster sampling. This is done from an *ad hoc* mini census, for instance, from maps. Cluster sampling is a territorial or a local unit. The sample taker selects his respondents directly on the spot. He walks along a street. He includes, say, every tenth house in the sample. This is a self-selection procedure. It works well unless the interviewer cuts corners and moves round about or here and there. It is useful when more reliable sampling frames are not available. This also saves operational costs.

4. Multi-stage sample : The sample is selected in different stages. Different types of sampling may be used at various stages. Generally, stratification is done at the first stage, while a random sample is taken at the second stage. The units at the first stage are known as primary sampling units (PSU). The units at the second stage are called secondary sampling units (SSU). The units at the final stage are known as the ultimate sampling units (USU). In other words, a multi-stage sample is selected in two or more stages. For example, we may select a few Lok Sabha constituencies (PSU) or primary sampling units in Punjab. At the second stage, we may select a few Vidhan Sabha constituencies or a secondary sampling unit within each Lok Sabha constituency. At the third stage, we may select a few villages (TSU or tertiary sampling unit) in each Vidhan Sabha constituency. In the fourth stage, we select a few heads of households or ultimate sampling units (USU) in each selected village. In other words, the interviewees are not chosen straightaway. The selection is done stepwise, in stages. It is difficult to calculate the sampling error for a multi-stage sample.

In *multi-phase sampling,* some data are collected in the first phase of sampling. Additional data are gathered from a sub-sample of the total sample.

Table 1
Quota controls

Gender	*Caste*				*Total*
	High		*Low*		
	Old	*Young*	*Old*	*Young*	
Male	20	40	15	15	90
Female	20	40	15	15	90
Total	40	80	30	30	180

Figure 1
Multi-stage sampling

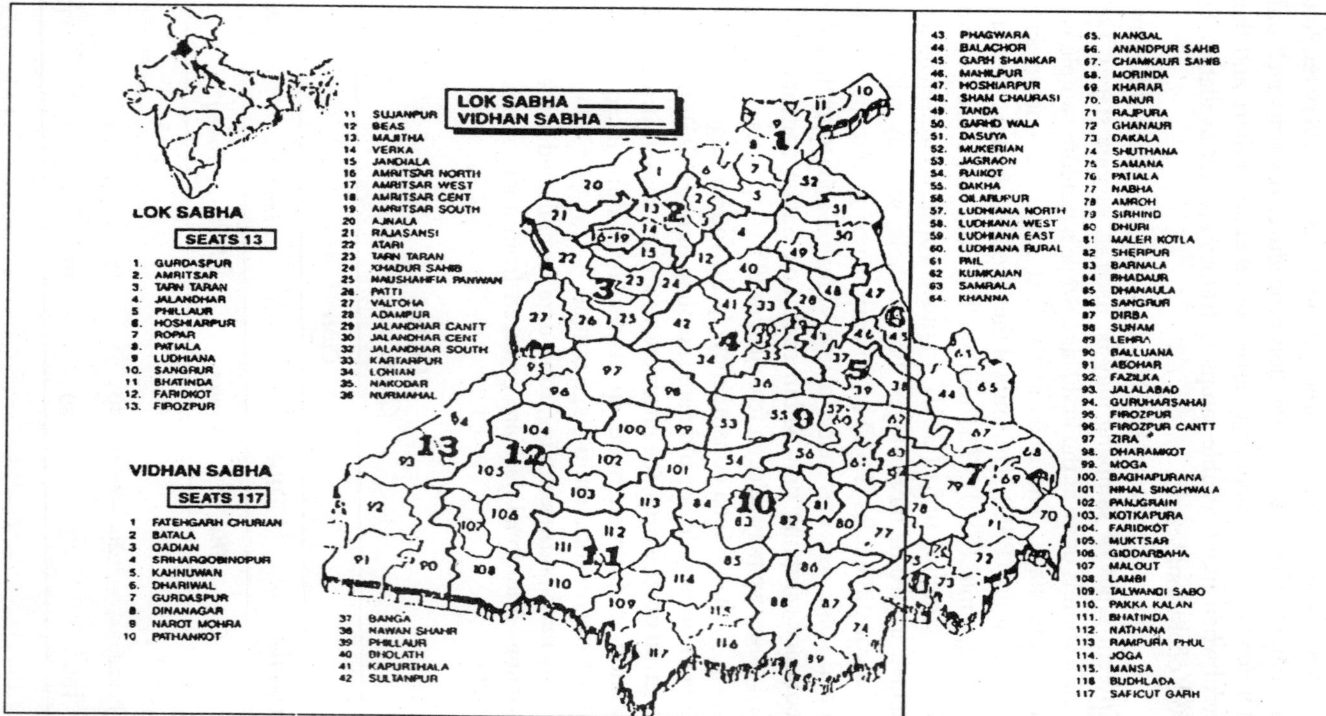

Source : *The Tribune*, Chandigarh.

5. *Quota sample :* In this type of sampling, the respondents to be contacted by the interviewers are not specified. The interviewers decide whom to interview and whom to leave out. They find their respondents in railway compartments, bus stands, street corners, and so on. While doing so, they are bound by the prescribed quota controls. In other words, such samples rely on the subjective judgement of the sample taker, within the limits set by quota controls. Such controls are laid down by the researcher in advance. The interviewer is given the freedom to select anybody who fulfils certain predetermined criteria.

In a way, quota samples are stratified samples. The only difference is that selection within strata is not random. On the basis of already available knowledge about the universe, the researcher carefully specifies certain proportions within each layer (like religion, linguistic region, caste, land ownership). Within these limits, the interviewees are selected on the spot by the interviewers according to their own convenience and subjective judgement. A quota represents the total population. For instance, three interrelated quota controls have been used in Table 1. These are gender, caste and age. The assumption is that the controlled and the uncontrolled variables are interrelated. This assumption can be verified statistically later on. The higher the coefficient of correlation between the two, the more representative will the sample be.

Quota controls, e.g., age, gender, caste are chosen in such a way that they exercise a general influence on the total universe. Moreover, they should be recognisable at first sight. They give good dispersion on the key background variables and attitudes. If many quota controls are used, the task before the interviewer becomes more difficult. If secondary data are available for verifying this assumption, so much the better.

Quota controls can be independent of each other or even correlated. We should be particularly careful, for example, that all old men are not urbanities and all young women are not ruralites.

Quota samples are less expensive. With them data collection is also made easy. They give us the benefits of stratification conveniently and quickly.

However, it is difficult to justify a quota sample on theoretical grounds. Various elements of the population do not find representation in it. The sampling error cannot be calculated. We cannot say with a known degree of confidence how representative it is. Therefore, the findings cannot be interpreted with surety. The interviewers have to select the respondents themselves. If they are in a hurry or are partisan then it can bias the results. If the rate of social change is fast, quota sampling has to be resorted to. However, research methodologists question their validity. Quota samples are not probability samples, because the sampling error cannot be calculated in their case. Their reliability can be checked by comparing the quota characteristics with other characteristics, and the overall results with materials from other sources.

Such samples are often taken by commercial researchers. They justify them on pragmatic grounds, by asserting that they work well. They yield satisfactory results. Often quota samples are the only way out because of the limited resources available to the researcher—financial stringency, manpower shortage, limited time budget and poor infrastructure. We can safely make use of quota sampling in exploratory studies.

6. *Snowball, dense, saturated samples :* There is a lot of scope for ingenuity in sampling. Snowball sampling may be used for studying those respondents who are spread far and wide or are not otherwise easily traceable. For instance, initially we take a small random sample of trade union leaders and later extend it by asking our respondents to provide additional names of informal leaders. Another instance is that of marginal groups like drug addicts. At first, we find out one or two such persons and interview them. Then they are asked to give the names of, say, 5 to 7 persons of their kind.

Table 2

Trend analysis of marital status (thousands)

Marital Status	*1994*	*1999*
Married	50	50
Unmarried	1	1
Total	51	51

They are located and interviewed. They in turn are also requested to give more names and addresses. We proceed in the same way and get chains of respondents. Thus, the cooperation obtained from the persons discovered earlier is made use of for finding additional specimens of the same type. This is like rolling a small ball of snow on a hill station in winter, and getting a larger and larger snowball. An additional advantage is that in such a sample we do not miss the inter-personal relations among individuals. In order to come to terms with the problem of sampling from such a fluid frame, we may take a saturated sample, a dense sample, or almost a total collection.

A dense sample is an approximation to a total collection of all the elements in a universe. We do not have to be concerned about the sampling error. It is irrelevant at this level.

A saturated sample is chosen in such a way that the sample size is slightly larger than a certain minimum optimum level. Therefore, the sampling error is irrelevant in this case too.

7. *Panels :* The sampling procedures given above are used at only one point of time. In contrast, panels are used to take into account two or more points over a period of time. The same persons are repeatedly asked more or less the same set of questions but at intervals. Such a procedure is useful for analysing the ongoing processes, change in attitude, voting behaviour, and so on.

Panel studies are different from synchronic studies. In the latter, several cases are taken at one and the same point of time. For example, we interview 20, 40 and 60 year old respondents on the same day. We may also analyse the matrimonial advertisements in, say, the Daily *Tribune* in 1951, 1961, 1971, 1981, 1991, 2001 and 2011. The results may be extrapolated for predicting the likely future trend.

Similarly, panel studies are different from trend studies. Like synchronic studies, trend analysis can be done with independent samples each time. Let us give an example. Table 3 shows the turnover between two points of time. As many as 53 per cent and 54 per cent favour Condoleeza Rice at points of time t_1, and t_2, respectively. There area a few changes. The turnover gives us the direction of change. It shows that nobody ceased to favour Condoleeza Rice and only one per cent changed their opinion between the two points of time. Panel studies provide data for comparing the answers to questions at various points of time.

Table 3

Turnover table of attitude towards Condoleeza Rice

Time Period t_1 (1990)	***Time Period t_2 (2000)***		***Total***
	Favourable	***Unfavourable***	***1990***
Favourable	53	0	53
Unfavourable	1	46	47
Total 2000	54	46	100

Like panel analysis, trend analysis is used to study change over a prolonged period. The difference between the two is that trend analysis studies only change. But panel analysis studies change as well as changers. It throws light on the process, direction, and causes of change.

Table 4 shows that the proportion of married persons has remained the same between the two points of time. However, there is no information about whether the same persons were married between the two points or there is some change in their marital status. Table 4 classifies the marital status simultaneously according to the two dimensions, viz., married and unmarried at two points of time, viz., 1990 and 1999.

Trend analysis shows net change. This means change in the frequency distribution between two points of time. But the net change does not show the changers. Panel analysis reveals change at the level of individuals who make up the aggregate. It clarifies the way in which the net change has taken place.

Table 4
Panel study of marital status (thousands)

1990	***Year 1999***		***Total***
	Married	***Unmarried***	
Married	49.5	**0.5**	50
Unmarried	**0.5**	0.5	1
Total 1999	50	1	51

The bold letters readings in Table 4 are the variant readings. They include all those people who have moved from one category to another between the two points of time. In this example, there are equal variations both ways. Thus, there was no effect on the net change. In other words, 500 were newly married, while another 500 were widowed, divorced, etc.

Once we have identified the changers from such a table, we can go ahead and ascertain their social background, factors responsible for the change, as also the direction of change. This is done with the help of other items included in our questionnaire at the time of designing the study. Suppose we find out that in case there is an election next Sunday, the upper class high caste Hindus intend to vote for the BJP, while the backward castes and Muslims intend to vote for the BSP. Those who are competing for their votes may be advised to look for wavers across these cleavages. They can get more votes by concentrating on the wavers rather than on those with firm voting intentions.

Panel studies are also different from time series analysis (Table 5). In the latter, one and the same case is taken into consideration at several points of time. Panel analysis studies many cases at a few (usually 3 to 5) points of time.

Table 5
Panel and time series

No. of cases	***Points of time***	
Time series	One	Many
Panels	Many	Few

Panel analysts come across certain difficulties. Bias due to mobility or migration of a part of the sample population is one of them. You do not meet some people again. Some elements of the sample chosen for repeated interview move away, become disinterested, or are otherwise no longer available. This is known as *panel mortality*. This difficulty can be overcome by making attempts to sustain their interest. If this is not possible, we replace them with others in a systematic way. Moreover, the learning effect from previous interviews holds on, or freezes, the responses. They may even become more critical. In order to appear to be consistent, they give the same old reply again and again. Thus, they do not remain representative of the universe under study. This can result in incorrect conclusions. Even this problem can be solved by regularly replacing some elements with others in a systematic way. We can reduce the inclination to appear consistent by spreading various related items in different parts of the questionnaire, rather than putting them together in one and the same lot. Furthermore, repeated measurement makes the cases different. They do not remain the same. Repeated questioning changes the meaning of what is being asked. Therefore, it is not proper to use the same panel over a prolonged period of time.

The panel technique is useful for a number of reasons. It helps us to study short-term changes. We can use it to find out the factors that facilitate or retard change. We can also ascertain the social background of those who are changing and those who are not changing. Panels cost much less in terms of money and effort than fresh samples every time we want to do a survey.

8. Replicated sample : Parallel samples are drawn. Two or more independent samples are taken with interpenetrating sub-samples. Among others, this enables us to check up eventual cheating by interviewers.

Sampling Bias

Bias means the tendency to reject the logic of rational evidence in favour of presumed beliefs. If a set of figures is such that all its errors tend to lie in the same direction, it is biased, e.g., elite regions are atypical of their geographical surroundings. Punjab and Haryana are atypical of India with respect to wheat production. Spring offensives in Japan are atypical of strikes in the rest of the world. AIIMS (All India Institute of Medical Sciences in Delhi) students are atypical of students in the ordinary medical colleges of the country. Merit scholarship holders are different from those students who have secured admission by paying capitation fee. Such cases are unsuitable for drawing broad-based generalisations. If the errors are not one-sided, they would cancel out each other and become unbiased. Inaccuracies or distortions may enter due to prejudice or errors of judgement. We can speak of two types of bias—sampling bias and non-sampling bias.

Sampling bias makes a sample unrepresentative by denying entry to some elements in the sample. They do not have adequate opportunity to appear in it. There are a number of reasons for this. These include the following:

1. Sample size: This refers to the number of elements covered by a sample. A large sample need not be without distortion. Representativeness depends upon the method of selection, not on the sample size as such. We cannot always take a large sample due to shortage of time, money and research assistance. The sample size depends upon degree of certainty desired, sub-tabulation needed, as well as no response.

2. Sampling frame: It is a list, map, an inventory, etc., of all the names and addresses in the population. For instance, voters list in an electoral constituency, a *patwari's* record of landholdings, attendance register in a school, establishment control register in a work organisation, zonal plans of a city, and so on. In some countries, the names of all inhabitants of a place are registered in a central office. Those who move from one place to another have to get themselves de-registered at the old place and re-registered at their new place of residence. In countries like India, there are no such arrangements. Decennial censuses have been held here for finding out how many people belonging to various cleavages are living in the country. In countries like Afghanistan, even this much is not being done. We have to look around for appropriate sampling frames in various situations. Where sampling frames are non-existent, we ourselves have to prepare substitutes with locally available resources. Distance, disorder, disturbances, doubts make it difficult to construct frames for drawing representative samples from the universe. In such eventualities, it becomes necessary to use purposive samples.

What are the qualities of an appropriate sampling frame? It should be adequate for the purpose. It should be complete. It should be free of duplication. It should be up-to-date. Its elements should be identifiable on the spot. Adequacy means that there should not be a lot of gap between the population and the universe. Membership of a trade union in India is not adequate for this purpose. This is because our trade unions are ad hoc bodies. They appear and disappear suddenly. Their membership is transitory. Lists based on the 1991 Census become inadequate in 1999. Sampling frames constructed from many sources have to be checked up for duplication. The sampling frame should be free of missing elements. In cities, especially in the Western countries, a lot of people move from one place to another every now and then. Consequently, mobile sections of the population are under-sampled. To avoid this, the sampling frame should not be old. If there are a number of households at one address, then all of them may be included in the sampling frame, or one of them may be selected methodically on the basis of consistent criteria.

3. *No response :* If many respondents cannot somehow be interviewed, such loss reduces the degree of certainty with which conclusions can be drawn. If no response can be estimated before hand, we can make good the loss by increasing the sample size. No response can be due to a number of reasons. These include the following :

(a) Not available : If some of the persons to be interviewed live in far off localities, it is not easy to approach them. One solution is to offer them incentives if they themselves come forward for being interviewed. The interviewers can be induced to identify them somehow and request them to fill in the forms. The time of the year (harvesting time, examinations, vacation, etc.) and the time of the day (working hours, popular TV serial timing, etc.) have to be taken care of in order to improve availability. Unless you are sure that the person will not mind it, do not disturb

anybody before breakfast, and after dinner as it may put him to inconvenience.

(b) Away from home : Some respondents are seldom available at home. They may be working a night shift and sleeping during the day time. They may be visiting friends or cinema or pubs. Repeated calls at convenient hours can solve this problem. However, the marginal utility of call backs goes down after three calls. The utility also depends upon seasonal variations.

(c) Do not understand : Sometimes the interviewees do not know the interviewer's language. Somebody may be deaf and dumb. Migrant workers from other parts of the country or from abroad may fall in a similar category. Somebody can be made to act as an interpreter in such a case.

(d) Refusal : Some respondents may not agree to cooperate. They refuse to get interviewed due to tiredness, lack of interest, mistrust, and a variety of other reasons. Some of them may answer some questions but refuse to answer others. They disclose a part of the information and withhold the rest of it. There could be a number of reasons for this. They may be tired of beggars, vote seekers, salesmen, advertisers and detectives. In some countries, too many interviewers are coming again and again to ask all sorts of questions. Many potential interviewees feel that it is not necessary to oblige everybody. Some amount of mistrust of strangers is always there. The respondents may have something to hide. Their apprehensions regarding infringement of privacy, etc., have to be tactfully put to rest. Rapport may be established with them through mutual acquaintances.

In case of questionnaires, write down the complete address on the envelope. Send them reminders, if necessary. If some respondents say that they have not received the questionnaire or have misplaced it, send them another copy thereof. The response rate for questionnaires is much less than personal interviews.

Good researchers know how to keep no response to the minimum. Another remedy is to find out some characteristics of those who cannot be interviewed. One can ask their neighbours. One can compare the results with secondary data.

By giving due weightage for missing data through systematic replacement and by collecting additional information later on, the effect of no response can be minimised.

Non-sampling Bias

Defective construction of the interview schedule, improper procedures for conducting interviews, use of whatever computer programmes are available, on data that do not fulfil the basic assumptions of statistics being applied, can confound the results. Design the interview schedule according to the prescribed procedure. Train the research assistants properly. Reward good workers. Beware of cheating. Choose the right time for doing the fieldwork. In this way, bias can be kept to the minimum.

Sampling Error

Sampling error means the type of errors caused by sampling. It measures the difference between the sample and the population. Often, it can be calculated. Sampling error (S.E.) is the standard deviation of the sampling mean. The following formula is used for calculating it:

$$\text{S.E.} = (1 - n/N)\,\frac{S}{N} = \frac{S}{n}$$

where,

n = Number of cases in the sample
N = Total number of cases in the population
S = Standard deviation

The proportion of population covered by a sample is known as the sampling fraction (n/N).

Sampling error cannot be worked out in case of purposive and quota samples. The outcome has to be justified by comparing it with other studies. Calculation of the sampling error is quite complicated for an ordinary sociologist without higher level training in statistics. The way out for a beginner is to restrict himself to systematic sampling from lists, or to take a dense sample. The latter is hardly effected by the sampling error.

Knowledge of the sampling error helps us to make a decision about the size of our sample. A large sample need not necessarily be more representative.

Conclusions

This chapter is aimed at targeting those readers who do not have a solid background in statistics. Surveys are undertaken by research teams. This is too much work for individuals. A large number of persons have to be interviewed. They have to be selected by taking a representative sample from a universe. Sophisticated sampling techniques are being made use of these days. It has become necessary for research teams to consult highly qualified experts in social statistics for this purpose. In order to make them understand our exact requirements, we have to grasp the broad features of the available sampling techniques.

REFERENCES

Chaudhury, A. and H. Stenger, *Survey Sampling: Theory and Methods*, Marcel Dekker, New York, 1992.

Cochran, W.G., *Sampling Techniques*, Wiley Eastern, New Delhi, 1984.

Kalton, Graham, *Introduction to Survey Sampling*, Sage Publications, New Delhi, 1984.

Moser, C. and G. Kalton, *Survey Methods in Social Investigation*, English Language Book Society, London, 1974.

Namboodiri, N.K. Krishna, *Survey Sampling and Measurement*, Academic Press, New York, 1978.

Scheuch, Erwin K., "Auswahlverfahren in der Sozialforschung", in René Koenig (ed.), *Handbuch der Empirischen Soziologie*, Ferdinand Enke Verlag, Stuttgart, 1967, pp. 309-47.

Sukhatme, P.V. and B.V. Sukhatme, *Sampling Theory of Surveys, with Applications*, Asia Publishing House, Bombay, 1970.

Yamane, T., *Elementary Sampling Theory*, Prentice-Hall, Englewood Cliffs (NJ.), 1967.

Yates, F., *Sampling Methods for Census and Surveys*, Hoffner, New York, 1960.

9

Data Processing and Analysis

What are Data?

Data (singular : datum) summarise a set of facts. Readings, scores, points, goals, measurements obtained from observation of the salient features of a certain reality, and systematically recorded in a standard from, are called data. Before recording, these are properly structured conceptually and theoretically interrelated. Irrelevant or meaningless observations are not data. Data are properly recorded observations. For instance, a particular respondent is 22 years old. He *speaks Telugu*. He is *suspicious* as well as *insecure*. He feels *insulted* on the slightest provocation. He finds it difficult to cope up with *stress*. He possesses a good *academic record*. *Performance appraisal* reports at his place of work are above average. These are data.

What do we do with data? We use them to draw conclusions. This helps us in understanding our environment. We use such information to adjust ourselves to the environment, or to change it. Or just for the sake of curiosity. Data facilitate comparison. Such knowledge may be useful sometimes later on, if not right now.

How do we distinguish between data and information? Signals from source are recorded. For example, by writing them in words or using symbols. These are data. When their significance becomes known, we call them information (see Figure 1).

Data are collected for testing hypotheses and constructing theories. Data possess certain features or characteristics. They refer to some event or phenomenon or object. For example, owner-cultivator in Kangra, trade union leader in Bangalore, child labour in Jaipur, or students in IIT

Written in collaboration with Satinder Kumar, Lovely University, Jalandhar.

Figure 1
Senders of signals and receivers of information

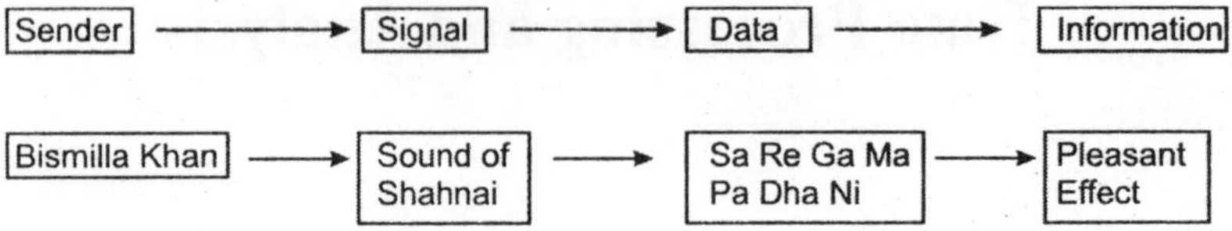

Mumbai. Data can be classified in a number of ways, depending upon the purpose for which a given classification is being done.

For the purpose of electronic processing, data may be divided into :

(i) alphabetical data, consisting of letters,
(ii) numerical data, consisting of digits,
(iii) alphanumerical data, consisting of a combination of alphabetical and numerical data, and
(iv) special characters like + – × ÷ () $ #.

For the purpose of analysis, data may be divided into primary and secondary. Primary data are used for the purpose for which they were originally collected. Secondary data are second-hand. These are used for analysing the old data for a purpose other than that for which they were originally collected. Thus, we can answer new questions about the old data, or look at the same old questions in a new way.

For the purpose of data analysis, data may be divided into nominal data and ordinal data. Nominal data are discrete. They consist of a set of alternatives. Somebody is either in a category or out of it. On the other hand, ordinal data arrange a category in some order between two extremes. They tell us to what extent something is like that.

Data are made up of variables. Variables may possess different values in different cases. A variable can increase or decrease. When variables remain unchanged, we have constants. A parameter is a constant quantity across a population. A variable pertains to several cases. But a parameter has only one value for each case. The values of a variable differ from one another in degree. A variable may vary between a lower and higher values. The relevance of variables and their values changes from time to time. Therefore, data collection is a dynamic endeavour.

Each variable refers to some feature of the unit under investigation. For example:

Variable 1	:	Ethnic affiliation
Variable 2	:	Education completed, in years
Variable 3	:	Subjective class identification
Variable 4	:	Score on religiosity
Variable 5	:	Intelligence quotient

Strictly speaking, variables are not attributes. An attribute is either present or absent. It either exists, or does not exist. Variables are quantitative, or numerical. Attributes are qualitative, non-numerical descriptors, like student, leader, sociologist, Kashmiri. When we are not speaking strictly, attributes are casually referred to as variables. Variables can be converted into attributes, and vice versa.

In other words, variables can be qualitative or quantitative. The former vary in kind. The latter vary in magnitude. Variables can be continuous, discrete, or serials. Continuous variables vary from a minimum to a maximum, more or less continuously. They can take several values within these limits. They are joined together. For example, the actual family income in rupees per month. Discrete variables are separate from each other. They can be counted. They can take only specific values. For example, income can be classified into three categories: High/average/low. Serials are multi-valued variables. They can only be ranked. For example, grades (O, A, B, C, D, E, F). In contrast to variables, attributes are dichotomous qualities. These have two values like man/ woman, authoritarian/liberal.

We can have unique variables as also summary variables. The former refer to specific individual units. For example, the annual income of a particular person. The latter refers to a set of individual units. For example, the mean per capita income of a country.

We may have dichotomous, trichotomous, or polytomous variables. Dichotomy means that the variable has two values or categories. Trichotomy means that the variable possesses three values or categories. Polytomy means that there are several values or categories of a variable.

Variables can also be independent, dependent, or intervening. An independent variable is used for explaining its dependent variables. An intervening variable shows an indirect relationship between two variables. If X causes Z, and Z causes Y, then Z is an intervening variable between X and Y.

For multi-level analysis, variables can be divided into four types. These are:

1. Individual variables : These are made up of the characteristics of individual members. They may refer to the answers of individuals in questionnaires regarding, age, gender, job satisfaction, migration, attitude towards something, etc.

2. Relational variables : These refer to the characteristics of the individual units relative to others in the same collection. For example 1. A relatively underdeveloped country amidst developed countries. Say, Portugal in Europe. 2. A student standing 4th in a class of 46 students. 3. Relatively affluent households in a slum area. 4. The topmost decile of the population in India in terms of income.

3. Aggregate variables : These are obtained by adding up individual elements in a collection. A change in the elements changes the collection too. For example, 1. Average marks of a school class. 2. Per capita income of a country. 3. The average number of hours per week spent by professors in a university on attending committee meetings. 4. A country with a Muslim majority.

4. Global variables : These are based upon the average qualities of groups. They are independent of the characteristics of elements within a collection. They cannot be obtained by adding up individual attributes. They cannot be reduced to the properties of other variables. They persist even after all the members of a group are no longer there. Members may come and go. But the global characteristics remain the same. For example 1. Drought-prone area, 2. Periphery of a metropolis, 3. Medieval poetry, 4. ILO headquarters in Geneva.

Figure 2
Variables and values

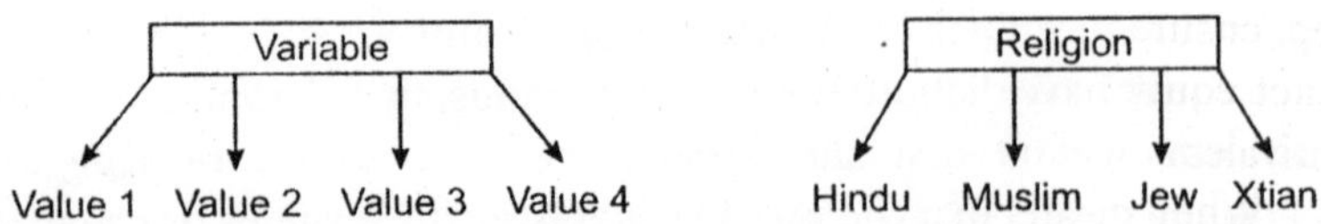

Variables have values. They can take a value from a number of values. Values are also known as categories. For example:

Variable class : Upper/Middle/Lower
Variable voting intention : Congress (I)/BJP/BSP— Any other (specify)

Similarly, middle-aged, resourceful, England-returned, unemployed, cunning may become values of the related variables. The point is that variables have values.

As already explained, dichotomy means that there are two values or categories for each variable. Trichotomous variables have three values. Polytomy means that there are several values : or categories for each variable. These values may be discrete (either... or) or continuous (to what extent?). Continuous variables may be converted into dichotomous variables, using meaningful cut off points for the latter. Values of a variable may often be collapsed with each other. Dichotomisation of categories is a pre-requisite for many statistical applications.

Collapsing can be done by reducing the number of categories, by combining them with each other. This is done by changing the cut-off points at the border. For this purpose, we break some categories, bend others to fit them together, using our technical competence as well as our creative imagination. Arbitrary cut-off points and unmindful lumping are sources of bias. These distort the findings. Collapsing has to be properly justified. The cut-off points need not necessarily be uniform for all data. The cut-off point for age groups usage differs from culture to culture. Age 45 means something in one culture, and something else in another. The cut-off points may differ from one situation to another according to the purpose in hand. For instance, in Bengal fish is a vegetarian diet, but in Punjab, fish is a non-vegetarian diet.

Re-categorisation may also be done while cumulating data from different sources for re-analysis. Do not re-categorise mindlessly. First consider why the earlier categorisation was done the way it was done. Find out what purpose it served. Then be clear about the new purpose(s). Change e.g. 5 into 2 categories, adjust the cut-off points accordingly. Collapse various categories to serve your purpose. Before taking such a step, ensure that no gaps are left between the old and the new categories. Exact equivalence is not always necessary. Sometimes even functional equivalents will do.

When data on some variable is missing from a particular data set, it can be replaced with functional equivalents. Both involve self-destruction. Brawl and abusive language are functionally equivalent. Wandering around and eating parched groundnuts are functionally equivalent, for passing time. An astrologer in India, a Shaman in Checheniya and a management consultant in the USA are functionally equivalent. Similarly, *pooja-archana* by Hindus, saying *namaz* by Muslims and church-going by Christians, are functionally equivalent activities, for measuring religiosity. The point is that when two or more variables produce the same result for a given purpose, these are functionally equivalent. Such equivalence is a matter of inference and not direct observation. Culture-fair and unbiased items have to be used for this purpose. Verify that the circumstances between the points of time under reference have remained unchanged. Interpolate the missing data with dummy data where it works without impairing validity.

Table 1
Units, variables and values

Units	***Variables***	***Values***
Employees of BEL, Bangalore	Their orientation towards work	Instrumental/Intrinsic
Progressive farmers of Himachal Pradesh	Use of bio-technology	Hybrid seeds used/Pesticides used/Chemical fertilisers Used*
Managers of SAIL, Bokaro	Their management style	Authoritarian/Democratic
Graduates of IIM, Ahmedabad	Their competence	High/Low

*Multiple responses permitted.

Let us summarise the discussion. Refer to Figure 2, data tell us about the values of cases or units for variables. The case or the unit is the object under study, e.g., a village, a factory, a person. A variable is an element of an aspect of a problem, e.g., voting intention, religious affiliation, leadership style. Units pertain to characteristics. What is the point? *Is mehfil mein aapko aana hai bar bar. Deewar au dar ko ghaur se pehchan leejiye!* Recognise what is what.

Data have to be adequately interpreted, while avoiding overinterpretation. This is done in order to find out the invariable sequence of events in social life, sets of conditions giving rise to such regularities, and so on. The same datasets can be analysed in a number of ways. The choice of variables does affect the results of research. The theoretical perspective and the creativity of a researcher have a big hand in his findings. Accumulation of large masses of data without adequate theoretical orientation in the hope that somehow something will come of it is called *data-dredging*.

Data Collection

Suitable data are collected with a view to solving the given problem. We may conduct a survey, or perform an experiment. The amount of data is neither more nor less than our requirements.

Why do we collect data?

With a view to analysing the same. Avoid unnecessarily cummulating large masses of data, hoping that something will somehow come out of them at last. Keeping this in mind at the time of preparation of a research design will stand us in good stead at the time of writing a research report.

Figure 3

Steps in doing surveys

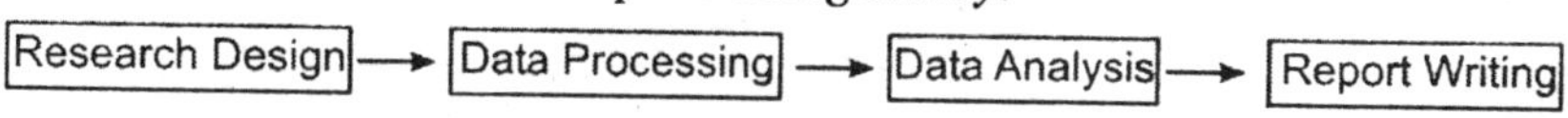

Data Analysis and Social Statistics

Empirical facts do not enable us to explain the total social phenomenon. Moreover, qualitative information does not guarantee the degree of certainty of the statements. That can be ascertained with adequately analysed quantitative data. Instruments of electronic data processing facilitate analysis. Application of proper statistical techniques, with an eye on their underlying assumptions, enables us to draw out statements with a known degree of reliability. This chapter provides us a bird's eye view of the related problems.

Data analysis goes hand in hand with data processing. It does make use of statistics. But this is not done with statistics alone. Qualitative consideration, visual inspection, graphic display are also used for this purpose. The underlying assumptions are examined. The data are broken up into their components. Their cutting points are readjusted. The categories are collapsed. These are given new names. The analyst plays with his data. He considers various alternatives. Their pros and cons are weighed. Appropriate measures are applied

Social statistics are very useful for this purpose. What are social statistics? These are tools for converting qualitative data into numbers, applying appropriate tests to them, and drawing meaningful conclusions. They enable us to say how big or small, how high or low various facts are with respect to each other, what is the strength of their mutual relationship, and a lot more. Statistics are applied with a view to making generalisations, constructing theories, and accumulating knowledge. They help us to analyse our data with a certain degree of precision and interpret the same.

Use and Abuse of Statistics

Development of statistics is associated with scientific advancement. Statistics play a supporting role for the method of science. It facilitates the task of arriving at reliable and valid inferences. It helps us in drawing logical inferences and then working out their implications, i.e., necessary connections. In this way, it helps us to eliminate ambiguity, clarify the given matter, and state it precisely. It helps us in classifying our data, shrinking large masses of data into a small amount of space, and separating information from noise. It enables us to reveal sequence and structure of our data. Knowledge of social statistics helps us in preparing and executing research designs.

Production of knowledge about various aspects of social life is increasing by leaps and bounds these days. A large number of books and even a larger number of articles in journals are coming out. It is not possible to grasp many of these publications without a modicum of acquaintance with social statistics. The use of statistics for scientific research is increasing day-by-day.

On the other hand, everything in social life cannot be stated mathematically. The connection between the two is weak. Instead of revealing information, statistics can serve to conceal it. It can be used for telling half-truths. It can be misused. Statistics are being used for confusing others, with a view to safeguarding the user's own interests. For instance, we would be concealing poverty in Taiwan and bestowing undeserved praise on the rulers of that country by asserting that the Taiwanese economy is growing twice as fast as that of Japan. Statistics can cover up reality even without telling lies. Of course, it should not be applied indiscriminately. For example, we do not need statistics to find out whether informal social networks are the locii of decision-making in particular work organisations. Qualitative social facts cannot always be quantified.

Often this can be done. Quantification facilitates handling large masses of data. For this purpose, they are first converted into symbols and formulas. Then they are processed with methods which are applicable to signs, but not to the facts behind them. Facts and their symbols cannot always be processed in the same way. Thus, instead of revealing information they serve to conceal the same. It is another point that statistics are not only liable to misuse they can also be put to good use. Of course, there are limits to their utility.

Many students of humanities and social sciences are at home in reading and writing rather than arithmetics. They are afraid of statistics. Most of them have not studied this subject at undergraduate level. They have a weak base. So they find it difficult to cope up with it. They are prone to making mistakes after applying statistics with a smile. Statistics with a smile is no statistics. Einstein used to say, "I haven't understood the theory of relativity myself ever since the mathematicians pounced on it."

The qualities of a group need not be applicable to each and every member of the group. Individuals have gone through different experiences. They have their own qualities. We can get false results by imposing the qualities of groups on all the individuals within them, and vice versa. Statistical conclusions are often based on probability. Again, statistical techniques are advancing much more rapidly these days than the methods of data collection. The point is that we have to be careful with statistical applications. It is not advisable to apply precise statistical tests on imprecise data. The data collected by social scientists seldom justify something more than ordinary percentages and four-fold tables.

In addition, raw cases are seldom smooth. Their coarseness has to be refined before we can understand them. Failure to take note of complexities will produce erroneous results.

Moreover, by collapsing various categories or changing their cutting points, by putting in or taking out marginal or outlying data, as well as in a number of other ways we can alter the statistical significance of our data. Such constructed significance can prop up our fancy conclusions and wishful thinking. If we fit preconceived results into tailored data without reason or rhyme, this would impair the validity of our results.

Furthermore, calculations are not always correct. There may be mistakes at several steps. These have to be checked up with each other, and with external details. All types of calculations cannot be applied to all types of data. It is not advisable to impose available computer programmes on whatever data are available, irrespective of the underlying assumptions.

Use of calculators and computers is increasing these days. Use of statistics has become common. There is no doubt about it that study of social statistics will help us to process a large mass of data in a small amount of time, keep us up-to-date and prevent us from becoming illiterate.

Types of Statistics

Typologies differ according to the purpose in hand. Depending upon the *Fundmentum divisions*, a basic consideration underlying the division in hand, we can classify statistics in different ways.

Population of a country, region, village, etc., under study is known as parameter. A sample drawn from it is known as statistic. In practice, there are always some gaps between the two. The method of drawing conclusions on the basis of a sample is known as non-parametric statistics. We also use this term when the variables are either nominal or ordinal. Parametric statistics are used only when the data are on a ratio or an interval scale.

Statistical research work can either be descriptive or explanatory. Descriptive data are facts collected through observation of various phenomena like voting behaviour, caste practices and political participation. For this purpose, we note down the nature and extent of a phenomenon under investigation. This is done as precisely as required stating its limits, central tendencies, outlying cases, notable exceptions, and so on. We accommodate a lot of data into a small amount of space. We make statements about them in general as well as in extraordinary cases.

Explanatory statistics make generalisations by taking a sample. We apply various tests like correlation, regression and factor analysis. These enable us to test hypotheses about the relationships between various elements of an entity. Explanatory statistics give us rules for explaining a broad universe in terms of its representative sample. This helps us to choose one among several alternatives. For instance, we can calculate the pros and cons of alternative policies, like whether it would be more profitable to construct thermal plants or plant more trees. Why did people vote for the Congress party rather than the BJP? The use of explanatory statistics is becoming common these days. In fact, both these types of statistics go hand in hand. Description precedes explanation.

While descriptive statistics take all the members of a population into consideration, the inferential statistics make use of samples in order to draw inferences about the entire population represented by the sample. This indicates whether the given variables are associated together, and if so how strong is their mutual relationship.

Some people are of the view that sociology is a purely descriptive subject. It is beyond its scope to make explanatory statements. To the extent a subject is descriptive in nature, it is less cumulative. Even otherwise, use of statistics is unnecessary when differences between two or more comparable groups are large. This is like seeing with a microscope what we cannot observe with a naked eye. Spectacles do not make up for insufficient knowledge of a language.

Table 2
Frequency of number of persons per household

No. of Persons	*Frequency*	*Cumulative frequency*
One	27.0	27.0
Two	24.0	51.0
Three	22.9	73.9
Four	10.1	84.0
Five	7.9	91.9
Six and above	8.1	100.0

Statistics are applied to data. The data collected by us are properly processed for analysis. Before we come to that again, let us have a look at elementary statistical measures.

Frequency Distribution

A frequency distribution tells us how frequently a particular value of the variable (class) is occurring. Cumulative frequency is obtained on successively adding up the frequencies of the values of the variable (or

Table 3
Cumulative frequency

Cumulative frequency	*Cumulative relative frequency*
0	0.00
10	0.08
60	0.50
80	0.67
120	1.00

classes) according to a certain law. Cumulative relative frequency is a proportion of the cumulative frequency. This enables us to compare the given cases with the total number of cases (see Tables 2 and 3).

Sampling distributions are shown by indicating their minimum and the maximum extent, averages and proportions, standard deviation (see further below), etc.

Diagrammatic and Graphic Representation

Diagrams and graphs are useful because they give a bird's eye view of the entire data, and information presented is easily understood. However, a distinction is there between diagram and graph. Graph brings the figures before us in concrete form. In constructing a graph, we generally make use of a graph paper, for representing frequency distributions and time series, graphs are more appropriate than diagrams. They indicate trends and relations, whereas a diagram is generally constructed on a plain paper. Diagrams are better suited for publicity and propaganda.

Steps for Constructing Diagram

1. Title : Diagram must be given a suitable title. The title should convey in as few a words as possible the main idea that the diagram intends to portray.
2. Proper proportion between width and height of the diagram should be maintained.
3. Selection of scale should be in even numbers or multiples of five. Odd values like 1,3,5,7 should be avoided.
4. Footnote should be given at the bottom of the diagram.
5. An index of different types of lines or different shades, colours should be given which helps in understanding the meaning of the diagram.

Technique of Construction of Graph

Graphs are drawn on a special type of paper known as graph paper which has a fine network of horizontal and vertical lines; the thick lines for each division of a centimeter or an inch measure and thin lines of small parts are the same. In a graph of any size, two straight lines are drawn at right angle to each other, intersecting at point 'O'. This is called origin. Two lines are called co-ordinate axis, horizontal line is called X-axis and is denoted by X'OX and vertical line is called Y-axis and is denoted by

Y'OY. Graph is divided in four quadrants. Generally, we use first quadrant unless negative magnitudes are to be displayed.

Figure 4
Frequency polygon

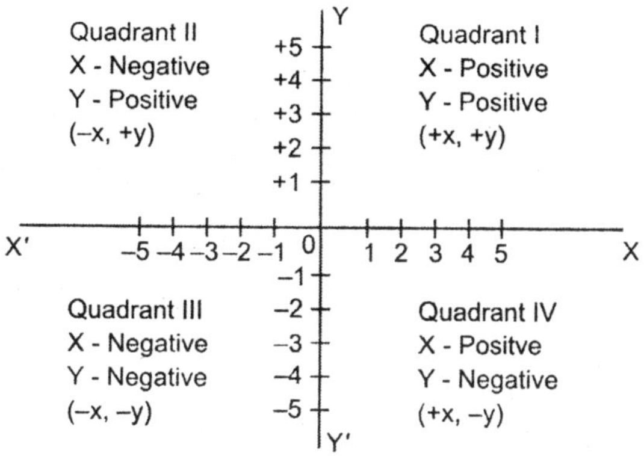

Scale along the axis should be so chosen that the entire data can be accommodated in the available space without crowding. If given data is irregular, use false line.

Bar Diagram

Bar diagrams are commonly used devices of presenting business and economic data. They are also called one-dimensional because in such diagrams only one dimension, i.e., height (or length) of the rectangles is taken into account to present the given values.

Types of Bar Diagram

Simple bar diagram : Simple bar diagram represents only one variable like production, sales, population, etc., for various years. Simple bar can be vertical or horizontal, but vertical bars are most popular, for example, the following data related to a firm from period 2000 to 2005.

Year	2000	2001	2002	2003	2004	2005
Production (Lakh mts)	20	30	35	45	55	40

Subdivided or component bar diagram : These are used to show the breakdown of a total into component parts. The length of the bar is proportional to the size of the item it represents, while the width of all the bars in the diagram remains the same. In order to distinguish the

Figure 5
Bar diagram

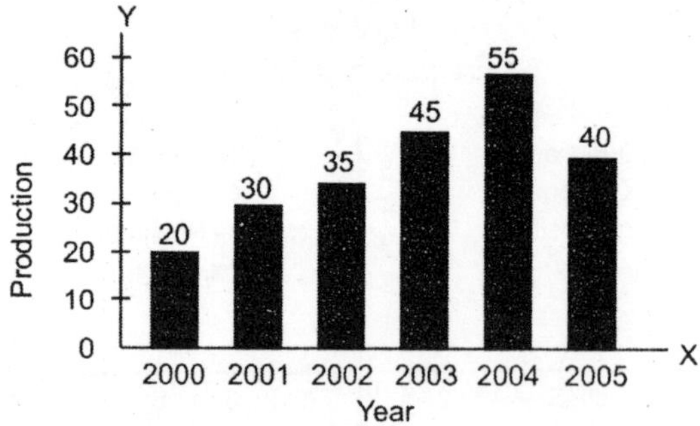

components of each bar, different shading, crossing or colours may be used. An index is given to represent the various components. The example represents the following data:

Table 4
Subdivided bar showing expenditure of two families

Items of expenditure	*Family A (Rs.)*	*Family B (Rs.)*
Food	150	150
Clothing	125	60
Education	25	50
Miscellaneous	190	70
Saving or Deficit	+10	–30
Total Income	Rs 500	Rs 300

Subdivided bar showing expenditure of two families:

Figure 6
Percentage bar diagram

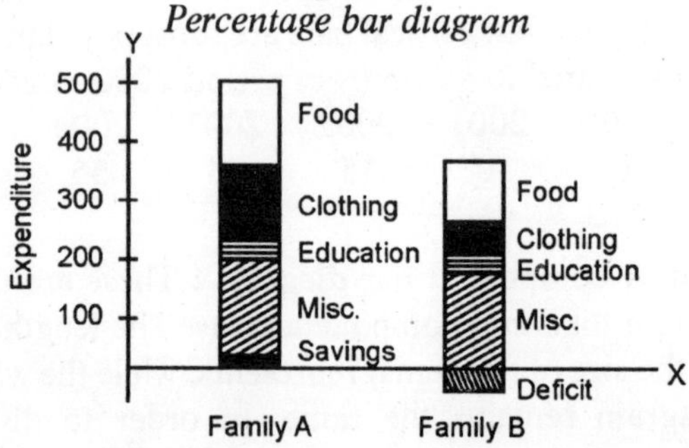

Percentage bar diagram : Subdivided bar diagrams presented graphically on percentage basis gives percentage bar diagrams. They are useful for the diagrammatic portrayal of relative change in the data. The total for each bar is taken as 100 and the value of each component is expressed as percentage of the respective totals. In percentage bar, diagram height of each bar will be the same, i.e., 100, whereas the various segments of the bar representing various components will vary in height depending on their percentage value of the total. These bars are helpful for comparing two or more sets of data. For example: percentage bar diagram represents the following data.

Table 5
Household expenditure

Item	*Expenditure (Rs)*	*Expenditure percentage*	*Cumulative percentage*
Food	100	$\frac{160}{400}\times 100 = 40$	40
Clothing	100	$\frac{100}{400}\times 100 = 25$	65
Education	70	$\frac{70}{400}\times 100 = 17.5$	82.5
Rent	40	$\frac{40}{400}\times 100 = 10$	92.5
Fuel and lighting	20	$\frac{20}{400}\times 100 = 5$	97.5
Miscellaneous	10	$\frac{10}{400}\times 100 = 2.5$	100.0
Total	Rs 400	100	

Figure 7
Percentage bar diagram

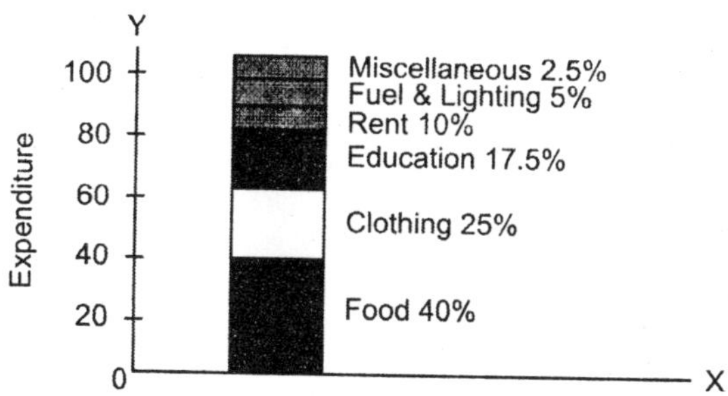

Multiple bar diagram : Multiple bar diagrams are used when two or more sets of interrelated phenomena or variables are to be presented graphically. Multiple bar diagrams are drawn in the same way as simple bar diagrams. In the case of adjacent bars, one of each variable is drawn. The example represents the following data of two firms A & B though multiple bar diagram.

Table 6
Figures for multiple bar diagram

Year	*Sale in ('000 Rs.)*	
	Firm A	*Firm B*
1993-94	120	80
1994-95	135	90
1995-96	140	110
1996-97	160	120

Figure 8
Multiple bar diagram

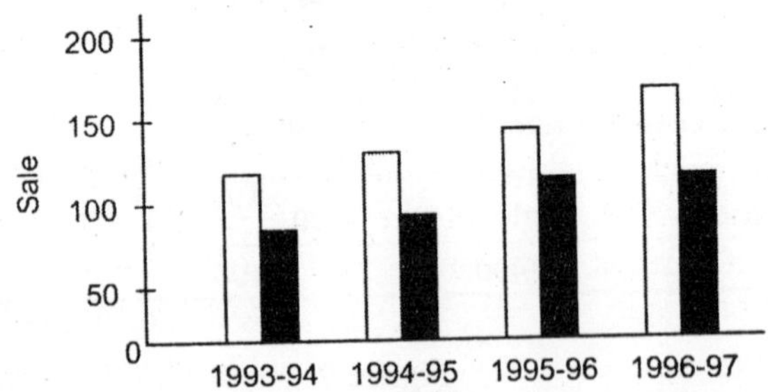

Histogram

This device is commonly used for charting continuous frequency distribution. It is also called two-dimensional because both height and length are taken into account. It is good for visual presentation.

Pie Chart

See Figure 10. It shows proportionate distribution of shares in reservations in the form of a cake. Comparability is made easy if we indicate percentages in each pie.

Figure 9
Histogram

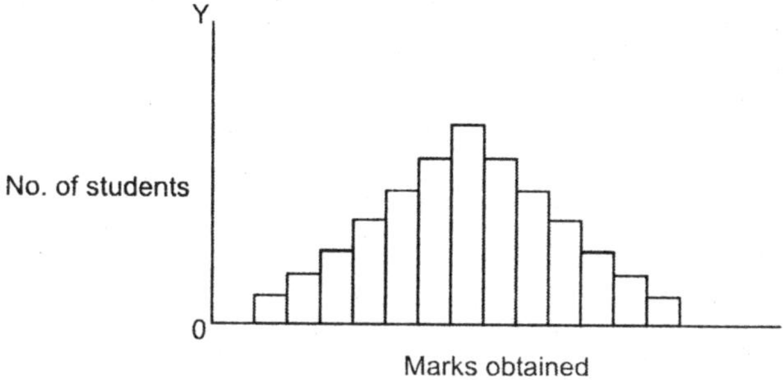

Figure 10
Pie chart

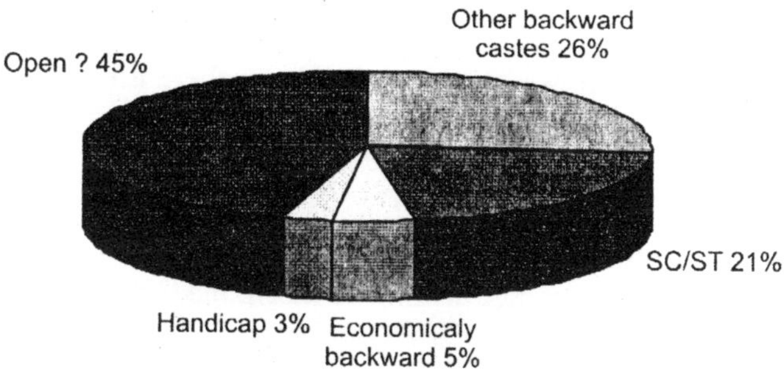

Steps for construction of pie diagrams:

Express each of the component values as a percentage of the respective total. The angle of the centre of the circle is 360°. The magnitude of various components is taken to be equal to 360°. Each component part is expressed proportionately in degrees, for instance, 1 per cent of the value is equal $\frac{360}{100} = 3.6°$. Similarly, other components can be converted to degree by multiplying each of them by 3.6°.

Frequency Polygon

Frequency distribution counts the number of times each value appears in a list. The data are measured with scores etc. These are arranged according to the values of the variables. These can be presented as such or graphically represented with a frequency polygon. Figure 11 shows one. The end points of the diagram are placed on the base-line (X-axis or abscissa) at the mid-points of intervals.

Figure 11

Frequency polygon

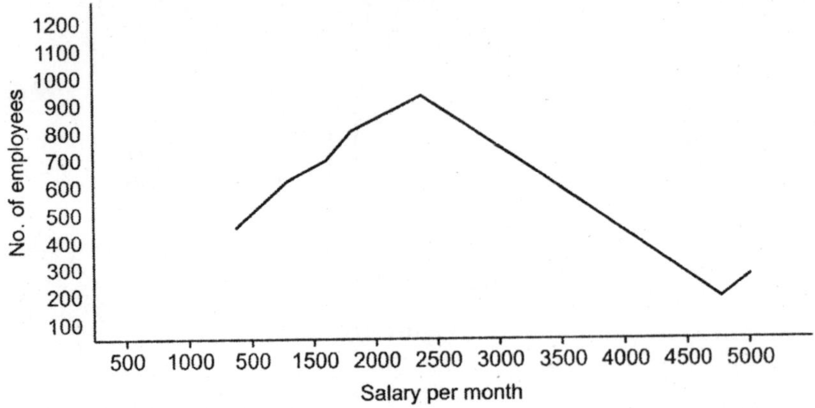

A frequency polygon can also be used to show cumulative frequency. This is known as an ogive. Where there are gaps, the ogive curve will be horizontal.

Average

An average is a single figure which represents the whole series. Following are the main types of average arithmetic mean, median, mode, geometric mean and harmonic mean.

Arithmetic Mean

A.M. of a given set of observations is their total divided by the number of observations. For example, the A.M. of 10, 12, 16, 14 and 8 is

$$\frac{10+12+16+14+8}{5} = \frac{60}{5} = 12$$

$$\text{Symbolically, } \overline{X} = \frac{x_1 + x_2 + x_3 + x_4 + \ldots x_n}{n}$$

i.e.,
$$\overline{X} = \frac{\text{Sum of items}}{\text{Total number of items}}$$

The arithmetic mean is of two types.

(i) Simple A.M. (ii) Weighted A.M.

In case of simple A.M., no weightage is given to any item, whereas in weighted A.M., weights are assigned according to the importance of the each variable.

Generally, there are three types of series.

Individual series :

$$\overline{X} = \frac{x_1 + x_2 + x_3 + x_4 + x_n}{n} = \frac{\Sigma x_1}{n}$$

Discrete series : In discrete series, frequency distribution is given and A.M. can be calculated as :

$$\overline{X} = \frac{f_1 x_1 + f_2 x_2 + f_3 x_3 + \ldots + f_n x_n}{n} = \frac{\Sigma f_x}{n}$$

where, n = Σ f is the total frequency.

Continuous Series

(i) the value of x is taken as the mid-value of the corresponding class.

(ii) multiply f with each value of x or the mid-value of the class by the corresponding frequency and obtain fx

(iii) Divide Σfx by n = Σf, i.e., by total frequency.

$$\overline{X} = \frac{\Sigma f_x}{***}$$

Averages are to be interpreted and applied wisely. Misinterpretation can lead to misleading results. Let us explain it like this. Once upon a time, a village patwari was transferred from one village to another, across a river. He left for that place with his wife and children. There was no bridge on the river. They could not swim. They had to cross the river by wading through its water on foot. The patwari calculated the average depth of the river. It was much less than the height of every member of his family. Thereupon he asked them to go ahead. When all of them were drowned, he was at his wit's end as to understand why such a tragedy had taken place. One has to be careful with arithmetic mean because it is much affected by extreme observations.

Mean is the most popular form of averages. It is based on all the observations. It is pure and reliable. Mean is easy to calculate and interpret. Mean is useful when extreme observations are not there. Mean is useful for further mathematical treatment, i.e., we can find combined mean. Mean is not applicable in case of qualitative data. It cannot be used in the case of open end classes.

Mean is much influenced by extreme observation. It can be illusive. For example, the per capita income of Kuwait or Brunei might give the impression that all the inhabitants of these countries are well-to-do. However, detailed examination reveals large gaps between the top and the bottom of the hierarchy. The influence of extreme cases (outliers) on the mean can be minimised by breaking down the population in different strata.

Difference of mean between two samples shows that they are unlike each other. We can apply an appropriate test of significance in order to check up whether this difference is symmetrical or not.

Mode

This measure of central tendency is made use of when we want to find out the most commonly used value. A uni-mode distribution possesses one maximum point. A bi-mode distribution possesses two humps, or two maximum points. Multi-mode distribution possesses more than two maximum points. It would be incorrect to assert that the mode represents the majority. Even a minority can be modal. It remains stable at a place. It is easy to find out. However, the mode ignores all the remaining values. If the readings are irregular, the mode can be delusive.

Figure 12
Modes

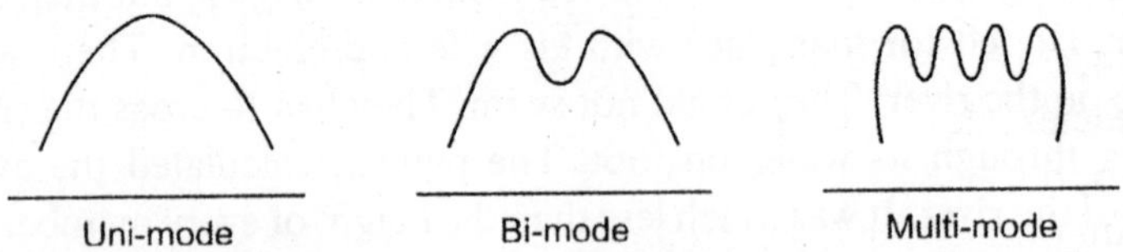

Generally, there are three types of series:

I. Individual series : In this case, the value which occurs more frequently is called mode. For example: find the mode from the following data:

Roll No.	1	2	3	4	5	6	7	8	9	10	11
Marks	10	12	12	9	8	9	12	12	13	10	11

From above data 12 occurs more frequently. So mode =12.

II. Discrete series : In discrete series, mode can be determined by inspection method or by judgement method, by looking for that value of the variable around which items are heavily concentrated. For example :

Income	40	50	60	70	80	90
No. of Persons	10	20	35	83	68	15

From the above value, modal size of income is 70, because the income 70 has occurred in case of the maximum number of persons, i.e., 83. However, finding mode by inspection method is problematic. Sometimes inspection method gives incorrect mode: (i) When frequencies are not systematic (ii) When the difference between the maximum frequency and the frequency preceding it or succeeding it is very small. (iii) When items are concentrated on either side.

In such cases, we use grouping method. For grouping method, figures should be arranged either in ascending order or descending order.

Steps : Forming Grouping Table

A grouping table has six columns. In the first column, write frequencies and mark maximum frequency. In the second column, write sum of two frequencies; for example, 1+2, 3+4, 5+6 and so on; in column three, ignore the first frequency. Write sum of frequencies taking two frequencies at a time. In the fourth column, group the frequencies in threes, for example, 1+2+3, 4+5+6, 7+8+9 and so on. In fifth column, leave the first frequency and group the remaining in threes, for instance, 2+3+4, 5+6+7 and so on and in the sixth column, ignore the first two frequencies and then group the remaining in threes. For example, 3+4+5, 6+7+8 and so on. In each column, mark the maximum total.

After preparing the grouping table, prepare an analysis table. In this table, put column number on the left hand side and various probable values of mode on the right hand side. The values against which frequencies are the highest are marked in the grouping table and then entered by means of bar in the relevant 'box' corresponding to the values they represented.

Example 1: Find out mode of the following data :

Variable	3	4	5	6	7	8	9	10	11
Frequency	5	4	6	8	9	7	5	9	4

Solution : The given statement is bi-modal. Inspection method is not suitable to find mode. We apply grouping method.

Table 7
Grouping table

	I	II	III	IV	V	VI
Variable	**Frequency**	**1+2**	**2+3**	**1+2+3**	**2+3+4**	**3+4+5**
3	5	—	—	—	—	—
4	4	9	10	15	—	—
5	6	14	—	—	18	—
6	8	—	(17)	—	—	23
7	(9)	—	—	(24)	—	—
8	7	(16)	—	—	21	—
9	5	—	12	—	—	21
10	(9)	14	—	18	—	—
11	4	—	13	—	—	—

Table 8
Probable modal value

Variable	I	II	III	IV	V	VI	Total
3	—	—	—	—	—	—	—
4	—	—	—	—	—	—	—
5	—	—	—	—	—	1	1
6	—	—	1	1	—	1	3
7	1	1	1	1	1	1	6
8	—	1	—	1	1	—	3
9	—	—	—	—	1	—	1
10	1	—	—	—	—	—	1
11	—	—	—	—	—	—	—

From the above, we find that the variable 7 occurs maximum times i.e., six times. So mode is 7.

Calculation of Mode: Continuous Series

Steps

(i) By applying inspection method or preparing grouping table and analysis table.

(ii) The value of mode determined by applying the following formula.

$$\text{Mode} = L + \frac{f_1 - f_0}{2f_1 - f_0 - f_2} \times C$$

where, L = lower limit
f_1 = frequency of the model class.
f_0 = frequency of the preceding model class.
f_2 = frequency of the succeeding model class.

Note: While applying the above formula for the calculation of mode, it is necessary to check that class intervals are equal. Throughout if class intervals are unequal, they should first be made equal by assuming that frequencies are equally distributed throughout the class.

However, in some cases there may be two values which occur with equal frequency. Such distribution is called bi-modal. In case of bi-modal distribution, the value of mode can not be determined by grouping method, i.e., where mode is ill-defined. Its value is determined by applying empirical formula.

That is, mode = 3 median – 2 mean.

Table 9
Mode of girls' dresses

Style	*No. of observations*
Frock	202
Salwar-kameez	240
Saree	272
Shirt and blouse	199
Pant and shirt	87
Total	1000

For grouped data,

$$\text{Mode} = L + \frac{d_1}{d_1 + d_2} \times i$$

where,
L = the lower limit of the class with the highest frequency.
d_1 = differences between the modal and the previous frequency.
d_2 = difference between the modal and the next frequency.
i = class interval (width of the class).

Median

Median is a positional measure. Median is the middle value of the given series after ascending or descending the given series. The median lies in between two extremes. It is the $\frac{n+1}{2}$ th value in individual and discrete series, whereas in continuous series median $= \frac{n}{2}$ th value. Such a sample is obtained by placing all the sums in an ascending or descending order. Half of the measurements are below the median and the remaining half are above it. Median is exactly in between.

The P_{50} percentile the 5th decile and the 2nd quartile are at the median. The observation one-fourth up the series is called the first quartile (Q_1). The observation three-fourths up the series is called the third quartile (Q_3). Median (Q_2) = 2nd quartile = 5th decile = 50th percentile. Quartile deviation $= \frac{Q_3 + Q_1}{2}$. Deciles divide the series into ten equal parts. Percentiles divide the series into 100 parts. Quartile divides the series in four equal parts and median divides the series in two equal parts. For grouped data,

$$\text{Median} = L + \frac{i}{f} \times \frac{n}{2} - Cf$$

where, C_f = Cumulative frequency of the group preceding the median group

f = frequency of the median group
L = the lower limit of the class in which median lies
n = total frequency
i = class interval

We use median when some of the observations are extreme or widespread. It can be calculated even when the extreme values of dispersion are unknown, i.e., in case of open end classes. Recall that the mean cannot be calculated in the absence of such information.

In a symmetric distribution, mean = mode = median. If their distribution is skewed towards left or right, mean-mode = 3 (mean – median), or mode = 3 median – 2 mean is called empirical formula. Thus, if we know two out of them, we can easily find out the third one.

Geometric Mean

Geometric mean or average is the *n*th root of the product of all observations comprising a group or items of a series. Geometric mean is used in the calculation of index numbers. It is very useful in dealing with ratios, i.e., averaging ratios, percentage and rates.

$$G = \sqrt[n]{x_1 \cdot x_2 \cdot x_3 \ldots x_n}$$

where, G = Geometric mean

$x_1\ x_2\ x_3 \ldots x_n$ are number of items.

Note : 1. If one of the items is zero. G.M. shall also be zero.

2. It cannot be calculated when any one item in the given series is missing.

The above said formula is applicable when the number of items is less. But if given number of observations are more we calculate G.M. with the help of log. The following method is used.

$$\log G = \frac{\log x_1 + \log x_2 + \log x_3 + \ldots + \log x_n}{n}$$

$$G = \text{antilog}\left\{\frac{\log x_1 + \log x_2 + \ldots + \log x_n}{n}\right\} = \text{A.L.}\left\{\frac{(\Sigma \log x)}{n}\right\}$$

For instance, find G.M. of the following data.

Marks	0-10	10-20	20-30	30-40	40-50
Students	5	9	10	16	4

Solution :

Let x = marks f = no. of students

x	*f*	*m. v.* $= \frac{L_1 + L_2}{2}$	*log m*	*f log m*
0-10	5	5	0.6990	3.4950
10-20	9	15	1.1761	10.5849
20-30	10	25	1.3979	13.9790
30-40	16	35	1.5441	24.7056
40-50	4	45	1.6532	6.6128
	n = 44		Σf log m = 59.3773	

$$\text{G.M.} = \text{A.L.}\left\{\frac{(\Sigma \log m)}{n}\right\} = \text{A.L.}\left\{\frac{59.3773}{44}\right\}$$

$$= \text{A.L.}\ (1.3495) = 22.37 \text{ Marks}$$

Harmonic Mean

Harmonic mean is computed by calculating the reciprocal of the arithmetic average of the reciprocals of the items of the series. It is used when it is desired to give more weight to the smallest items. It is applicable in averaging rates, time, average speed, etc.

$$\text{H.M.} = \frac{N}{\frac{1}{x_1} + \frac{1}{x_2} + \frac{1}{x_3} + \ldots + \frac{1}{x_n}} = \frac{N}{\Sigma - \frac{1}{x}}$$

or

$$\text{H.M.} = \frac{N}{\Sigma\left(\frac{f}{x}\right)}$$

where, H.M. = harmonic mean.

$x_1, x_2, x_3 \ldots.. x_n$ are values of the variable

f = frequency.

Note : Relationship between G.M., H.M. and A.M.

(i) AM > GM > H.M. when items are not equal in value.

(ii) AM = GM = H.M. when items are of equal value.

(iii) $GM^2 = .HM$ or $GM = \sqrt{\bar{X} \times H.M.}$

Dispersion

Dispersion is the measure of the variations of the items. Measures of dispersion tell us how widespread or compact the observations are from their mean. Range, mean deviation, standard deviation and variance express dispersion.

Range

The difference between the maximum and the minimum values of a series is known as the range. Range shows the largest and the smallest points of a scatter. For example, if the age of the oldest farmer in a village is 91 years and the age of the youngest farmer there is 21 years, then the range would be 70 years. Range = maximum age – minimum age = 91 – 21. Range can be quickly calculated and easily understood. However, it is not a precise measure. With the change in one extreme value, the value of range also changes. However, range can not be used in case of open end classes.

Knowledge of range can be used to find out the coefficient of dispersion. In the example of age of farmers given above, the coefficient of range $= \frac{91-21}{91+21} = \frac{70}{112} = 0.625$. We can compare two series of coefficients of dispersion and interpret the difference between the two.

Variability

Variance, mean deviation and standard deviation are measures of variability. They tell us how far two or more groups are dissimilar from each other. Let us take these into consideration one by one.

Variance is the sum of the squared deviations about the mean, divided by n.

$$\sigma^2 = \text{Variance} = \frac{\text{Sum of (deviations)}^2}{\text{n}} = \frac{\Sigma(x-\bar{x})^2}{\text{n}}$$

Standard deviation (see hereunder) is the square root of variance. Conversely, variance is the square of standard deviation.

In case of normal distribution :

$$\text{Q : D : MD : S.D. : : } -\frac{2}{3}\sigma : -\frac{4}{5}\sigma : \sigma :: \frac{2}{3} : \frac{4}{5} : 1$$

$$= \text{Q.D : M:D : S.D. :: } 10 : 12 : 15$$

or $$4 \text{ S.D.} = 5 \text{ M.D.} = 6 \text{ Q.D.}$$

Mean Deviation or Average Deviation

Average deviation is the average amount of scatter of the items in a distribution from either the mean or the median, ignoring the signs of the deviations. The average that is taken of the scatter is an arithmetic mean, which accounts for the fact that this measure is often called the mean deviation.

Steps : First of all, calculate arithmetic mean or median of the distribution. Then take the deviation $\{d = x - \overline{X} \text{ or x-med}\}$ of each observation from the mean or median. Ignoring sign obtain the sum of absolute deviation in case of individual series and in case of discrete or continuous series. Multiply the absolute deviation by corresponding frequency and then obtain sum, i.e., $\Sigma f(X - \overline{X})$ or $\Sigma f(X - \text{med})$ and divide it by n to find mean deviation.

Note : In mean deviation, we take absolute value of the deviations. So mean deviation is mathematically unsound and illogical.

$$\text{Coeff. of mean deviation} = \frac{\text{Mean deviation}}{\text{Average about which it is calculated}}$$

Standard Deviation

Standard deviation is the positive square root of the arithmetic mean of the squares of the deviations of the given observations from their arithmetic mean. Thus, if x_1, x_2, x_3,....x_n is a set of n observations then its standard deviation is given by

$$\sigma = \text{S.D.} = \sqrt{\frac{1}{n}\Sigma(x - \bar{x})^2}$$

Steps : Compute arithmetic mean and deviation $(Xi - \bar{x})$ of each observation from arithmetic mean i.e. $X_1 - \bar{x}, X_2 - \bar{x}, \ldots X_n - \bar{x}$. Square the sum of the deviations, i.e., $(x_1 - \bar{x})^2, (x_2 - \bar{x})^2, \ldots (x_n - \bar{x})^2$ and find sum, i.e., $\frac{1}{n}[\Sigma(X - \bar{x})^2]$, and divide the sum by n, i.e., $\Sigma(x - \bar{x})^2$, and in case of discrete and continuous series the formula becomes

$$\frac{1}{n}[\Sigma f(X - \bar{x})^2]$$

Note : Standard deviation is independent of the change of origin but not of the scale.

$$\text{Coefficient of variance} = \frac{\sigma}{x} \times 100$$

Coefficient of variance measures the relative homogeneity or heterogeneity of variables.

Probability

Probability is the chance of occurrence of an event. Let us try to understand what probability is by distinguishing it from what it is not. Probability is not determinism. Determinism explains everything in terms of the overpowering effect of a single factor above everything else. Probability implies that such a factor has no more or less, a modicum of, influence. Thus, apart from the dominant factor, some others have also to be taken into consideration. Probability is the likelihood of something being there or not being there. Probable conclusions indicate tendencies. These are not applicable in each and every case. Probability tells us whether a hypothesis is plausible, or otherwise. More than that, we can say with so much probability that in, say, 95 or 99 out of 100 cases, the relationship holds. Estimate of probability facilitates decision-making. If the probability is large, the danger of making wrong decisions can be avoided.

Figure 13
Normal probability curve

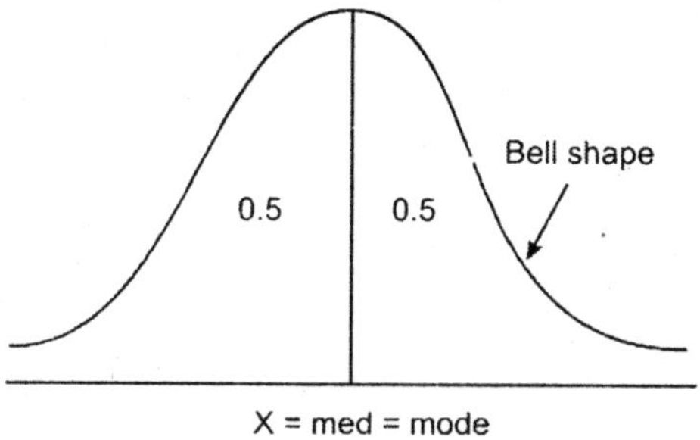

The probability of an event taking place is a relative portion of the total number of such events. The probability of a tossed coin falling down heads or tails is 50 out of 100, or 0.5. The probability of getting one out of a pack of 52 cards is 1/52. There is one chance out of a hundred that we will get a certain pass percentage. Probability varies between 0 (not at all) and 1 (has to be, sure). The probability of an event E is E (p). If we accumulate a large number of figures, they are likely to be distributed according to a normal probability curve. It is also known as a bell-shaped or a Gauss curve (after Laplace Gauses). Cent per cent events are normally probable. Such a curve is symmetrical. It is made up of many units. If we know the total figure, the normal probability distribution can be found out. When the distribution is normal, mean, mode and median are equal. They lie exactly in the middle of the distribution. If the distance from the mean is known, the probable number of cases in between can be found out. (see Table 10).

Table 10
Percentage distribution of cases in normal probability

Distance from mean ordinates in terms of $\pm\ \sigma$	***Area under the curve***
$z = \pm\ 0.6745$	50% = 0.5
$z = \pm\ 1.00$	68.26% = 0.6826
$z = \pm\ 1.96$	95% = 0.95
$z = \pm\ 2.0$	95.44% = 0.9544
$z = \pm\ 2.58$	99% = 0.99
$z = \pm\ 3.0$	99.73% = 0.9973

Figure 14
Normal probability curve

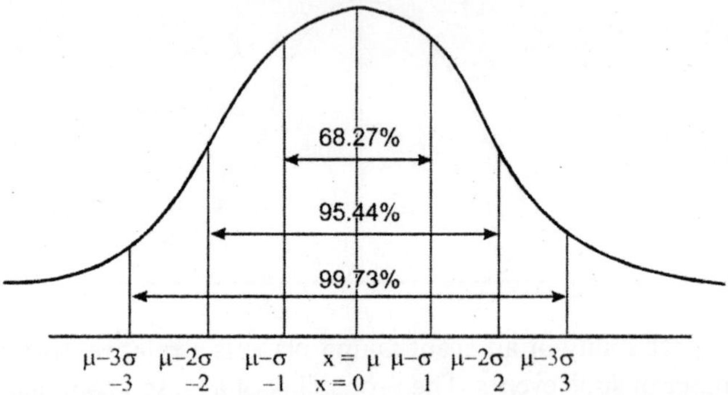

Kurtosis : Kurtosis enables us to have an idea about the shape and nature of the hump (middle part) of frequency distribution. Kurtosis deals with flatness or peakedness of the frequency curve. In the following graph, mesokurtic is called normal curve. A curve with peakedness or bulging is called leptokurtic. Flatter curves are called platykurtic and are said to possess kurtosis in excess or have positive kurtosis.

Figure 15
Kurtosis

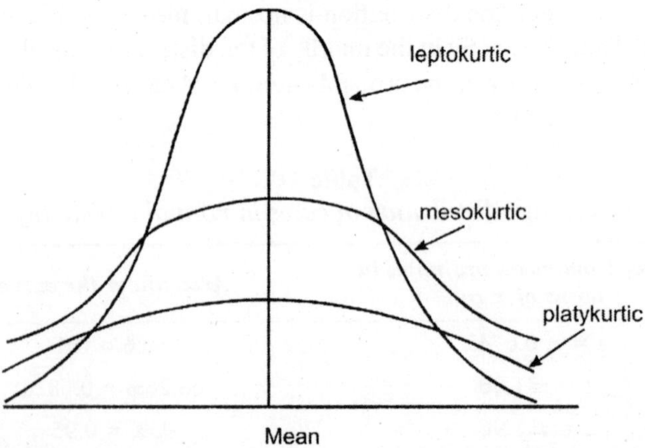

Skewness refers to lack of symmetry. In a positively skewed curve, the right tail is longer. In a negatively skewed curve, the left tail is longer. (See Figures 16 and 17).

Figure 16
Negative skewness

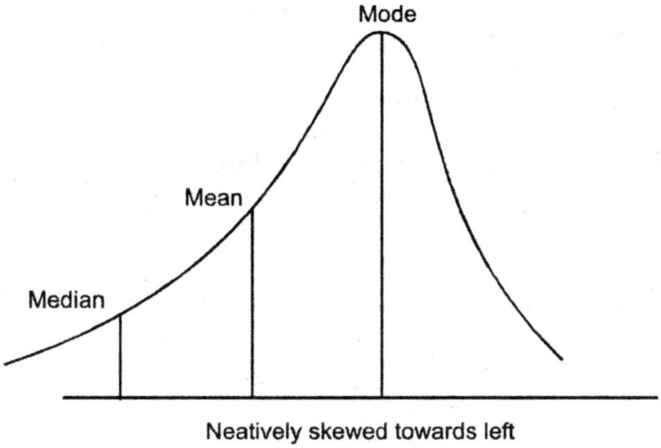

Figure 17
Positive skewness

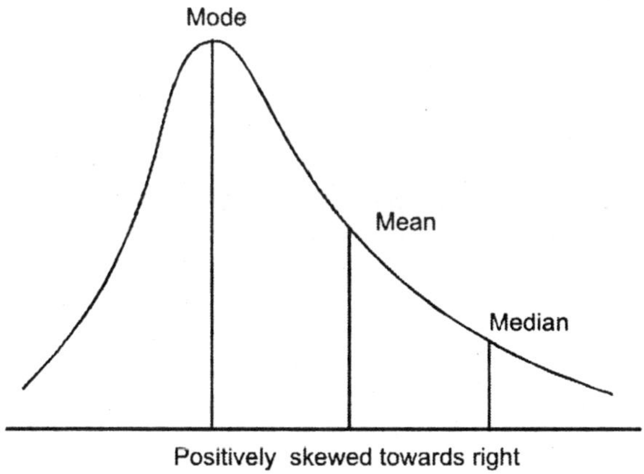

Data Processing

The data collected by us with interview schedule, etc., have to be properly processed before we can analyse and interpret the same. For this purpose, we have to turn over the matter in our mind before-hand and make the necessary preparations so that the data can be suitably coded and tabulated.

Preparation of Data

What does observation do? It takes note of whatever is considered relevant for a given purpose. Characteristics like somebody's voting behaviour, expression of confidence, attitude towards work, etc. What are data? Data are recorded observations, readings, goals, scores, points, victory or defeat in a match, or utilising one way or another in a questionnaire, are known as data. When their significance becomes known, data become information. We apply our mind before hand and collect neither more nor less data than we need. Then we reduce them to smaller size with a view to facilitating data processing and analysis.

The questionnaires, etc., are properly edited. Errors and inconsistencies are culled out. Cases with too much of missing data are eliminated. Where it is possible, the missing data are filled in. If it is found out that a particular interviewer has resorted to cheating by carrying out fake interviews with some fictitious persons, all the data collected by him may have to be discarded. Then we do the coding. Prepare a data file. Computer programmes for collapsing categories and building scales with alternative combination of items are available these days. They facilitate statistical applications.

Coding

Coding facilitates data processing by quantifying statements. How do we code our data? For this purpose, a code design is prepared beforehand. The code-book contains the names and numbers of various items and variables. Often a variable is made up of several items. Variables are given names like VAR001 OCCUPATION, VAR002 EDUCATION, VAR003 INCOME, and so on. In case of open-ended items, sometimes the interviewers record long statements. This makes coding difficult. In order to facilitate matters, only the first response is to be coded. Latter responses are ignored. If some data are missing, keep the cell empty. Do not use that cell for storing data from other columns. The code book should also contain special instructions for coders and secondary analysts. Later analysts cannot always refer back to the researcher's memory and implicit assumptions for finding out the missing links.

The data are carefully entered on code sheets or code cards. Hasty work by coders leads to many errors later on. A part of the coded data is checked by research supervisors with a view to verifying consistency. Inter-rater reliability also eliminates the effects of a coder's preconceptions. The coded data are fed to a computer-readable medium like a card, a tape or a floppy disc. The data are meticulously cleaned by removing the errors and preparing duly debugged data sets. Illogical entries are checked. This is often a strenuous task. It needs a lot of cross-checking, search for missing entries, recording, collapsing with or without alternative cutting points, and so on, with due attention. Verify and correct the punches (data entries). Run them on a computer and check marginals. Take care that there is only one code in a column. See that all the data are within a valid coding range. Filter check ensures that only those persons who have replied a filter question positively have answered the subsequent connected item(s). Eventual errors are rectified. Instead of having to correct a bundle of mistakes later on, it is better to punch carefully in the very beginning. Data prepared and cleaned in this way are ready for statistical applications.

Table 11
Data sheet

Unit	***Gender***	***Age***	***Class***	***Political preference***	***Job satisfaction***
First	Male	19	Middle	Congress	Yes
Second	Male	35	Middle	Congress	Yes
Third	Male	51	Lower	JD	No
Fourth	Female	25	Upper	Akali	Yes
Fifth	Male	87	Middle	JD	Yes
Sixth	Male	66	Middle	JD	Yes
Seventh	Male	27	Upper	BJP	Yes
Eighth	Male	19	Lower	JD	No
Ninth	Male	55	Lower	Congress	Yes
Tenth	Male	29	Lower	Akali	Yes
Eleventh	Male	62	Lower	JD	No
Twelfth	Male	19	Lower	SJP	Yes
Thirteenth	Male	32	Lower	SJP	Yes
Fourteenth	Male	21	Lower	Congress	Yes
Fifteenth	Male	47	Lower	Congress	Yes
Sixteenth	Male	32	Lower	Congress	Yes
Eighteenth	Male	18	Lower	SJP	Yes
Nineteenth	Male	43	Lower	Congress	Yes
Hundredth	Male	49	Lower	Congress	Yes

Data processing may be done (i) manually, (ii) mechanically, or (iii) electronically. While (ii) may be done with sorters, reproducers and tabulators, using punching cards, (iii) is carried on with computers. There are three steps for doing this. Firstly, the cleaned decks of job cards, programme cards, and data cards are arranged in proper order and made ready for input. Job cards let the others gain entry into the computer. Secondly, the programme cards let the central processing unit of the computer do specified calculations, or logical operations. Thirdly, the output tables, charts, etc., are printed out. Micro computers have enabled us to carry on these operations on a single window. These are to be interpreted by the researcher.

Which variables are to be cross-tabulated with each other? It is costly and useless to blindly run all variables with each other. A decision in this regard is made at the time of preparing the research design. Such decisions are built into the questionnaire. Unless appropriate hypotheses, concepts, operational definitions have been provided at proper places in time, data analysis would be useless. Facts do not speak for themselves. In order to ascertain their meanings, we have to make necessary preparations before hand. Open mind towards the data, freedom and facility to do so, make meaningful data processing easy.

Table 12

Code design

Col No.	*Item No.*	*Variable*	*Identification*	*Code*	*Category*
1.	0.2	VAR001	Registration	1	Registered
				2	Unregistered
				9	No response
2.	0.4	VAR002	Affiliation	1	AITUC
				2	BMS
				3	HMP
				4	HMS
				5	INTUC
				6	SSF
				7	AIBEA
				8	NFPTE
				9	IND-MISC
3.	0.5	VAR003	Year	1	upto 1947
			established	2	1948–52

...Cont'd

...Cont'd

				3	1953–57
				4	1958–62
				5	1963–65
				6	1966
				7	1967
				9	No response
4.	0.8	VAR004	Enrolment	1	100–499
				2	500–999
				3	1001–1999
				4	2000 and above
				9	No response
5.	0.3 (1-5)	VAR005	Employer attitude score	1	Yes on 1 point
				2	Yes on 2 points
				3	Yes on 3 points
				4	Yes on 4 points
				5	Yes on 5 points
				6	No on all points
				9	No response
6.	4.1.1	VAR006	Participation in meetings	1	All or most
				2	Three-fourths
				3	One half
				4	One-fourth
				9	No response
7.	4.7.2	VAR007	Participation in strikes	1	All or most
				2	Three-fourths
				3	One half
				4	One-fourth
				9	No response
8.	4.8	VAR008	Role of unions	1	Raising production
				2	Implementing norms
				3	Social change
				4	No response

Code Design: A Study on Trade Unions in Amritsar

Total pre-planning for data processing is neither possible nor desirable. A researcher has to playfully interact with his data. Count marginals. Suspect relations between relevant variables. Do not cross-tabulate everything with everything else. Construct the required tables and check up your suspicions. Overproduction of output is counter-productive. Before operating a computer, switch on your brain first. Garbage in brings garbage out. Gold in brings gold out. For productive utilisation of research work, understand the method first. Everything is not applicable everywhere. The underlying assumptions must be met before applying particular statistical techniques.

Interact with your data. Think intensively with focused attention. Redefine your categories. Change their borders and cutting points. Collapse them together whenever necessary. Introduce additional data. Try and try again, keeping an eye on the theoretical linkages.

Tabulation

Small tables are prepared manually. Large tables are constructed with computers. Computers facilitate statistical calculations. However, we have to read and interpret them ourselves. Applicability of the given computer programmes as well as their underlying assumptions have also to be closely examined.

Tables are prepared in such a way that they facilitate data analysis. Number of units, their size, dispersion, difference of means, come handy for explaining facts. The presence of a relationship, and its strength, can be ascertained by applying the chi square test and an appropriate coefficient of correlation. Factor analysis is a tool for finding out various dimensions of a problem. Regression is useful for synthesising facts into a whole. Prepare the tables in such a way that they are easy to read. It helps to present tables in the text at the top or bottom of a page, than at the end of an article.

Layout of a table can facilitate or retard the task before a reader. Proper display, spacing, separating lines or blank spaces, proper labelling, etc., improve readability and understandability. Visually bring out the focus of attention. Round off surplus digits after the decimal point. The figures to be compared are placed near each other. Let us look at the structure of a table. Each table has a particular identification number as well as a title. The number is quoted while referring to a table. Rows lie horizontally across the table. These are also known as the turn-out. Columns lie vertically up and down a table. Boxes are known as cells. Numbers in the boxes are known as cell frequencies. In a cross-table, each cell shows the respondents' score on both the variables under consideration. Numbers in edges below are called column marginals. These are obtained by adding up all levels of the row variables. Numbers in the columns on the extreme right side of a table are called row marginals. These are obtained by adding up all levels of the column variables. In large tables, various totals in the body of a table are summed up to show the grand total. The total number of cases is represented with a (capital) N. The number of cases in a sub-table or a sample is represented with a (small) n. Elaborate titles, labels, variables, missing elements, etc. Give reasons for, and break up of, the missing data. This can be done with the help of asterisks or stars(*) and similar other signs. These draw the readers' attention to footnotes at the bottom of a table regarding source of the table, details, missing data, limitations, etc. This keeps a reader well-informed about the necessary details.

Rounding off decimal points introduces a small amount of inaccuracy. Thus, the total may not add up to exactly 100.00. A modicum of imprecision has to be tolerated in the interest of understandability. This can be improved by rearranging the format. Thus, row and columns

Table 13
Tally sheet

Class intervals (Income)	Tally signs	(Rs/month) (Frequency)
Upto 1000	|||	3
1001-2000	卌 卌 卌 卌 |||	23
2001-3000	卌 卌 卌 卌 卌 卌	30
3001-4000	卌 卌 |||	13
4001-5000	卌 卌 卌 卌 卌 ||	27
5001-6000	卌 卌 卌 卌		21
6001-7000	卌 卌 卌 |||	18
7001-8000	卌	5
8001-9000	|||	3
9001-10000	卌 卌 卌		16
10001-11000			1
11001 and above	卌 ||	7

can be interchanged with one another. Arrangement is done in some viable ascending or descending numerical, alphabetical or psychological or logical order. For this purpose, some overriding consideration is kept in view.

Table 14
Structure of a table

Stub (dependent variable)	***Title***			***Total***
	Heading (independent variable)			
	Column 1	***Column 2***	***Column 3***	
Row 1	Cell	Cell	Cell	Row
Row 2	Cell	Cell	Cell	Marginals
Row 3	Cell	Cell	Cell	
Row 4	Cell	Cell	Cell	
Total	Column Marginals			

Data Analysis

Data sets are analysed and synthesised with a view to making generalisations. Analysis involves breaking up into meaningful parts. Its opposite, synthesis, involves combining parts into a whole. This enables us to show interactions and structures. These are linked up into theories and put in the wider perspective. Data analysis bridges the gap between data and theory.

Data are symbols. They do not speak for themselves. We have to read them ourselves and unfold their meanings. They have to be interpreted. How is this done? First of all smooth out the rough. Refine the raw data. Do not throw away the baby with the bath tub. In other words, do not oversimplify. Summarise the data. The summary ought to be precise, complete, and useable. Shuttle to and fro between raw data and test scores. Inspect, get a comprehensive view of the matter. Describe. List the essential features of an object with a view to differentiating it from similar objects. Explain how exactly the units are linked with each other. For example, how political preference is related to ethnic background, or how job satisfaction is related to organisational hierarchy. Avoid hasty generalisations. Be aware of the existing theories in the field. Point out what is new in them. Present the old in a new light.

Data analysis can be of two types. Exploratory data analysis helps us in finding out and revealing relevant clues. It explains the interrelationship between variables and their underlying dimensions. Confirmatory data analysis enables us to assess the strength of evidence.

Interpretation means assessing the meaning of something and relating it to something else. Interpret the data as adequately as you can. But avoid over-interpretation. Do not bestow greater reliability and validity on the data than is justified. Do not forget that interpretations from statistics are applicable to groups. These may not be true of each and every individual in the group. Generalisations based on a sample from a village are applicable to that village. These need not necessarily be true of each and every individual in the village.

Statistics is a handmaid of data analysis. Statistical tables can be divided into three types : (i) univariate, (ii) bivariate and (iii) multivariate. Let us deal with them one by one.

Univariate Tables

Tables can be constructed in a number of ways. They do not speak for themselves. The analyst has to read them and bring out significant conclusions. Therefore the tables should be presented in such a manner that their analysis is facilitated.

Reading a table means talking through the table. Break up larger tables into smaller ones. Concentrate your attention on the details. Inspect the data. Examine their location, spread and shape. Apply descriptive statistics. State the magnitude of the variables. Translate absolute numbers, percentages and proportions into properly worded statements. Examine their effects on each other, and their mutual differences.

Table can be read according to the frequency of absolute numbers as well as according to percentages, or even proportions. Their rank order also tells us about their relative significance. The shape of distribution reveals the structure of data in the table. Data are explained in terms of other data. Their implications are drawn for policy-making. It is often remarked that particularistic considerations play their part in recruitment to jobs in traditionalistic societies. It is noticed from Table 15 that a combination of technical skills, professional qualifications, as well as influence of relatives, friends and community leaders plays its part in recruiting incumbents for jobs in the organisations under study. An implication of this inference is that professional qualifications are least important in the process of recruitment.

Table 15
Factors in recruitment

Factors	*No.*	*Percent*
Technical skills	37	$\frac{37}{214}\times 100 = 17.3$
Influence	29	$\frac{29}{214}\times 100 = 13.6$
Professional qualifications	14	$\frac{14}{214}\times 100 = 6.3$
Combination of above	128	$\frac{128}{214}\times 100 = 59.8$
No response	6	$\frac{6}{214}\times 100 = 2.8$
Total	214	99.8

That technical skills do not go hand in hand with formal educational qualifications, reflects lack of rationality as well as low quality of professional education. Intermingling of influence and power in the broader community with the functioning of goal-oriented organisations can only hinder their overall effectiveness.

Various categories in a table can be collapsed together. Two or more values on a variable can be merged with each other. This is done if we have substantive reasons for doing so. Our previous knowledge about the background of the matter facilitates this operation.

Analysis is as good as the sample it is based on. Some data may be missing due to refusal or inaccessibility of some elements in the sample. Some respondents may have given incomplete or irrelevant response. The sampling frame itself may be inadequate. Data may be missing due to wrong entries. Whatever reasons are there, if there are not too many missing numbers, they can be imputed qualities of similar people in other meaningful categories.

Percentage

These are easy to understand. Percentages are obtained by dividing the number of cases with the total frequency. The result is multiplied by 100. In this way, the absolute numbers are expressed as parts of one hundred. This improves their comparability. Proportions are obtained by dividing the number of cases in a cell with the total number of cases. The outcome is multiplied with 100 in order to get percentage.

Table 16
Parts of a hundred

Part	*Name*
1	Centile
2	Two centiles
10	Decile
1-25	Lower quartile (Q1)
50	Median
75-100	Upper quartile (Q3)

Prominent percentile are given special names. These are shown in Table 16. One part of a hundred is one per cent (1%).

We may also calculate per thousand, per million, etc. Percentages are not to be used uncritically. If the total number of cases is small, say less than 50, we refrain from using percentages. In that case, it is better to use absolute numbers. For that matter the number of cases on which percentages are based must also be indicated in the table. It may be necessary to indicate how much no response is due to non-availability of the respondents, their refusal to give replies, inapplicability of the matter to them, or to the available data being somehow unreliable. Apart from these, even when multiple responses are permitted, the total percentage will not add upto 100.

It is easy to construct percentage tables. If there are not too many of them, it can be assumed that such cases are more or less evenly distributed over the remaining categories. Otherwise, take care of them while interpreting. Differential 'no response' in various items of a study hinder comparability of data.

Rounding off decimal points serves a double purpose. On the one hand, it enables us to avoid exaggerated precision. On the other hand, it saves loss of information. While putting a decimal point in a percentage, ensure that the data are precise enough for the purpose. Avoid pseudo-precision. One place after decimal is good enough for survey data. Round off the figures after the decimal. For instance, 6.69 will become 6.7, 17.85 will become 17.8, and 43.37 will become 43.4. Rounding off may involve double precision. This means that the calculations are done with two digits after the decimal, while the outcome is rounded off to only one digit after the decimal.

Per cent increase or decrease is obtained by dividing the increase or decrease with the total number of cases. The result is multiplied by 100. Thus, $\frac{\text{Increase}}{\text{Total number}} \times 100$ or $\frac{\text{Decrease}}{\text{Total number}} \times 100$. For instance, if the price of a vegetable falls down from Rs. 1.50 to Rs. 0.90 per 100 gm., this would be a decline of 60 per cent. In such cases, the earlier and the larger figure provides the base for calculating the percentage.

Percentage can also be presented as rate. So 16 per cent increase is at the rate of 16.

Table 17

Employees' training and job satisfaction

Job satisfaction (V2)	***Training (V1)***		***Total***
	Trained	***Untrained***	
Satisfied	400	200	600
Dissatisfied	100	300	400
Total	500	500	1000

How are percentages interpreted? Compare them across the rows and down the columns. Examine the breakdown of different categories. Small differences in percentages can be due to chance. We have to reveal the meaning of large differences.

Percentaging can be done both ways, and even on the basis of grand totals. There is no hard and fast rule about it. Convenience for interpretation is what matters. However, they are often calculated in the direction of causation. Table 17 is a bivariate frequency table. Again, Table 18 is a bivariate percentage table. It shows percentages for the absolute numbers from the previous table, in the vertical direction. These add up to 100, vertically. These are to be compared vertically. A difference in percentages indicates that the two variables (training and job satisfaction) are interrelated.

Table 19 indicated perfect association between the two variables. Thus, each and every value of the variable V_1 is related with each and every value of the variable V_2. Similarly, Table 20 shows complete (but not perfect) association between the given variables. The figures in Tables 17 to 20 are fictitious. These have been put up here in order to bring home interpretation of tables.

Table 18

Employees's training and job satisfaction

Job satisfaction (V2)	*Training (V1)*		*Total (per cent)*
	Trained	*Untrained*	
Satisfied	80	40	60
Dissatisfied	20	60	40
Total	100	100	100

Table 19

Employees's training and job satisfaction

Job satisfaction (V2)	*Training (V1)*		*Total*
	Trained	*Untrained*	
Satisfied	500	0	500
Dissatisfied	0	500	500
Total	500	500	1000

How do we interpret percentage differences between two or more categories, say nations? If India and Pakistan differ from each other, what does this mean? So what? Some people explain too much in terms of religion alone. Political system, class composition, ideology, size, etc., may also be used as explanatory variables. Our theoretical knowledge and creative imagination tell us how we are going to decide what is to be done, or what is to be cross-tabulated with what.

Bivariate Tables

Tables 17–21 are bivariate tables. These are also known as cross or contingency or dependence or 2 × 2 tables. Here two variables are classified together with each other. Then various statistical tests are applied with a view to finding out whether the two variables are dependent upon or independent of each other. This can help us to predict a dependent variable from a second one (independent variable).

Dichotomous variables are two-pronged. They have two categories each like satisfied/dissatisfied, and employed/unemployed. Trichotomous variables are three-pronged. Polytomy means that a variable is divided into several categories. Dichotomisation reduces complexity. This makes it easy to deal with the tables. However, the cutting point should be meaningful. Thoughtless dichotomisation can conceal relations instead of revealing them.

Table 20

Employees's training and job satisfaction

Job satisfaction (V2)	***Training (V1)***		***Total***
	Trained	***Untrained***	
Satisfied	450	10	460
Dissatisfied	50	490	540
Total	500	500	1000

Table 21

Relationship between dependent and independent variables

Dependent variable	***Independent variable***		***Total***
	Column 1	***Column 2***	
Row 1	Cell 1	Cell 2	Row
Row 2	Cell 3	Cell 4	Marginals
	Column marginals		Grand total

Table 21 is a bivariate table. If both the variables are dichotomous, i.e. contain two categories each, we get a 2 × 2 table. This has four cells. The body of a table is made up of these cells. One of the variables is a column variable. The other one is a row variable. The column variable lies vertically up and down. The row variable lies horizontally across the page. In tables 17-20, training is a column variable, while job satisfaction is a row variable. Generally, the column variable is independent, while the row variable is dependent. This need not always be so. Percentages are often calculated in the direction of the independent variable. (Once more : the vertical columns contain the independent variable, while the horizontal columns contain the dependent variable.) Cells make up the body of a table. Right side totals are called row marginals. Bottom totals are called column marginals.

We can interpret a two-way table in several ways. Some of them are given below.

(a) Inspection

How do we inspect a table? Examine intuitively. Look at the table with focussed attention. This is also known as eyeballing. Get into the matter. Comprehend. This is a subjective operation. What do the various categories look like? Note down the form, the overall pattern, the underlying structure. Examine the contents. Speak out, express precisely, compare with prior findings by various researchers under different conditions. Draw implications, with reference to your own point of view.

Overcrossing props up inspection. If sub-groups across rows and columns significantly differ from each other, the given variables are mutually related. If in a 2 × 2 table, the larger and the smaller sums of both the columns overcross each other, then the variables are mutually related. Look at Table 19 with careful attention. It shows that trained persons are satisfied with their jobs. Untrained persons are dissatisfied with their jobs. We can say that training promotes job satisfaction. Had the differences across the lines been small, the variables would have been unrelated.

(b) Association

Two variables are related or associated together if they are fellow travellers. Thus, change in the value of one variable will be accompanied by change in the value of the other variable. One of these can be used for predicting the other. Refer back to Table 18. It shows that 80 per cent of the trained employees express satisfaction with their jobs. On the other

Table 22
Measures of association

(i)	Perfect	150	0	150
		0	50	50
	Total	150	50	200
(ii)	Conditional	50	25	75
		0	125	125
	Total	50	150	200
(iii)	Imperfect	40	35	75
		60	65	125
	Total	100	100	200

hand, 60 per cent untrained employees expressed dissatisfaction with their jobs. In other words, we can say with a probability of $p=0.8$ that training and job satisfaction are related together. Similarly, we can say with $p=0.6$ that lack of training is associated with lack of job satisfaction.

(c) Odds Ratio

An odd is the chance of being in a category or not being in it. The ratio between the frequency of being or not being in a category is called odds ratio. This is also known as cross-product ratio.

There are two types of odds. The marginal odds refer to the total frequency in one margin of a table. The conditional odds correspond to percentages. Odds ratio is obtained by dividing one conditional odd with the other. Anything divided by zero is equal to infinity. In case the frequency in any cell is zero, odds cannot be calculated. In that case add a constant, say 1, to each cell. Then calculate odds. If all the conditional odds are more or less identical, the two variables are unrelated. The higher (or lower) the departure from 1.00, the stronger the direct (or inverse) relationship. In case it is negative, the two variables are inversely related. If the two variables are only nominal, i.e., without any order, the increase relationship is also interpreted as a direct relationship.

Even if we interchange the rows and columns, the odds ratio does not change. Odds ratio of 1.00 shows lack of any relationship between the two variables. In other words, the odds are the same in both the categories. The odds ratio varies from zero to infinity.

Let us compare the odds of being satisfied. Look at Table 17 again. The table shows that the odds that a person is satisfied with his training are 600 ÷ 400 = 1.5 or three to two. These are the marginal odds. These pertain to the total frequency in the margin of the table without taking the effect of any other variable into consideration. The conditional odds in the body of the table correspond to percentages. These are the chances of satisfaction or dissatisfaction with one's job, given being trained or untrained. For trained employees, the odds ratio is 400 to 100 or 400 ÷ 100 = 4.00. For untrained employees, the odds ratio is 200 ÷ 300 = 0.67. If there had been no relationship, the two odds would have been the same for trained as well as untrained employees. The ratio of the two odds is 4.00 ÷ 0.67 = 5.97. If the odds had been the same for both the categories, their ratio would have been 1.00. In that case, there would have been no relationship. As it is, 5.97 is much more than 1.00. In other words, the two variables are mutually related. Thus, trained employees are more likely to be satisfied with their jobs than untrained employees. The larger the odds ratio, the stronger the relationship between variables. In case the odds ratio had been negative (minus), the relationship between the two variables would have been inverse. The odds ratio tells us how strongly two variables are related with each other. It can be further used for building up log-linear models for causal analysis.

The odds ratio is also used for calculating Yule's coefficient of association. *(Yule's Q)*. This provides us a measure of association for a 2 × 2 Table case,

Thus,
$$\text{Yule's Q} = \frac{\text{Odds ratio} - 1}{\text{Odds ratio} + 1}$$

This may vary between ± 1.00. Zero means lack of relationship between the variables. For Table 17

$$\text{Yule's Q} = \frac{5.97 - 1}{5.97 + 1} = .71$$

This shows, once more, that the two variables are highly correlated.

(d) Difference of Proportions

Proportion can be calculated by dividing the cell frequency with the category total. Difference of proportions may vary between ±1. In between the two extremes, 0 means lack of any relationship between the variables. See Table 23. The difference of proportions between the values of the two variables shows that they are interrelated. If the value is high or low in both cases, the relationship is positive or direct. However, if the values were high on one, and low on the other, the relationship would have been negative, or inverse.

Table 23

Difference of proportion between variable

Variable 2	*Variable 1*		*Difference (partial association for variable 1)*
	High	*Low*	
High	0.63	0.81	–0.18
Low	0.08	0.49	–0.41
Difference (partial association for variable 2)	0.55	0.32	

(e) Percentages

Overcrossing can be tried with absolute numbers, and also with percentages. Calculate percentages within categories of the independent variables. Compare these percentages across the categories of the independent variable. In case the percentages are more or less identical at all levels of the independent variable, the two variables are unrelated. If the percentages between or across the categories differ significantly from one another, the variables are related to each other.

(f) Chi-square

Chi pronounced as ki, (Sky without S) is a letter of the Greek alphabet. The square of the standard normal variable is called chi square variate with 1 degree of freedom abbreviated as df. Thus, x is random variable following normal distribution with mean μ and standard deviation σ then $\frac{(x-\mu)}{\sigma}$ is standard normal variate and its square is chi-square, i.e. $\frac{(x-\mu)^2}{\sigma}$ with 1 df.

Chi-square test is used for analysing contingency tables. It finds out whether two variables are independent of each other. If they are independent of each other, they will not go hand in hand. If they are dependent upon one another, the presence of one of them can be predicted from the presence of the other. This is seen by taking note of the difference between the expected frequency and the observed frequency. It tells how much they fit each other. It measures their goodness of fit. Specifically, it shows the difference between the frequencies obtained from the collected (observed) data and those expected on the basis of some theory (expected). The expected frequencies show that the table should have looked like if the variables had not been related together. If the difference is large, the two variables are significantly related together. Attention : This test does not say anything about the strength of such a relationship.

How to calculate the chi square?

$$\chi^2 = \text{chi-square}$$

$$\chi^2 = \sum \frac{(O-E)^2}{E}$$

where O = observed frequency
E = expected frequency.

Example : Suppose the numbers of automobile accidents per week in a certain community were as follows :

12, 8, 20, 2, 13

Solution : H_0 : Set up null hypothesis that the given frequencies are consistent with the belief that the accident conditions were the same during five-week period.

Sum of total accidents over the five weeks is :

$$12+8+20+2+13=55$$

Under null hypothesis, these accidents should be uniformly distributed over the five weeks. Hence, expected frequency = $\frac{55}{5}$ = 11.

Table 24

Calculation of chi-square

Week	*Observed no. of accidents*	*Expected frequency (E)*	*O-E*	*(O-E)²*	*(O-E)²/E*
1	12	11	1	1	0.0909
2	8	11	–3	9	0.8182
3	20	11	9	81	7.3636
4	2	11	–9	81	7.3636
5	13	11	2	4	0.3636

$$\sum\left(\frac{O-E^2}{E}\right)=15.999$$

$$\chi^2=15.999$$

Since the frequency is 5, therefore, df = n.1, i.e., 5 – 1 =4 tabulated value of χ^2 for 4 df at 5 per cent level of significance is 11.070 is less than calculated χ^2. So it is highly significant and Ho is rejected at 5per cent level of significance.

E means value expected if the variables are unrelated. These are hypothetical, not real. These provide us anchorage for comparison with the actually observed data. Expected values are constructed by multiplying the marginals corresponding to cells and dividing the same with the number of cases. Thus, we use the formula $\frac{(a+b)(a+c)}{N}$. Actually observed (O) data are contrasted with the expected (E) data. If O=E, chi-square is zero. Chi-square can never be negative (minus). It is always positive (plus). If O is not equal to E, that is the observed and the expected values differ from each other, then the two variables are mutually related. The larger the difference between the two values, more significant will be the value of chi-square.

This test can be applied to data on all types of scales. However, the data must satisfy certain assumptions. Chi-square is to be calculated from absolute frequencies. Percentages or proportions can not be used for this purpose. The categories must be mutually exclusive and collectively exhaustive. If multiple responses are permissible, chi-square test can not be applied. We have to ensure that the sample is not only random but also large. How large? Opinion differs. Some statisticians say 30 is large enough. Others insist upon total collection. The chi-square test is not applicable to small samples. Better use Fisher's f-test test for them. Alternative tests are available for non-random samples. On the other hand, larger samples invariably yield significant results. Significance can be easily manipulated. Thus, it can yield illusive results. Question wording, cutting points of categories, marginals are chosen on the basis of subjective judgement of the researcher. These can be sources of bias. Thus, the statistical significance need not necessarily be theoretical importance. One has to ascertain why and how a particular relation exists. Knowledge of time, place, conditions, is necessary for this purpose. For that matter, the problem under study has to be well- formulated in advance. Moreover, the number of cases in any single cell of the table under analysis should not be very small (5 or lesser). In order to increase the number of cases in a single cell, we may pool our data in one lot, and collapse various categories. Meaningful dichotomisation yields significant results from 2×2 tables. However, misclassification of cases leads to misinterpretation of data even if the chi-square appears to be significant. The point is that forcible imposition yields erroneous results.

The chi-square test is used for testing hypotheses. It helps us to choose between one of the alternative hypotheses. This shows that the difference between two means is not significant. Thus, the two variables are not related to each other. They are independent of each other. Rejecting the null hypothesis means that the variables are significantly interrelated. This is known as an alternate hypothesis (H_1). There can be two different types of errors in accepting or rejecting a hypothesis. Type I error is made by failing to accept what is true by not claiming a relationship which is there. If we reject a true hypothesis, Type II errors can be made by accepting what is false by claiming a relationship which is not there. We accept a false hypothesis. We reject a true hypothesis. The chance of making a Type II error can not be calculated. Level of significance represents the probability of making a Type I error.

How do we interpret the chi-square? The chi-square for Table 17 is 116.6, df = 1, $p \leq .001$. The null hypothesis can be rejected with 99.9 per cent probability. In other words, training and job satisfaction go hand in hand.

How do we ascertain df (degree of freedom)? It (df) = (no. of rows − 1) × (no. of columns − 1). In a 2 × 2 table, df would be (n − 1)(c − 1) i.e., (2 − 1) × (2 − 1) = 1 × 1 = 1. Similarly, in a 3 × 2 table, df = 2, and in a 4 × 3 table, d.f. = 6. Then we look at the relevant statistical tables. These are given at the end of text books of statistics.

The table shows that given so much chi-square and so much df, p would be this much. Suppose that in a particular case, p.≤. 001. Then we can say with 99 per cent certainty that the given variables are interrelated. Even then, if in the remaining 1 out of every 100 cases, the two variables are not interrelated inspite of the chi-square being significant overall. Once more, the probability statement p=≤. 05 means that in 5 out of 100 cases the results could have been obtained by chance. In the remaining 95 cases, the results have not been obtained by chance.

Some of the limitations of the chi-square test can be covered up with other tests like Phi, Cramer's V, Gamma, Eta, etc., Chi-square is affected by the number of cases in the sample. The larger the number of cases, the higher the chi-square. In order to remove the confounding effect of a large sample size, the ± chi-square table is standardised or smoothened. This can be done, sometimes, by calculating percentages. These are treated as if these are row frequencies.

Let it be emphasised that the chi-square test does not tell us about the strength of relationship, or its form, or about other factors involved in the relationship. At best it can indicate whether a relationship exists or does not exist, not even about how large or how small it is. In order to find out the strength, we can calculate an appropriate coefficient of correlation (r). Even there (see further below) when r is high, we are not in a position to assert without any doubt that the given variables are infact causally connected. Detailed knowledge of the underlying assumptions is indispensable for this purpose. For that we have to go beyond correlation to the theoretical background of the matter under consideration.

(g) Coefficient of contingency : This is a variant of the chi-square test. It is calculated as follows :

$$C = \frac{\chi^2}{\chi^2 + N}$$

This varies between 0 and 1. Zero means absence of association. One means perfect association. However, the upper limit varies, depending upon the number of rows and columns in a table. The coefficient of contingency is not independent of the chi-square test. Similarly, some varieties of correlation bank upon the chi-square test. Thus:

$$\phi^2 = \frac{\chi^2}{N}$$

$$T^2 = \frac{\chi^2}{N(r-1)(c-1)} = \frac{\phi^2}{(r-1)(c-1)}$$

All these measures are zero when independent.

Correlation

The coefficient of correlation was put to use first of all by biologists. Even nowadays this method is more often used by economists and psychologists rather than students of sociology. It tells us the strength of relationships between two or more variables. It summarises relationships between large sets of data. If the coefficient of correlation between two variables is high, the existence of one will predict the existence of the other. If both of them go together, they are bound by positive, or direct, relationship. If the one goes up the other goes down, their relationship is negative or inverse. If two variables (X and Y) are correlated together, then one of them can be an independent variable (causal) and the other one a dependent variable (effect). If the relationship is deterministic, then the existence of one will predict the other. Such a relationship can be reversible ($X \leftrightarrow Y$) or irreversible ($X \rightarrow Y$). It can be probable. It can be deterministic. It can be successive. It can be only associative.

Cause-effect relationships are successive, irreversible and interdependent. Other variables cannot spoil their relationship. These are ruled out. Cause-effect relationships can not be assigned on the basis of statistical correlations alone. These have to be further interpreted. We have to go beyond statistical correlations to show that a theoretical connection is really there. In order to get divorced, you have got to get married first. But for example, marriage is not the cause of divorce, even though the former precedes the latter, then the independent variable precedes the dependent variable. The error terms are not correlated. In other words, confounding variables do not intervene between the cause and the effect. The independent variable accounts for the dependent variable. In case it can be asserted with full confidence that these assumptions have been met, then correlation can be accepted as proof of causation. It is difficult to be sure about cause-effect relations without conducting experiments. There can be many reasons for two variables being correlated together.

Figure 18
Cause-effect relationship

Liberalisation	→	Competitive costs

(i) Types of Correlations

Depending upon their qualities, correlations can be of several mutually overlapping types. Some of them are being discussed here.

(a) Conditional relationship : An unconditional relationship is true under all circumstances. Thus, Y=f(X) is a conditional relationship. The presence, direction and intensity of an unconditional variable is dependent upon some other variable. Thus, R (X,Y) = f (T). In other words, the relationship between X and Y is modified by a third variable (T).

(b) Intervening variable : X produces Z, and Z in turn produces Y. It appears as if X is producing Y. But the intervening variable is also there in between. The apparently direct relationship between X and Y is mediated by Z.

Pilot having piano lessons as a child	→	Eye-hand coordination developed	→	Fighter plane success
Independent variable	→	Intervening variable	→	Dependent variable

It is not easy to distinguish between an intervening and a spurious relationship.

X	→	Z	→	Y

An intervening variable is not a moderator variable.

Figure 19
Types of variables

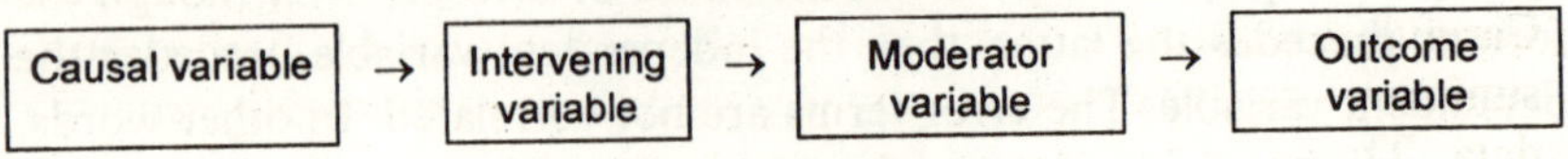

Figure 20
Multicausality

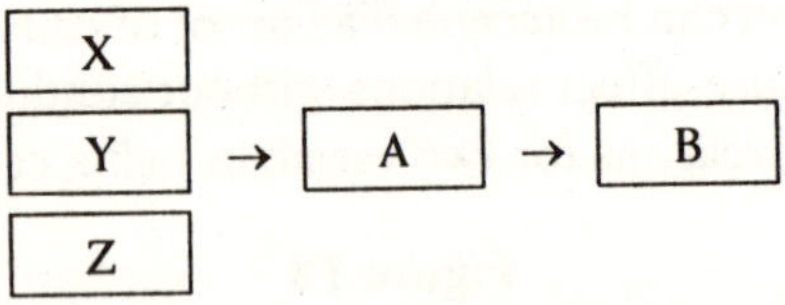

(c) Symptomatic correlations : If ladies who use lipstick participate in political activities more often than those who do not use it, then use of lipstick will be correlated with political participation. Infact, this is only a symptomatic relationship. The real cause is somewhere else. Women who use lipstick tend to be better off. They can spare time for such activities. They are wives, sisters and daughters of big men. Poor women do not possess the required resources for enabling them to participate in political activities. Such a relationship between variables conceals the real causes behind their symptoms. These are symptomatic, not causal variables. Superficial symptoms are different from their causes lying down below.

(d) Multicausality : X and Z act together to produce Y. Y produces A. A produces B, they cannot produce these results by themselves alone. This is a case of multicausation.

(e) Lack of correlation : Sometimes theoretical considerations show that correlation is there, but tabulation shows that it is not there. This can be checked up by bringing a third variable and holding it in between the two. Keep it constant. This will clearly bring out the relationship between the first two variables.

(f) Spurious correlation : It appears as if two variables (X and Y) are related together. Infact, they are not. Their apparent relationship is produced by the common effect of a third variable (Z) on both of them. They are connected together by dint of variable Z. By controlling or removing the confounding effect of Z, the relationship between X and Y vanishes. For instance, when it appears that the birth rate is higher in villages than in towns, because there are many more storks in villages.

How do we detect a spurious relationship? Apply your mind. Calmly put yourself on the alert and be ready for taking appropriate action. Carefully examine the details in the data. Do not confine your attention to summary statistics alone. Summaries are based on smooth aspects of data. These cannot always be fitted together. They ignore the rough aspects. Deviations from the smooth are called residuals. Residuals alone yield distorting and misleading results. Intuitively grasp the rough as well as the smooth. Suspect spurious relationships. Check them up objectively. This can be done by applying some control.

Figure 21
Correlation

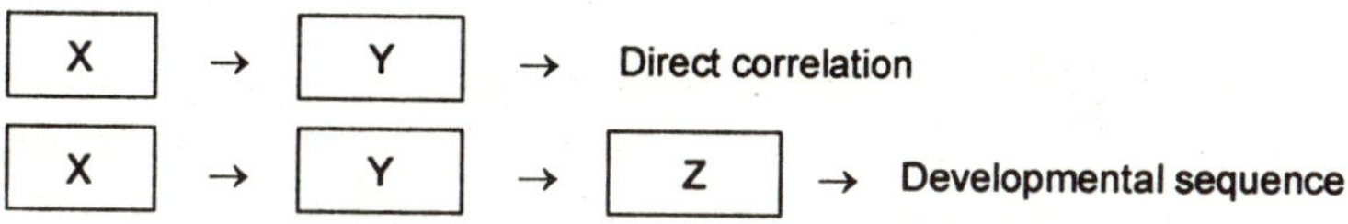

How can we control the effect of Z on the relationship between X and Y? Divide the respondents into mutually exclusive categories according to the value of the control variable (Z). Examine the relationship between X and Y for each value of the control variable. If the relationship continues to exist in all categories of Z, it is genuine. If imposition of control weakens the original relationship between X and Y, this means that their mutual relationship is spurious. Thus, the original association was caused by the intervening variable.

Spurious correlations can be checked up by understanding the underlying mechanism. For this purpose, we elaborate the relationship between the two variables (X and Y). One way of doing this by controlling the intervening variable (Z) has been clarified above. An alternative procedure by exercising control is by collecting data from respondents who are homogeneous on Z. Such elaboration can be done through matching. Thus, X is matched with different categories of Y.

We can also hold the control variable constant or fixed. Then we sub-classify on it. If the relationship between X and Y remains the same on all values of Z, then Z has no bearing on the relationship between X and Y. In this case, X and Y are interrelated. In case the relationship between X and Y is strong in some categories of Z and weak in others, then X and Y are related together. We can say that if there is a spurious correlation, the percentages in each column of the sub-table remain the same. Once more, if elaboration shows that X and Y are not affected by variation in Z, then Z is a spurious variable.

Presence of some extreme cases (or outliers) in the data also creates spurious correlations. Identify such cases. This can be done by closely examining a variable which has an unduly large correlation with everything else. Scattergrams can also be made use of for this purpose. In order to grasp the structure of the data, keep deviant cases apart. But do not hide them.

Figure 22

Spurious and intervening correlations

Spurious correlations can also be partialed out. How is this done? Gross or zero-order correlation is calculated from all the cases of a table, without controlling for the effect of other variables. Net correlation is calculated from all the cells of a table while controlling for the effect of other variables. When more than two variables are given and we study the relationship between two variables keeping all other variables constant it is called partial correlation, e.g., production of wheat depends upon rainfall, seeds, fertilizers etc. When we study the relationship between production of wheat and seeds, keep other factor constant.

In multiple correlation, more than two variables are given and we study all variables simultaneously. This is called multiple correlation, for example, relationship among production of wheat and rainfall, seeds, fertilizers etc. A partial correlation is calculated from only some cells of a table, controlling for the effect of other variables. We calculate partial correlation between each independent variable and the dependent variable. These are compared with each other. The control variable is kept constant when the particular association between other variables is being calculated.

A partial correlation means association between two variables in a control group. It explains the relationship between the independent and dependent variable by partialling out the impact of the moderator variable.

It measures the relationship between the dependent and the independent variables as well as the relationship between the independent

Figure 23

Multiple and partial correlations

variables themselves. This enables us to examine the relationship between two variables by removing (partialling out) the effect of the other variables by holding them constant. For this purpose, we calculate **partial correlations** between the dependent variable and the independent variable. These are compared with each other. The control variable is kept constant when the partial association between two other variables is being calculated. Suppose X_1= class, X_2=caste, X_3=education, and X_4=income. Further suppose that their partial correlations are $r_{43.12}=.4$, $r_{41.32}=1.3$, $r_{42.31}=0.1$. These show that the variables appearing after the decimal point have been correlated with the variables appearing before the point. In the above example, education and income are strongly correlated together (.4). The coefficient of correlation r_{xy} between X and Y keeping Z under control is (r_{xy}.3). Ideally, the partial correlation r_{xy}.3 ought to be zero. In practice, it is not altogether zero. It is round about zero or very small. In other words, the partial correlation is used for detecting spurious relationships between variables.

Some points of clarification. What is a **control group**? The set of units with similar values on the control variable(s) from which a partial association with other variables is being calculated is known as a control group. The net association between two variables while controlling the other variables influencing the dependent variable is known as the direct effect. The component of association between two variables which is due to the intervening variable is known as the indirect effect. The varying partial association (weaker in one, stronger in the other) between control groups is known as their **interaction**. That means the relationship is different in the two groups. After detecting interaction, we go ahead and specify the conditions under which the relationship holds. Attention : Never control a dependent variable.

(ii) Coefficient of Correlation

This tests the actual strength of relationship between variables and coefficient of correlation is denoted by r. Depending upon the assumptions underlying the data, we calculate different types of coefficients in different situations. It is not proper to apply a coefficient without knowing the underlying assumptions. The following assumptions hold for many (not all) coefficients of correlation. Both variables are on an appropriate (say ordinal) scale, sample size is adequate, both variables are distributed according to a normal probability curve, are (say) bivariate, and their mutual relationship is (say) linear. For example, if Pearson's 'r' is very low, it means the absence of a, linear relationship between the variables. If the value of 'r' is high, it means high degree positive correlation. The value of coefficient of correlation always lies between ± 1.

The higher the correlation, the more significant it is. The lower the correlation, the less significant it is. If $r_{xy} = 1$ this means that the relationship between X an Y is perfect positive. The two are necessary and sufficient conditions for each other's existence. If r_{xy} is near zero, it means that the relationship between X and Y is trivial. If it is zero, this means that there is no linear relationship between the variables. Their relationship may be curvilinear. Again, perfect positive correlation shows that the connection is direct and complete. As one of them goes up, the other goes up too. As one goes down, the other goes down too. Perfect negative relation shows that the connection between the two variables is inverse and complete. Thus, we can use one of the variables for predicting the other. If the coefficient is away from unity (± 1), this means that the relationship is not deterministic (either... or), it is probablistic (to what extent). If this is so, we can predict with a probability of that where there is X, there will also be Y.

Significance may be illusory if it is not true for ascertaining its truth, we have to go beyond statistics to their underlying theoretical connections.

Another method of understanding the coefficient of correlation relies on calculating its square is called coefficient of determination i.e.,

Figure 24
Coefficient of correlation

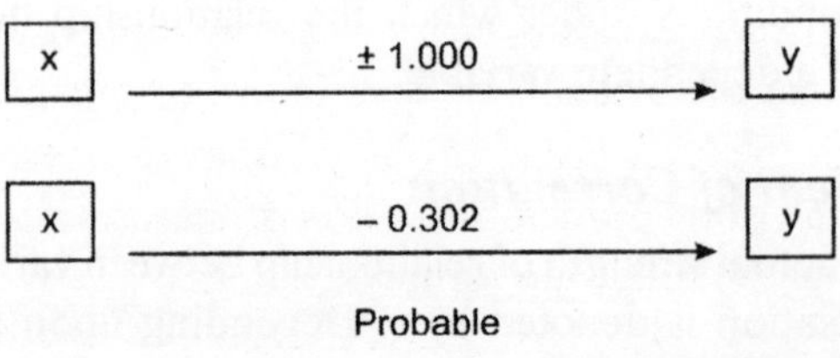

r^2. If r = 0.700, r^2 would be 0.49. This can be interpreted by saying that this relationship explains 49 per cent of the variation. We will have to explain the remaining $(1 - r^2)$ is called coefficient of non-determinations $(1 - r^2{=}51$ per cent) variation by examining the remaining variables. Conversely, while 49 per cent of their variance is common, the remaining 51 per cent remains unexplained variance. This has to be explained in some other way.

(iii) Karl Pearson's r

Pearson's product moment coefficient of correlation can be applied when both the variables are on a rational or an interval scale, and are normally distributed. This can be calculated by the following formula :

$$r = \frac{n\Sigma(x-\overline{x})(y-\overline{y})}{\sqrt{n\Sigma(x-\overline{x})^2}\cdot\sqrt{n\Sigma(y-\overline{y})^2}}$$

$$r = \frac{\Sigma xy}{\sqrt{\Sigma x^2}\cdot\sqrt{\Sigma y^2}}$$

where, $x = (x - x)$
$y = (y - y)$
$\Sigma x^2 = \Sigma(x - x)^2$
$\Sigma y^2 = \Sigma(y - y)^2$

where, X and Y are given variables.

x and y are their respective mean.

Nominal or ordinal data can be converted into interval data by introducing dummy variables in between. If Pearson's r is low, this means the absence of linear relationship between variables. In order to check up whether curvilinear relationship is there, calculate η, which measures linear as well as non-linear association. $\eta^2 - r^2$=non-linear variance.

(iv) Spearman's r

Spearman's rank order coefficient of correlation measures the strength of relationship between two variables. It can be applied when both the variables are ordinal or cardinal, i.e., qualitative or quantitative. We do this by comparing the rank order of observations of one variable to the corresponding rank of the same observation of the second variable. This is done by applying the following formula:

$$r = 1 - \frac{6\Sigma d^2}{n(n^2 - 1)}$$

where, d = difference between pairs of ranks
n = number of pairs of ranks.

Suppose we want to find out the association between rural and urban scores on ranking castes in an area. Collect the data with a scale. Calculate scores for each caste separately. Assign marks to all the castes, starting with 1 for the caste with the lowest score. Calculate r, using the formula given above. This would show the association between the ways caste is ranked in rural and urban areas. r is calculated in the following ways : Arrange the scores in a descending order with reference to either rural or urban scores for different castes. Calculate d by subtracting the ranks for (say) urban areas from the ranks for the rural areas. Minus signs are automatically ignored when d is squared. Then go ahead and interpret r.

It has to be emphasised that correlations are heuristic devices for the purpose of research. For interpreting them, go beyond correlations to the underlying theoretical relations. However, if equal ranks occur, then following formula is used.

$$r = 1 - \frac{6(\Sigma d^2 + 1/12(m^3 - m) + 1/12(m^3 - m) + \ldots)}{n(n^2 - 1)}$$

where m = number of time repeated value in X series and Y series.

For example:

x	y	R_x	R_y	D $R_x - R_y$	D_2
10	7	4.5	4	+0.5	0.25
15	3	6	1	+5	25.00
8	8	2	6	–4	16.00
10	7	4.5	4	+0.5	0.25
9	5	3	2	+1	1.00
7	7	1	4	–3	9.00

$$\Sigma D^2 = 51.50$$

Solution : In x series 10 occurs twice so m = 2 and rank

$$= \frac{4+5}{2} = 4.5$$

Similarly, in y series 7 occurs thrice, m = 3. Its position rank

$$= \frac{3+4+5}{3} = 4$$

$$r = 1 - \frac{6(\Sigma d^2 + 1/12\,(m^3 - m) + 1/12\,(m^3 - m)}{n\,(n^2 - 1)}$$

$$r = 1 - \frac{6(51.50^2 + 1/12\,(2^3 - 2) + 1/12\,(3^3 - 3)}{6\,(6^2 - 1)}$$

$$r = 1 - \frac{6(51.50^2 + 1/12\,(8 - 2) + 1/12\,(27 - 3)}{210}$$

$$r = 1 - \frac{6(51.50 + 0.5 + 2)}{210} = 1 - \frac{324}{210}$$

$$= 1 - 1.54 = -0.54$$

$$r = 0.54$$

Scatter Diagram Method

A scatter diagram summarises a lot of data in a small amount of space. It visually presents the relationship between two variables.

These are represented as points or dots. See Figure 25. The horizontal (X) axis, or abscissa, represents the independent variable. The vertical (Y) axis, or the ordinate, represents the dependent variable. The values of the two variables meet each other at a coordinate point. The data are plotted with dots showing joint distribution of both the variables under study. Each and every point in the scatter diagram does not necessarily fit into a pattern. The general direction can be identified and presented in the form of a curve or the line of the best fit. The nearness or spread of the points around the curve indicates strength of relationship between variables. The nearer the points along the curve, the stronger their 'r' relationship. A number of procedures are available for finding out the best fitting line connecting different points.

Before interpreting a scatter diagram, we have to check up whether, just in case, some errors have been left out somewhere. Find out how these have crept in. See that all the data have been gathered in the same way. These might be due to mistakes in transcribing, punching, inadvertent mix-up, or otherwise. Ensure that the various categories are comparable. See that all the percentages etc., have been calculated on the same basis. Rectify eventual errors. Pull out suspicious outliers. These

Figure 25
Scatter diagrams

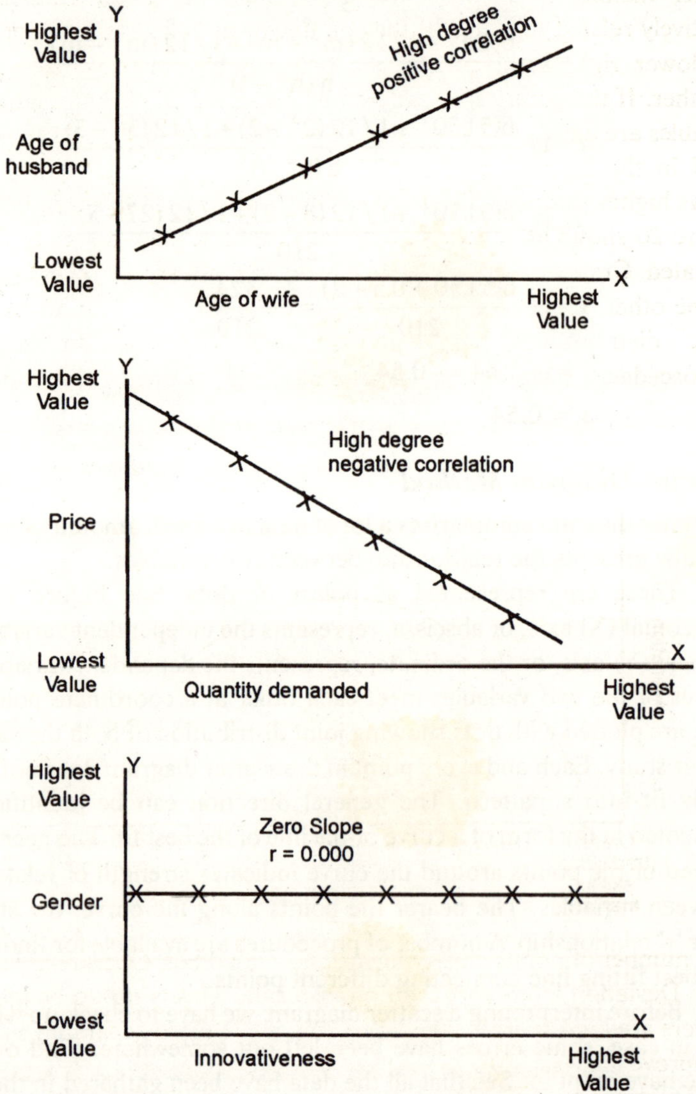

are extreme points, deviant points or unusual cases that stand apart from their company. These distort the general pattern and make it difficult to understand the same. These have to be interpreted separately. Look out for gaps and overlaps. The point is to understand the matter yourself, and then explain it for others. How do we interpret a scatter diagram? If the pointed line goes upwards from the lower left to the upper right hand corner making a unilinear trajectory, then the given variables are positively related together. If they go downwards from the upper left to the lower right hand corner, the two variables are inversely related together. If the points are scattered or dispersed all over the graph, the variables are unrelated. The curve shows the shape of the relationship. A bend in the curve shows curvilinearity. An inverted U-shaped curve shows higher values at the start and finish, and lower values in between. Figure 26 shows an inverted U-curve. Assembly line workers are highly alienated. Craft workers on the one hand, and chemical process workers on the other, are least alienated. A fan, with thin distribution here and thick distribution there, shows heteroscedacity. In contrast, homoscedacity involves equal scatter all along the line. A cloud means a

Figure 26

Automation and alienation (after R. Baluner)

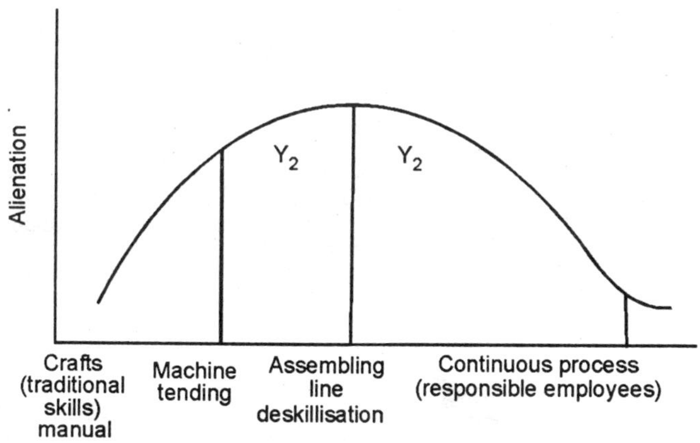

large number of points clustering around each other. Outliers are exceptions. Deviation from norm can prove a rule. This is not to be ignored. Outliers are kept apart for the time being and treated separately in order to improve analysis.

Different procedures are used for calculating linear and curvilinear relations. If we assume a linear relationship where there is curvilinearlity, this would lead to erroneous results. By showing whether the relationship is linear or curvilinear, it helps us to choose an appropriate coefficient of correlation or another statistical procedure and apply the same.

Extrapolation can be done by extending a scattergram or a curve in an expected direction. Understand and summarise the structure of the given data within the given conditions. Then extrapolate, going beyond the range of actual observations, carefully avoiding over-generalisation. We have to place the matter in proper perspective. Sometimes, extrapolation yields delusive results. It gives us the illusion that we know more than we actually do.

We often infer future developments in India from the present ones in the UK or Pakistan. Again, census data show that the population of Delhi doubles up every ten years. We can extrapolate this trend and predict the growth of the population of the city during the coming days. The inference can be used for drawing implications, for the policy makers and administrators, among others.

Regression

This is a flexible analytical tool. It can help us to analyse various types of dichotomous as well as continuous data. It accounts for the effect of one

Table 25
Regression

Trade union membership (Y)	(X) All respondents job satisfaction			Control (Z)								
				High income job satisfaction			Medium income job satisfaction			Low income job satisfaction		
	High	Medium	Low	High	Medium	Low	High	Medium	Low	High	Medium	Low
High	70	50	40	80	60	50	70	50	40	60	40	30
Low	30	50	60	20	40	50	30	50	60	40	60	70
X and Y above are interrelated												
High	70	50	40	70	70	70	50	50	50	40	40	40
Low	30	50	60	30	30	30	50	50	50	60	60	60

or more independent (=predictor) variables on a dependent (=response) variable. Thus, as independent variable X increases or decreases this much, the dependent variable Y will also do that much. To begin with, possible effects of a control variable make a scattergram. Examine the relationship between X and Y. Loosely fit the points. This enables us to find a rough line of fit. The slope of the line enables us to ascertain the structure underlying our data.

Linear regression is calculated by using the algebraic equation :

$$Y = a + bx + u$$

where,
Y = the dependent variable
X = the independent variable
a = is "Y-intercept"
b = regression coefficient. It is always expressed in terms of a value of the Y axis.
u = disturbance term (unknown variables)

If we know a and b, then we can predict the value of the dependent variable Y for any value of the independent variable(s) X.

Regression equation of X on Y is not necessarily the same as regression of Y and X. This property of regression makes it a useful tool for explaining asymmetric relations.

Each category of every variable is treated as a separate variable. Each of them is transformed and put into the equation. We create a series of K dichotomous dummy variables. Superfluous variables are excluded. K – 1 variables are included in the equation. The interaction between two variables with I and J categories needs (I – 1) (J – 1) dummy variables.

Two main methods of regression are being discussed below :

(a) Ordinary least square method : This is an exploratory technique. The least square line estimates the expected value, the line of best fit (regression line) joins the points. It is drawn in such a way that the sum of the squared vertical deviations in different directions between the bivariate points and the line is minimum. This method minimises the sum of squared deviations from the fitted line.

(b) Multiple regression : This is used to predict the relationship between a dependent variables (Y) and two or more independent variables, (X_1, X_2, X_3 ... X_n). It controls various independent variables and finds out the influence of the remaining ones in the dependent variable.

Regression is based on a number of assumptions :

1. Unilinear, additive equations are assumed. Fitting linear equation to curvilinear or multilinear data creates problems. Curvilinearity can be checked up with a scattergram. It can also be calculated. Non-linear curve may be convex or concave, like lenses. A convex curve faces upwards. It increases the distance in the upper range, and decreases it in the lower range. A concave curve faces downwards towards the larger values.
2. Symmetry : Each point in the scattergram comes from a normal distribution curve. Variance is uniform.
3. The errors are symmetrical and mutually unrelated. The error term has constant variance for all values of the independent variable. The variance is small. This means it is BLUE, the best linear, unbiased estimate.
4. The independent variable and the error term are unrelated.
5. There is no bias. Apart from the above assumptions for OLS, (ordinary least square), multiple regression falls back upon further assumptions too. These are as under :
6. Insignificant variables have been culled out.
7. There is no interaction among independent variables.

In practice, the assumptions are not always met. If the assumptions are violated, remedial action is called for. This can also be done with transformation. One must also guard against pseudo-precision. Large sample size increases significance. This produces illusory results. Again, bivariate and multivariate relations are hardly equally important.

Interpretation of regression has to be done carefully. Alpha, beta, gamma are used for populations, while a, b, r are used for samples where a = constant, b=regression coefficient, r=coefficient of correlation, r=1 means perfect fit of the regression line. If r=0, this means that there is no

Figure 27
Least square

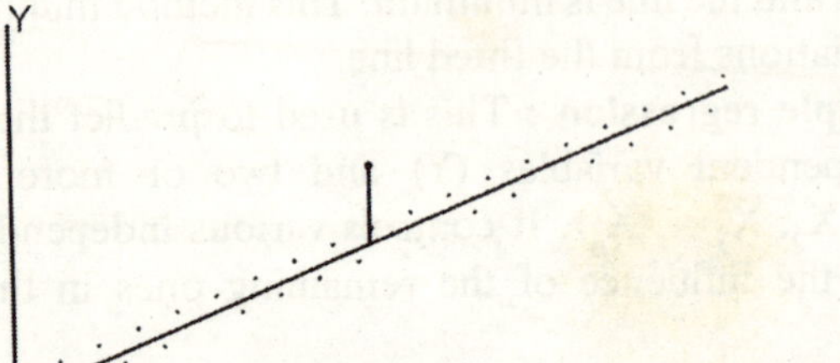

relationship between the variables $R^2 = \frac{\text{Explained variance}}{\text{Total variance}}$. This is also called the coefficient of determination. It measures the model's fit. It shows the percentage of variance explained by the regression. However, it does not guarantee causal connection.

R^2 alone is not enough to predict the strength of relationship. Standard error of estimate (SE estimate) is also needed for this purpose. It is the standard error of the predicted Y for given values of X.

$$F = \frac{\text{Mean square due to regression}}{\text{Mean square due to residue}}$$

statistical significance of R^2 at a given (say.001) level of significance.

t-statistic shows whether the regression coefficient is significant or not. Roughly speaking, if t-statistic is 0, we can not accept Ho : (Null hypothesis) at 95 per cent level of confidence.

We encounter some analytical problems in regression. Homoscedacity means that the variance of the error term is constant. The magnitude of error is not related to the independent variable. All over X, the spread of the residuals is constant. Heteroscedacity means that as X increases or decreases, spread of residuals on X increases.

Some points in a scattergram are isolated deviations away from the ordinary pattern. For instance, Brunei, Kuwait and Paris are so different from the company they keep. They stand apart. These are to be kept away from the main body of the data, and handled separately.

ANOVA and MANOVA

Difference of means between two interval-level variables can be compared in order to find out significant variation between two groups. Analysis of variance (ANOVA) is used for this purpose. This yields F-statistic and its level of significance. Thus, we can compare the incomes of migrant workers with the sons of the soil and point out their significant difference.

Multiple Analysis of Variance (MANOVA) is a tool for Multivariate Analysis. For example, we can point out how Gujarat and Punjab are following different paths of development. Interval level scales being rare in sociology, this technique is more often used by economists.

Multivariate Analysis

Variables in a table are also known as its dimensions. Analysis of tables with more than two cross-classified variables is known as multivariate analysis. Multivariate analysis helps us to study the impact of several variables on each other. Factor analysis, multiple regression, path analysis, discriminant analysis are often used for this purpose. Multivariate analysis is often done by simplifying the data. Large tables are broken up into sub-tables. The generalisations are combined into a viable mosaic. Separate noise from information. Do not throw away the baby in the bath tub. All data analysis involves systematic throwing away of information that is not needed for the time being.

Three-way Tables

A two-way table has two rows and two columns. It is also called a 2 × 2 table. It presents a zero-order relationship between an independent and a dependent variable without any other variable being partialled out (held constant). This makes a clear visual distinction between variables. A two-way table is simpler to read than a three-way table. Such a table has three rows and three columns. It is also called a 3 × 3 table. The latter presents partial relationship between two variables, holding a third one constant, i.e., removing its effect. Thus, the three variables are classified together. The latter helps us to elaborate the relationship between the independent and the dependent variables.

Rows and columns are laid out according to control variables. By convention, X is an independent variable, while Y is a dependent variable. Z is a control variable, or layer. An important point to be noted here is that we should never control a dependent variable. That will give us erroneous results. Entries in the cells show percentage differences in the dependent variable produced by the independent variable.

How do we read such a table? Specify zero-order relationships. Compare adjacent numbers. Elaborate their links.

Percentage tables can be used for elaborating the relationship between different variables. We want to find out whether the relationship between X and Y is genuine, or is it spurious because of the effect of Z on both of them. Table 26 physically divides the respondents into different categories according to the values of the control variable. Thus, as many sub-tables have been prepared as there are values in the control variable. If the original relationship between X and Y disappears when Z is taken into account, then that relationship is spurious. The upper hypothetical sub-table in Table 26 shows that the original 30 per cent difference between various categories of job satisfaction disappears when we take income into account. Thus, the (lower) sub-table indicates that job

Table 26

Correlation matrix of qualities of leadership

	(1)	(2)	(3)	(4)	(5)	(6)	(7)	(8)	(9)	(10)	(11)	(12)	(13)	(14)	(15)	(16)
1. Leadership	1.000	648	638	631	569	559	540	526	497	482	475	434	430	423	218	160
2. Resourcefulness		1.000	734	568	613	611	508	438	578	428	359	615	651	348	128	126
3. Exercising Control			1.000	668	608	622	529	490	741	433	428	508	639	492	255	188
4. Initiative				1.000	544	503	509	410	555	493	304	336	474	462	293	191
5. Intelligence					1.000	660	646	424	532	438	463	616	607	245	380	225
6. Self-confidence						1.000	767	532	771	639	427	704	621	322	190	236
7. Persistence							1.000	375	496	554	274	587	565	336	141	197
8. Negotiations								1.000	660	344	555	361	411	347	095	194
9. Decision-making									1.000	502	411	415	684	364	236	154
10. Dedication										1.000	273	678	497	365	087	041
11. Making speeches											1.000	231	448	629	291	162
12. Honesty												1.000	496	235	109	-007
13. Persuasiveness													1.000	487	351	149

...Cont'd

...Cont'd

14. Organising														1.000	230	290
15. Correspondence															1.000	223
16. Court work																1.000
F-1	560	713	636	547	736	832	789	358	621	734	146	855	637	141	134	013
F-2	520	362	507	412	190	288	136	708	517	198	800	037	376	741	064	184
F-3	−115	−062	−196	−274	−377	−106	−156	066	−093	094	−192	079	−282	−253	−818	−641
h2	596	644	700	543	721	787	665	633	661	586	698	738	627	633	691	444

In order to save space, coefficients of correlation have been written here without decimal points, i.e. only with the quantities after the decimal points and +ve signs satisfaction has no effect on trade union membership when we control income. Differences in trade union membership are caused by income differences. These patterns can be summarised by calculating chi-square, gamma, or other statistical measures for sub-tables with different values of income.

We have already discussed elaboration through partial correlation in the above section.

Factor Analysis

Regression and factor analysis do the same thing from two opposite directions. Regression breaks down dimensions into their components. Factor analysis brings together variables into dimensions. The results of factor analysis can be verified with regression.

What exactly is factor analysis? This is one of the techniques of multivariate analysis. It improves our comprehension and interpretation of data. It does so by bringing an adequate, but not very large, number of the underlying variables under a few dimensions. A factor is a weighted linear combination of variables under study. Factors are meaningful bundles of variables with strong + or – correlations. Factor analysis is done by ascertaining the linear combinations best predicting the variance in a set of variables. Small sets are combined into larger sets, along dimensions. The statistical operation enables us to grasp the pattern of interrelations between the given variables along the related dimensions. This makes it possible for us to describe our respondents with, say, three factors instead of, say, 34 variables.

It may be necessary to transform the data to meet the assumptions of factor analysis. For example, responses on a five-point scale can be dichotomised in order to fulfil the assumptions behind the point biserial coefficient of correlation between variables.

Before applying factor analysis, the given data are inter-correlated with other variables. Let us recapitulate what we have said earlier. Correlation means the strength of relationship between two variables. It lies between $\pm$ 1. Both ends represent perfect correlation. Positive correlations are direct relationships between the variables, while the negative ones signify inverse relationship. In between, 0.000 means that there is no relationship between the variables. Higher correlation between the two variables can be interpreted as association between the two variables, subject to reasonable theoretical assumptions beyond a statistical significance. Sometimes the correlation between the two variables may be due to both of them being mutually related through a third or an intervening variable.

Factor matrix is, so to say, the juice from the correlation matrix. Inter-correlated variables are bunched into clusters of factors. These explain that so much percentage of the variability of a phenomenon conceptualised as, e.g., leadership can be explained in terms of factors I, II, III respectively, the rest being due to uniqueness of the phenomenon under study. Uniqueness in turn is composed of specific variance and error variance. The latter can be attributed to error in the measurement. Similarly, communality represents the contribution of all the factors to the total variance. Thus, the total variance = communality + specific variance + error variance.

A number of steps have to be taken for extracting factors. The first step is to collect data from a representative sample of the population under study, say, by interviewing them. While preparing the interview schedule, we have to be careful about the choice of relevant variables. Inclusion of unrelated variables or exclusion of relevant variables is a source of error. The researcher has to exercise his judgement to avoid it. The variables have to be meticulously selected. They should be theoretically meaningful as well as measurable. Mechanical selection creates confusion. The results can be improved by incorporating new variables in the later runs and/or refining the old variables. The point is to carefully calculate the coefficient of correlation between all pairs of variables. These are arranged in a matrix.

Before feeding the coefficient of correlation into a computer, we have to exercise our choice in favour of one of the alternative procedures for factor analysis. These produce slightly different results. These include the principal component, maximum likelihood, canonical, centroid, generalised least squares, maximum likelihood, etc. Each one of them is useful for different purposes. For this purpose, we have to take into consideration basic assumptions behind each of them. The procedure used by us has to be explicitly stated in our research report. Different versions yield different results. The principal components method involves linear combination of the observed variables. The succeeding components represent larger to smaller variance on the common factors. This enables us to ascertain the number of factors required to explain most of the variables in a set of variables. This is too cumbersome a task to be done manually. Obtain the factor loadings. These are the correlations of factors with other factors. Drop out variables with low coefficients of correlation, in case this is theoretically possible. Extract the factors again. How many factors are to be extracted? Usually, three of them. Each factor accounts for a certain percentage of variance in the set of variables therein. The first factor explains a larger percentage of the variance in the given set of variables than the second one. The second factor accounts for a larger percentage of variance than the third one, and so on.

As already mentioned, we retain only the most important factors. Usually 3, 5, 7 of them. The remaining ones are often ignored. A rule of the thumb method is to retain factors with an eigenvalue 1. Their communalities are estimated, starting with the R^2 value between a given variable and other variables, and ending with values to which successive estimates converge.

In case the initial extraction does not yield satisfying results, we seek alternatives by rotating or transforming them. This involves changing over from one set of components to another. Shift in the angle of vision provides us a better fit in the cluster of variables. Unrotated factors define the general pattern of relations in the data. Rotated factors explain more variance than in the first attempt. Such a procedure makes it easy to grasp the problem under study. Rotation yields simpler structure of factor loadings. It provides a better fit for the factors. Rotation facilitates interpretation. Where do we rotate? This depends on theoretical considerations. While selecting variables for factor analysis, anticipate an underlying configuration. Rotate accordingly. Then check up. Rotated factors are easier to interpret. However, it does not improve the degree of fit between the data and the factor structure. Moreover, before rotating we should carefully take note of the assumptions behind various types of rotation.

The orthogonal rotation defines only the uncorrelated patterns. The orthogonal factors are not correlated with each other. They are simpler to understand and interpret. Communality values (see further below) for the unrotated factors do not change with the orthogonal rotation.

The varimax rotation is a variety of the orthogonal rotation. It improves the fit by maximising the variance of squared loadings for each factor.

The oblique rotation generates additional information. It traces patterns irrespective of their correlation. It defines the boundaries of clusters precisely. Thus, the central variables in a cluster can be identified by their high loadings.

Tailpiece : Neither communality nor eigenvalues should be given in a rotated factor matrix.

The factors so obtained have to be interpreted. This means conceptualising or verbalising the factors, or giving them names. This is a creative activity. For this purpose, we attentively inspect the factor loadings. See which of them have higher correlation with the given factors. Find out what they share in common. Give them a common name. We have to judge ourselves what they have in common. This requires a lot of background information and analytical ability. Be precise. Do not use the name of a single variable for a factor. The resulting hypothesis has to be tested and verified. Evidence of factor analysis alone is not firmly conclusive.

In case of simple structure, each factor is significantly associated with a single variable. It leaves other variables unaffected. In case of the social sciences, unidimensionality is rare. When this is so, cent percent of the variance between variables is explained by a single factor. A unique factor affects only a single observable variable.

Interpretation of factor analysis tells us how much variance of a phenomenon can be explained in terms of its specific aspects, i.e., its latent dimensions.

We have to understand the following terms for interpreting factors :

1. **Factor loading** means the strength of relationship of the variable with the pattern. It is the correlation between a factor and a variable. It measures how well a factor fits a variable. A loading of 0.2 is insignificant, 0.2–0.3 is low, 0.3 – 0.5 is moderate and 0.5 – 0.7 is high. Higher the loading, better the fit. Lower the loading, poorer the fit. Its square denotes the contribution of the factor to the total variance of the variable.

2. **Variance** is the extent to which a measure discriminates between individual differences. Total variance is of three types. Common variance correlates with other variables. Specific variance does not correlate with other variables. It is related only to itself. Error variance is due to chance, sampling error, measuring mistakes etc. Common variance + specific variance = reliable variance. Reliable variance+error variance = 1.00.

3. **Communality** (h^2) is obtained by summing the squared factor loadings in each row. It shows the variance accounted for by a factor. The higher the communality, the more a variable is explained by a factor. Communality × 100 is the variation of a variable in common with each pattern, in percentage. Thus, the multiple correlation coefficient of .700 of a variable X with the remaining variables in a pattern is squared and

multiplied by 100. Example, $(0.700)^2 \times 100 = 49$. This gives us communality. On this basis, we can say that 49 per cent of variance of X can be explained.

4. Eigen value is the sum of the column of squared factor loadings. It indicates how well each factor fits the data on all the variables. It serves as a criterion for determining the number of factors to be extracted. Size of its eigenvalue indicates the significance of a factor. E.g., eigenvalue of F_1=.4177 shows that it explains 41.17 per cent of the variance from all the variables. Add $F_1+F_2+F_3+$...and find the factors. Eigen values are extracted only if the principal axis method of factor analysis is used.

5. Uniqueness component $(1 - h^2)$ is the proportion that is unique to each variable. Uniqueness of a variable = 100 percentage of variation in common with the given pattern. This indicates the extent to which a variable is unrelated to others in a given pattern, and cannot be predicted from them.

Tables in this section show a concrete example of factor analysis. Social psychologists have suggested a number of traits as explanations for the process of leadership. Here 15 such traits are intuitively selected from various publications for follow-up operations. In order to check up the relevant significance of variables selected and to reduce 15 variables to a smaller number of dimensions, the dichotomised answers of 279 trade union leaders on an original five-point scale, were subjected to factor analysis. The dimensions themselves are not included in the interview schedule at start. These are not even known at that time. These are extracted afterwards, statistically. Dimensions, or factors, are sets of variables. These are brought together with the help of statistical operations. Here data pertaining to 279 respondents i.e., $279 \times 16=4{,}464$ readings have been reduced to three dimensions. Table 28 shows coefficient of correlation, between pairs of variables in the upper half. Three factors, constructed after rectilinear rotation of these correlations are shown in the lower half of the table. Through rotations one looks for a favourable situation for the factor axes. In the present case, the rotated version corresponds with the original value (deviation $\pm$ 0.0000). In order to interpret the correlations, the same are squared and multiplied with 100. This process yields a percentage of variables involved in each correlation. A γ =0.648 between leadership and resourcefulness signifies that $(0.648^2) \times 100=42$ per cent of the variation in case of 279 interviewees on these two characteristics is common. It follows that in case of these persons 42 per cent of their leadership is explained by their resourcefulness. An extreme case of a coefficient of correlation = $\pm$ 1.000 would mean that the variation of one of these characteristics can be fully explained when the other one is held constant. But even then one can not immediately conclude that one of these two is necessarily a dependent variable of the other. Their theoretical independence is an assumption. It has to be justified on the basis of validity of the prognosis. In other words, a statistical significance alone does not necessarily imply or justify the conclusion that leadership is either a cause or a consequence of resourcefulness. This might well be the case. But not necessarily. Two variables may be connected to each other through known immediate variables. A deductive test for such an inductive procedure would be to conduct regression analysis in the reverse direction of factor analysis. This must show clumping. If every person were to be described with the values of all the 15 variables on all the underlying factors, i.e., in case of a normal distribution of persons in the factor space, the resulting typology would not be valid.

An interpretation of the factors, i.e., verbalisation of the behaviour defined by the factor, indicates :

F_1 – *Sarpanch* (= village leader)

F_2 – *Jathedar* (= agitator)

F_3 – *Vakil* (= pleader)

These represent three different styles of leadership. An interpretation of F_1 is justified by a higher correlation of the key dimension with all the variables, except those included in F_2 and F_3. The interpretation of F_2 is justified by a strong correlation of the key dimension with speech making, organising agitations and demonstrations, and skill in negotiations. F_3 covers court work and correspondence. In fact F_3 is a case of pseudo-leadership, i.e., persons holding offices in trade unions without being real leaders. This fact reflects lack of confidence of the followers in a person possessing bureaucratic qualities. This implies an obstacle in the way of rational organisation of trade unions. For leadership, F_1 is more important than F_2, while the latter is more important than F_3. They explain 31,27 and 11 per cent of the variance respectively. With respect to all the 4,664 readings, F_1, F_2 and F_3 represent 35,20 and 11 per cent of the variation respectively. In all, 65 per cent of the total readings could be reduced to the three underlying dimensions, while 35 per cent of the variance remains unexplained.

Path Analysis

Path analysis is used for building up causal models.

This can be done with correlation as well as regression. This helps us in pinpointing the causal connections by specifying the direct and indirect influences of many variables on each other. This can be done to show only one-way causation (recursive model), or to show reciprocal effect of variables on each other (non-recursive model). A model being recursive means that there is no arrow in the reverse direction. Thus, all causal arrows are in the same (right) direction. There is no feedback loop. Path analysis shows the magnitude of linkages between variables. These helps us to understand the underlying causes.

Path analysis can be done with regression, if the necessary conditions are fulfilled. One of the conditions is that the residual and the explanatory variables are not interconnected. We make a series of regression equations with each variable in the model acting in turn as a dependent variable. A dependent variable in one equation may become independent in others.

Discriminant Analysis

Ordinarily, student's t, F-test and analysis of variance (ANOVA) are used for distinguishing between groups. These techniques become cumbersome if the dependent variable is multi-dimensional. It changes multi-pronged variables into univariate ones. It predicts membership in two or more mutually exclusive groups from a set of predictors. It identifies the most effective variables that discriminate between groups. This knowledge can be used for meaningfully regrouping categories. Besides, similarities and differences among various groups on given counts can be identified.

Report Writing

Inaccuracies easily creep up into tables at various stages of their preparation. Do not hastily throw away rough papers. These may have to be referred back for verification of mistakes later on. Check up accuracy of facts, formulations in the text, and figures in the tables. See that the percentages add up to 100, unless multiple responses have been permitted. Ensure that the figures in the tables and the text tally with each other. Remove typing errors and printing mistakes from tables.

The manuscript should indicate a proper place for putting the given tables and figures somewhere around. Footnotes and appendices should contain full details according to a consistent format of the publication.

Conclusions

In this chapter, we have given an elementary introduction to adequate analysis of systematically collected data with social statistics. Numbers are to be used carefully. First of all, understand the underlying assumptions. For example, chi-square can not be applied on very small samples. Similarly, Pearson's product moment coefficient of correlation is applicable only to the ratio-type data. Misapplication of statistics brings out erroneous results. We learn data analysis by repeatedly processing the data, applying appropriate statistical measures, precisely interpreting the results, and fitting the outcome into theories. Data analysis is a matter of theory, as well as practice with focussed attention, in dialogue with accomplished scholars in the field. In any case, there is no doubt about it that various instruments of research do tilt the results one way or another.

Why do we collect data? With a view to analysing the same. Avoid unnecessarily accumulating large masses of data, hoping that something will somehow come out of them at last. Keeping this in mind at the time of preparing a research design will stand us in good stead at the time of report writing. Let us clinch the issue. Some people know a lot of social statistics without knowing what society is. We cannot afford to neglect the man behind the statistics.

References

Allen, R.G.D., *Statistics for Economists*, Hutchinson Publisher, London, 1949.

Blalock, H.M., *Social Statistics*, McGraw Hill, Tokyo, 1988.

de Vaus, D.A., *Surveys in Social Research*, Sage, London, 2002.

Elhance, D.N., *Fundamentals of Statistics*, Kitab Mahal, Allahabad, 1976.

Gupta, S.C. and V.K. Kapoor, *Fundamentals of Applied Statistics*, Sultan Chand & Sons, New Delhi, 2003.

Gupta, S.P., *Statistical Methods*, Sultan Chand & Sons, New Delhi, 2004.

Kumar, Satinder, *Statistical Methods*, K.G. Publishers, Amritsar, 2005.

Montagnes, Ian, *Editing and Publication*, International Rice Research Institute, Manila, Philippines, 1988.

Shenoy, G.V. and Madan Pant, *Statistical Methods in Business & Social Sciences*, Macmillan India, Delhi, 1994.

Series, *Contributions to Empirical Social Research*, Campus Verlag, Frankfurt.

Series, *Quantitative Applications in the Social Sciences*, A Sage University paper series, Sage Publications, New Delhi.

Simran, Kang-Sidhu, *Elementary Education in Rural Punjab, A Sociological Perspective*, Department of Economics & Sociology, Punjab Agricultural University, Ludhiana, 2003 (with Harnek Singh).

Singh, Jaspal, *Methodology and Techniques of Social Research*, Kanishka, New Delhi, 2001.

Singh, Jaspal and Satinder Kumar, *Data Collection and Analysis*, Workshop for Young Writers, Indian Sociological Society, Chennai, 2006.

Yamane, Taro, *Statistics: An Introductory Analysis*, Harper & Row, New York.

10

Report Writing

Report writing involves expressing in black and blue why we started the project under study, and proceeded to complete it. Initially, we give our readers a broad perspective of the subject matter. The title has to be chosen after due consideration. It should make some sense, even if it is controversial. Some people conclude what is in a book just by reading the title. This improves the salability of the book. The topic under study is placed in its proper perspective. We tell our readers what it is all about. We explain why the topic is important. Then we give the details of what is done in the study. We write down a clear, complete, and simple account of how we went about the study and what our findings are. We tell the readers about the difficulties encountered during the course of our work. First of all, we write down the outline of our study. We define our terms. We state our hypotheses in a verifiable or falsifiable form. Then we write down a rough draft of the report. We go through it repeatedly with extreme concentration. We revise the draft. We put everything in proper format. We polish it. All errors are corrected. Then the matter is given for typing.

Regular exercise in writing improves our ability to write well. We should keep our pen in working order, so that it writes smoothly. We should keep sufficient writing paper at hand. We should search a cosy corner with proper lighting, where we can work with concentration and without disturbance. Then we sit down comfortably and systematically put down everything on paper.

Contents

Our report begins with an introduction. The introduction informs the readers what the study is about. It gives an account of the nature and scope of the study and why it was undertaken. Here we must clearly define the purpose of writing the report. What we write must lead to the achievement of the defined objective. The introduction answers a number of preliminary questions. Who sponsored the project? When was the fieldwork done? What procedures were made use of for carrying out the study? Who assisted in doing the work? If it is a survey-based study, how many interviewers were employed? How was the sample selected? What was the nature and extent of 'no response'? In order to be able to specify the extent to which the findings of the sample survey are representative of a larger universe, the writer compares the key figures with the available secondary sources.

In this section, the author also tells his readers about the theoretical importance and the practical significance of the study. Its aims and objectives are made clear. Project reports, monographs, dissertations, theses, are partially overlapping and interchangeable terms. A project report is a write-up on a project assigned to a researcher on a given topic. A monograph gives the details of a particular item. A dissertation or a thesis is written independently by a scholar, under the supervision of a research guide. The report shows the writer's grasp of the contents as well as the format. One is supposed to bring out new facts or fresh insights on already known facts.

Originality is not expected at the post-graduate level. However, a student is expected to be thoroughly conversant with the form of academic work, not necessarily with all its contents. Marks are deducted for mistakes in format. At the doctorate level, originality is also expected.

Sections

A researcher has to present the data collected and analysed by him before an audience. For specialised articles, fellow sociologists and scholars from the neighbouring disciplines are the main audience. For general articles, the general public or laymen are the readers. The contents and the style of the reports have to be oriented to the needs of the readers.

Our findings have to be properly organised. For this purpose, we prepare an outline scheme. We arrange the various items on our agenda in a logical order. The article is divided into sections, sub-sections, and paragraphs. These are coherently inter-connected with one another. As we go ahead, we may have to revise the original plan.

The contents of each chapter are divided into three parts the introduction, the main body of the chapter, and the conclusions. The introduction states what is being dealt with in the chapter. The purpose is to evoke the interest of the readers and to make them read further. The conclusions refer the reader back to the introduction. It clinches the issue being discussed in the chapter and presents the main findings and their implications. It may provide suggestions and make recommendations. It may also include suggestions for further research.

Review of Literature

Review of relevant literature in the field is based on library work. Research means finding something new. A researcher does so by standing on the shoulders of giants whose works are available in libraries.

There is no point in rediscovering what is already known. We have to carry out a thorough search in the library for this purpose. We discuss the matter with others working in the same field. Scientists working on similar problems exchange off-prints of their articles. These are often available in their private collections and in departmental libraries. Abstracts of articles appear regularly in such publications as *Sociological Abstracts*. Available bibliographies have to be thoroughly scanned. Book reviews and review articles of recent developments in the area are published in many periodicals from time to time. We are supposed to be fully conversant with the available literature in our filed. Unfortunately, the infrastructure for research is underdeveloped in our country. Under the given circumstances, we have to make the best use of whatever can be effectively obtained. The available literature must be reviewed meaningfully. It may be organised logically, chronologically, or otherwise. The research methods and the findings of the earlier writers are critically evaluated and related to the study in hand.

Libraries are extremely important for researchers. Research activity starts and ends in a library. A library is essentially a storehouse of printed matter. Nowadays libraries also include video cassettes and CDs. Already known facts are contained in books. New knowledge is brought to us by journals. Those who create new knowledge have been well-conversant with the already available knowledge. A library is the place to go to for this purpose.

Books alongwith journals, magazines and newspapers appearing at regular intervals (known as periodicals) are the core material.

The list of available books in a library is known as a catalogue. Catalogues are available authorwise, subjectwise, and even language or regionwise. The incoming periodicals are properly indexed before they are placed on the library shelves. Backdated ones are kept on the stacks. Apart from catalogues and indices on cards, bibliographies on a variety of topics are also prepared by subject-matter specialists from time to time. An annotated bibliography contains a brief note on the given material. Abstracts contain details about the recently published articles on a wide range of specialisations in various subjects. *Encyclopaedia Britannica, Encyclopaedia of Social Sciences*, and so on, contain brief articles on key concepts. Dictionaries of sociology and other subjects contain definitions of the key concepts. Researchers look around libraries, documentation centres, archives for available information on topics of their choice. Details of recently completed dissertations on various topics are available in *Dissertation Abstracts*. Prior consultation of the above before starting an assignment prevents unnecessary duplication.

As we go through the important books and periodicals, we make relevant notes from them. Depending upon our needs, we may summarise an entire book or article, or note down important passages from it. Passages which are meant for being quoted verbatim later on are placed within quotes. The exact pages on which they occur are noted down. It is not permissible to change the original wording of material within inverted commas. Paraphrasing may be done when a direct quotation is not required. This means restating the given ideas in one's own words. References to the context may be given directly in the text, or in footnotes. A summary is much shorter than a paraphrase. It contains a list of what is stated in the original version.

Footnotes, references should be complete in all respects according to a standard format. References may be arranged in an alphabetical order, or numerically.

After pointing out what others have done in the field under study, we move over to our own problem and tell the readers what techniques and procedures we have used for arriving at the conclusions stated later on in the report.

Method of Research

Research work is done methodically. A researcher tells his readers which techniques he has used for carrying out the work: participant observation, interviewing, experiment, or some other technique. He gives the details of the procedures for selecting a sample. He describes the scales used by him and the problems encountered in collecting and analysing the data.

Results and Discussion

Verify that the readings have been sufficiently scientifically interpreted. Ensure that the results presented earlier are adequately supported by facts observed in the field. After that select a few salient features of the matter under discussion. Succinctly state what you have found out. Clinch the issue firmly at the end, like the falling down of a hammer. If there are any negative findings, do not discard them or conceal them. Connect the findings with the hypotheses stated in the introductory part of the article/book. Place them within the context of the article/book. Place them within the context of the existing body of theory. Bring out the implications of what you have found out. Point out why the matter is important. Suggest leads for future researchers in the field. If you find yourself unable to bring the report to a fruitful end, give it a beautiful turn and leave it there.

Elaborate concise statements with appropriate instances, anecdotes, or cases to drive home your point.

Summary and Conclusions

Concluding means wrapping things up. Towards the end of an article, the main points in the article are brought together in this section under common names. They are placed within a framework. They are linked to the available theories in the field. Their implications are drawn for policy-making. Suggestions are made for further research in the field.

New data are not brought in this section. A summary is not an abstract. Unlike the latter, it may even refer to tables and figures in the main body of a report.

Some journals publish an abstract at the beginning, others at the end. An abstract briefly states the salient features of the article, in about 200-250 words. It elaborates the information given in the title by giving key terms. It briefly tells us about the substantial and methodological issues involved, and the key conclusions. Acronyms and abbreviations are excluded from abstracts. The same is true of references to tables or diagrams.

Acknowledgements

This is the place to thank all the people who have helped us in carrying out our study, in one way or the other. Courtesy costs nothing, but earns much credit. One may thank the sponsors for providing the required funds. Thanks are due to the respondents and their leaders for sparing their time for providing the required information. Thank the research supervisor for his advice and guidance. Friends and colleagues who went through the earlier drafts and gave suggestions for improvements, deserve to be thanked. One may also like to express appreciation for one's family members. Do not be thankless. But at the same time do not go on dropping in big names unnecessarily with a view to impressing some readers.

Footnotes

In the past, footnotes used to be given with symbols or numbers at the bottom of the relevant page. Nowadays, footnotes are given at the end of each chapter, or even towards the end of the book, lest they should hinder the flow of material in the main body of the article/book. If it is necessary to refer to them earlier, place them within brackets in the main body of the article etc.

Bibliography

This is the list of all the documents having a bearing on the study in hand. References are the sources actually used by an author for carrying out his work. In case of books, state the author(s), title, publisher, place of publication and year of publication. For articles, mention the author(s), title, journal, volume, number, date and pages. Use a standardised format for doing so. Various journals/institutions often lay down their own formats for this purpose. Put the references in the prescribed order. All the citations in the text must find a place in the list of references. Avoid giving too many references. Avoid the temptation of unnecessarily citing your own or your friends' work unless the study demands.

Appendix

In a book or a communication, some tables are superfluous in the text. These are appended at the end, for record and reference by a few interested readers.

When we write a research report, we must first understand the matter ourselves before explaining it to others. The point is not just having something to say (content), but also saying it as best as we can (format). The contents are important. So is the style.

Style

Scientists are not supposed to take sides. They are expected to write impartially and impersonally. They avoid using ornamental language. They write clearly and precisely in a matter of fact way. Not that they have to use telegraphic language. But redundancy is out of place here. They proceed systematically.

Audience

A writer has to orient his language to the needs of his audience. Research work brings out primary material. Its contents are original. These are to be published for the first time. Before accepting an article for publication, the editors of a journal refer it to qualified subject matter specialists for reviewing who certify that it is something significant, and is worth publishing. Primary materials are written by researchers for their professional colleagues. The articles are indexed and cited in bibliographies. On the other hand, secondary publications are meant for the general public. They are in the form of magazines, textbooks, and so on. *Guru Nanak Journal of Sociology* is a primary publication. *India Today* is a secondary publication. Whether the work is primary or secondary, a writer systematically makes each point, keeping his audience in view. That enables them to bring home the matter intelligibly.

Plagiarism

It is not honourable for a scholar to strut around with others' feathers in his cap. Plagiarism means stealing words and ideas from others, and passing them on as one's own. However, common knowledge does not fall in this category. We do not have to rediscover the wheel anew. However, ideas taken from others have to be acknowledged in a proper way. Scholars are expected to say things in their own words. If they fail to do so, they can be easily found out. Uneven expressions will be obvious to anyone going through the study.

Organising Ideas

A writer arranges everything systematically. Chaos, disorder, or lack of proper organisation prevent us from conveying what we want to say. Therefore, we have to put together the ideas in a coherent form in such a way that they can be easily grasped by those interested. Present them in a proper order. Arrange the details logically. Specify their breadth and depth. Let the matter flow smoothly from the start to the end. Keep some points in mind. Put them in black and white, if you like it that way. Gradually move through the material towards the last point in some order, ascending or descending, alphabetical, numerical, logical, or psychological order. Those who have dealt with computers can think in terms of flow charts and algorithms for this purpose.

Words, Sentences and Paragraphs

We have to use proper words, at the right place and at the right time. Do not use big words. Do not use any word without understanding its full meaning, including its connotations and denotations. If there are any gaps in between their objective, subjective and conventional intentions, get rid of them. Select your words with great care. Do not use difficult words where a simple one will do.

Remove spelling mistakes and grammatical errors. Consistently use British or American spellings, depending upon the journal etc. for which you are writing. One may spell utilisation with an 's' or a 'z'. However, this should be done uniformly throughout the study.

Combine proper words to put together straightforward sentences. Knit the sentences together into logical arguments. Weigh the arguments in your own mind. Reconsider and reformulate. Sentences should be short. Break up large complex sentences with a number of clauses into smaller simpler ones. Maintain continuity from sentence to sentence. Do not leave gaps in-between. Let the sentences flow smoothly into paragraphs. These are merged together to form sub-sections and sections.

Each paragraph contains one central idea. Sentences in a paragraph are coherently bound together in unity around this idea. One sentence states the topic. It is located either at the start or at the end of a paragraph. The preceding sentences smoothly flow into the succeeding ones. They keep pace with each other. Jumping here and there from one idea to another creates confusion. Do not digress or beat about the bush. Come to the point. Keep the discussion under control. Coherence may be achieved with words and phrases like again, moreover, therefore, and however. Short sentences are knitted together into brief and to the point paragraphs. Long paragraphs are broken up into shorter ones.

Different paragraphs are methodically put together, with chains of reasoning, into sub-sections and sections. The topic has to be narrowed down to a manageable level within the available time. The point at issue finds mention in the topical or thematic sentence. This may stay at the start, middle, or the end of a paragraph.

Revision

We can seldom make use of all the data we have collected. At some point, short of hiding relevant facts, we have to call it a day. Then we go through what we have written with complete concentration and revise the draft report with a view to getting rid of all the errors and unnecessary material. While doing so, we desist from clinging to unwanted words, sentences, paragraphs, and details. We improve our formulations. State everything precisely and concisely. Ambiguity impairs precision. Equivocal expressions yield unintended meanings. Conciseness means that there is no redundance. Correct all spelling mistakes. Get rid of grammatical errors. Replace inaccurate words with more precise ones. Do not insert the same words and phrases again and again. Use the right words at the right place. Cull out vague words. We cannot do much without our professional terminology. However, avoid unnecessary jargon.

Simplify complex sentences. Bring together sentences on the same theme under the same paragraph. Reorganise paragraphs in order to improve understandability. Rearrange the ideas where necessary. Watch out for gaps, slips or duplications. Things that belong together are to be put together. Write the words, sentences, paragraphs, themes in your article very carefully. Check for consistency and flow of arguments. Remove errors of reasoning.

Polish your statements. Read with full concentration what you have written, again and again. Carefully improve your choice of words, sentences, sequence of the material throughout the report. When you reach a stage where you have reason to believe that you cannot make further improvements, call it a day. Again take up the report the next day. When you are no longer able to think of any more improvements, keep your draft aside for a few days. Do not be in undue hurry to get rid of it by despatching it for publication. Meanwhile, unconscious incubation takes place in your mind. When you pick it up again, new ideas will flow to your mind. Think with due concentration. Critically assess the manuscript, as if somebody else had written it. Impersonality sharpens one's critical abilities.

Request some competent and willing colleague or friend to go through what you have written. Give due consideration to his constructive criticism. Present your article in a seminar or a conference.

Incorporate acceptable suggestions from those present on such occasions.

Typing: Submission of Report

An author is supposed to submit a debugged meticulously typed and, depending upon its size, nicely tagged or bound copy of the manuscript of his work, to the editors of an appropriate journal etc. For getting it typed, the author establishes contact with a competent typist possessing or having access to a good typing machine. He works out a time schedule and books the typist on the due dates. It is not advisable to blame the typist for the typing mistakes or the book-binder for poor binding. The author is supposed to instruct them properly and get the desired quality of work done from them. The world is not interested in the storms you encountered, but did you bring in the ship.

The writer prepares a legible manuscript. He carefully goes through the manuscript for spelling mistakes, omission of material/ pages etc. If he has used some abbreviations or made some insertions in his manuscript, these have to be made clear to the typist. It is not advisable to assume that the typist is a good person and a competent worker, and therefore he will not make any mistakes. Trust is good, but control is indispensable. The author carefully goes through the typed manuscript, makes the corrections and checks that all mistakes are corrected in each copy. He also sees to it that all the pages have not only been correctly numbered, but also placed in a proper sequence. It is more convenient for the typist to avoid mistakes than to carry out corrections.

The typist has to be clearly informed beforehand as to how many copies of the document are required. In case of articles, two copies have to be submitted to a journal—each co-author is to be given one copy, while one copy is to be kept on file in the office for record. When passing on paper to others for comments, or sending it for publication by post, make duplicate copies and retain one in case the original is lost in transit. In case of dissertations etc. for examinations, often 5-6 copies are needed. In case of project reports, the sponsors want to get several copies for reference and record or circulation at various levels. Carefully go through the letters granting funds, before starting the typing work.

Good old-fashioned mechanical typing costs lesser. But make sure that the machine is not rickety. Its letters should not be dented. Before using it, get its keys cleaned with spirit and brush or some other cleaning agent available in the local market. Electronic typing costs more. But it gives an even and beautiful display. Better machines even possess letters with different sized boldness. These can give us as many corrected and original copies as we need. Word processors facilitate editing on the machine. Computers have facilitated the editing of manuscripts. Several computer programmes are available for this purpose. Computers are increasingly becoming popular in India nowadays. But one can also use a typewriter.

Typing ribbons must be fresh. Better use silk ribbons. Paper ribbons, when available, produce even better results. Faint ribbons yield illegible copies, especially when reproduced through photo-copying.

Use good quality carbon paper. Do not go on putting it to use again and again. Ensure that the typist washes his hands properly, lest the carbon copies of the paper should get smudged with finger-prints while he is handling the carbon paper. The eraser or erasing-medium are to be used sparingly.

Use bond paper for typing work. Thin, brittle or porous paper creates problems for the editors and compositors. If something is to be reproduced through photo-copying, use paper without water marked brand names. Otherwise it may leave its shadow on the copies.

Headings, spacing, margins must be uniform in the report. Get the manuscript typed in double space, only on one side of the paper. The space in between is to be utilised for making corrections. This is for the convenience of the editors and the compositors. Indicate the title, main headlines, and sub-headings uniformly all over, as per the design and layout actually followed by the journal. Leave a 1.5 inch margin at the top and the left side of each sheet. Leave a 0.5 inch margin on the right side as well as at the bottom. If it is necessary to split a word between two lines, keep the syllables intact. Put a hyphen in between. Remind the typist not to create difficulties for the book-binder by transgressing the prescribed space for typing each page.

When typing, the abstract is given in the front page. Then comes the cover page. It shows the name (s) of the author(s). It also gives their institutional affiliation alongwith their postal address. The names of the authors appear according to their contribution to the article/book. This may also be done according to the prevalent local usage.

When quoting others, put the quoted material within quotes. If something is to be put in italics while printing, underline it. Emphases are to be underlined, and later on italicised. Explain abbreviations or acronyms when these appear in an article etc. for the first time.

Mention in the text where a particular table is to be inserted. See that the tables are well-displayed as well as intelligible. The matter should be in some logical, numerical, or other order. As pointed out earlier, the main body of the paper, ending with the summary and the conclusions, is followed by acknowledgements, footnotes and references. Append the tables numberwise at the end.

Binding

The concerned organisation may have prescribed a certain type of binding. Check this up in the departmental office or the library. Give the binding enough time to become dry and get set. Do not be in a hurry to submit your thesis before the binding is ready. It should be dry. A stitch in time saves nine. Otherwise, fungus might spoil the whole impression. The examiners and others would not even like to touch it, what to speak of reading it.

Dissertation and Thesis

There are different requirements and procedures for this purpose in different countries and institutions for various examinations. Before starting the work, one has to get registered for a degree under an approved research supervisor. The proposal is thrashed out and approved in various committees. After the work has been completed, copies are sent to a duly constituted board of examiners. They are expected to evaluate the thesis technically and otherwise. They examine whether the already available literature in the field has been properly reviewed. They check up whether appropriate techniques of research have been applied. They ensure that the candidate has applied his mind. The conclusions have been validly drawn, and the results have been drawn methodically. Tables have been adequately interpreted. Overgeneralisations have been avoided. Illustrations are appropriate. Then examine whether the expression is clear. Not only the contents, but also the form is sober. That grammatical errors have been eliminated. That typing mistakes have been duly corrected. The candidate has used his own words. Citations are neither too many nor too few. The research student has put forth problems for further investigation. If the board of examiners is satisfied, it recommends to the authorities that the dissertation/thesis may be accepted for the grant of the same or a lower degree.

Otherwise, the same may be sent back for revision or rejected outright. Good institutions refrain from lowering down their standards by granting degrees when the work is not up to the mark, because of other than academic considerations, e.g., compassionate grounds.

Publication

Sometimes the sponsors, who provide the required funds, do not allow the findings to be made public. They want to use the same themselves in order to take care of their interests. One who pays the piper also calls the tune. Lack of academic freedom impairs objectivity. If you are in favour of freedom of science, do not accept secret contracts. With a view to controlling the quality of output, many universities do not allow the researchers to publish their theses without permission from the higher authorities. Wherever necessary, get the required permission.

If you want to publish your findings, submit your work to various journals in the form of articles. Later on, you may put the articles together and bring them out in the form of a book. Choose an appropriate journal which usually publishes such articles. Decipher its style and proceed accordingly. One may also go through the instructions to contributors. These are issued by the editors from time to time for the benefit of the contributors. These are often reproduced inside the front cover or in the first few pages or inside the back page. If typing has been done electronically, ask the typist to transfer the complete paper on to a computer floppy/diskette. The floppy should be properly packed and enclosed with the required number of copies of your manuscript.

Do not submit an article for consideration to more than one journal at a time.

Summary and Conclusions

Report writing is best learnt by writing reports. Preparatory work in the library, contents, style, typing and printing are all important to write a good report. Have something to say, and say it in the best manner you can. *Jago sone walo, sun lo meri kahani.* Do not let the medium become the message. Clinch the issue at the end, like the moral of a story or the falling down of a hammer. E.g. : Let us cultivate our garden. Man is a social animal. Workers of the world, unite ! Educate, organise and agitate. And so on and so forth.

References

Altbach, Philip G. (ed.), *Publishing and Development in the Third World*, Sage Publications, New Delhi, 1992.

Barass, R., *Scientists Must Write*, Chapman and Hall, London, 1978.

Madsen, David, *Successful Dissertations and Theses*, Jossey-Bass, San Francisco, 1992.

Montagness, Ian, *Editing and Publishing*, International Rice Research Institute, Manila (The Philippines), 1991.

Shah, Vimal P., *Reporting Research*, Rachna Prakashan, Allahabad, 1977.

Singh, Jaspal, *Methodology and Techniques of Social Research*, Kanishka, New Delhi, 2001.

Appendix

<u>Confidential</u> Serial No. :

Interview Schedule on Trade Union Leadership

0.0	Block 1	:	Union Background
0.1	Name of the Union :		0.2 Regd./Unregd.
0.3	Office address :		
0.4	Affiliation (Single or Double) : AITUC/HMP/HMS/INTUC/Unaffiliated/Any other		
0.5	Year of establishment :		
0.6	Who took initiative in establishing it? Insiders : Employer/One of the employees/A group of employees. Outsiders : A political party/Another TU/An individual ( )		
0.7	Eligibility of membership :		
0.8	Actual enrolment :	0.8.1	Possible enrolment :
0.9	Any rival TUs : 0/1/2/3/4+	0.9.1	Their total membership :
0.10	Annual subscription :		
0.11	No. of active members : Paid : Unpaid :	Insider	Outsider (Whole-/Part-time)
0.12	How would you describe the attitude of the following to TU movement in India on the whole? Are you (1) Highly satisfied, (2) Satisfied, (3) No response, (4) Dissatisfied, (5) Highly dissatisfied?		

Party	Response	Please give reason	What specific measures would you suggest to create more favourable climate for TUs?
Central government			
Punjab government			
Management			
Workers			
Intelligentsia			
General Public			

0.13.1 Is this TU recognised by the management? Yes/No

0.13.2 Are TU notices allowed to be put upon the notice board? Yes/No

0.13.3 Are replies to the TU letters regular and prompt? Yes/No

0.13.4 Are TU representatives received by the management for negotiations? Yes/No

0.13.5 Are you allowed to collect subscriptions within the premises? Yes/No

1.0 Block 2 : Personal and Social Background

1.1 Name : 1.2 Office held :

1.3 Sex : Man/Woman 1.4 Marital status : Married/Unmarried/ Any other

1.5 Age : 1.4.1 If married, age at the time of the first marriage :

1.6 Home community

1.6.1 Which is the nearest town to your home community?

1.6.2 Give distance :

1.7 Since how long have you been living in this town?

1.8 Religion : Christian/Hindu/Muslim/Sikh/Any other :

1.9 Caste : 1.9.1 Gotra :

1.10 Educational level attained :

1.11 Languages known : English/Hindi/Punjabi/Any other :

1.12 If you attended any colleges, which ?

1.13 A brief biographical note :

1.14 At what age were you first employed?

1.14.1 Please give details of your employment right from the beginning upto the present job :

S.No.	Job	Salary	Name of organisation	Period employed	Reasons for leaving
1.					
2.					
3.					
4.					
5.					

1.14.2 At present any source of income other than the primary job? Yes/No

1.14.2.1 If yes, mention source : amount (PM)

1.14.3 Do you think your present job is what you really deserve?

1.14.4 If not, what job do you think you deserve?

1.15 Please give the following information about your family :

S.No.	Relative	Education	Occupation	Income	Marital status	Living with you/not	Economically dependant on you/not
1.	Father (alive/not)						
2.	Mother (alive/not)						
3.	Brothers, sisters, wife, children:						
4.							
5.							
6.							
7.							
8.							
9.							
10.	Father-in-law						

1.16 Has any relative of yours ever held a TU or political office? Yes/No.

If yes, please state:

S.No.	Relation with you	Position attained	Organisatio n	Dates	Sacrifices made
1.					
2.					
3.					

1.17 What is the reaction of your family to the amount of time you spend on TU work?

Highly pleased/Pleased/Displeased/Highly displeased

1.17.1 Is/was your father a TU member? Yes/No

1.17.2 Would you like your son to become a TU functionary?

1.17.2.1 Why? Yes/No

1.18 How would you rate the present economic condition of your family?

Very well to do/Well to do/Average/Poor/Very poor

1.19 To which social class, in this town, do you think you belong?

Upper/Middle/Lower

1.20 Have you ever been detained or imprisoned? Yes/No

If yes, state :

S.No.	Dates	Reasons given
1.		
2.		
3.		
4.		

2.0 Block 3 : Functioning

2.1 Approximately how many hours per week do you devote to TU work?

2.2 Are you a member of any of the following committees?

1. ESIC Committee — Any other :
2. Minimum Wages Advisory Committee — 7.
3. Provident Fund Committee — 8.
4. Wage Board — 9.
5. Works Committee — 10.
6. Workers Education Committee — 11.

2.3 Which of the TU activities make the greatest demand on your time?

Attending courts or offices/meetings/collecting subscriptions/

negotiations/paper work/helping members with individual problems

2.4 Of the persons/officials whom you have to contact in the course of your work, with whom do you spend most of your time? Members/Management/Govt. officers/Other leaders.

2.5 During the last one year, how many of the following activities did you engage in?

Court cases			Meetings etc. attended				Articles written	Rallies, etc., organised
Tribunal	Conciliation	Argued without lawyer	Executive	General body	Gate	Seminars Conferences		

2.6 What are the immediate objectives of your TU?

2.7 What difficulties stand in the way of attaining these objectives?

2.8 In your judgement, what are the long-term goals of TU movement?

2.9 What are the most remarkable achievements to the credit of your TU during the last three years?

2.10 Do you think your TU members want you to do the same things as you wish to do? Yes/No 2.10 (a) Why?

2.11 What is the best way your TU can adopt to serve the best interests of its members?

2.12 Which considerations should be kept foremost in organising and running a TU?

2.13 What considerations would you keep foremost in taking a strike decision?

2.14 What role do TUs have in resolving these problems?

2.15 What was the most difficult problem which you faced as a TU functionary?

2.15.1 How did you resolve it?

2.16 Can you recount any event in which your skill in mediation was pivotal in resolving a crisis?

3.0 Block 4 : Recruitment and Succession

3.1 At what age did you first become associated with a TU?

3.1.1 How did you come to be associated with that TU?

3.1.2 At what age did you first hold an office in a TU?

3.2 Please give an account of your association with various TUs :

S.No.	Name of the TU	Office held	Period	Your Contribution	If left, why?
1.					
2.					
3.					
4.					
5.					

3.3 Insider/Outsider

3.1.I If outsider, whether ex-actual worker in this line? Yes/No

3.3.2 What are the advantages and disadvantages of outsider participation in TUs?

Advantages Disadvantages

3.4 Have you any training, formal or informal, in TU?

Yes/No

Please state :

Training agency/person	Period of training	Has this training been useful to you?	If training courses for TU functionaries are arranged, what subjects should be taught?
		Highly useful/ Useful/Useless/ Highly useless	

3.5 When was the last election held in your union?

3.6 Factors leading to your first appointment as office-bearer of a TU : Founder of the Union/Emerged during a crisis/Victimised or frustrated worker/Any other :

3.7 Please account some significant event in your early life which roused your interest in TU movement.

3.8 Are you satisfied with the support you receive from your members? Highly satisfied/Satisfied/Dissatisfied/ Highly dissatisfied.

3.9 How do you explain the confidence which your members repose in you?

3.10 Are you aware of any case of victimisation of TU office in your establishment/department during the past three years? Yes/No. If yes,

Victim	Punishment	Any struggle conducted for this, and the outcome
Self		
Other members and office-bearers		
TU		

3.11 Please mention some common reasons for cleavages and factions in TUs.

3.12 Do you know whether some TU leaders augment their incomes from certain illegitimate sources? Yes/No

3.12.1 If yes, to which category of unions do they belong?

3.12.2 What sources do they tap?

4.0 Block 5 : TU Membership

4.1 How many general body meetings of your TU were held during the last year?

4.1.1 How many of the members usually attend the general body meetings? All or most/Three-fourth/One half/A quarter or lesser.

4.2 How do you inform the members about the time and place of a meeting? Personal communication/Loud speaker/Notice Board/Leaflets/Any other :

4.3 Reasons for some members not regularly attending meetings : Their inadequate education/Their inadequate experience/ Lack of interest/Lack of time/Fear of employer/Any other:

4.4 Leaders want large attendance because...

4.5 What, in your opinion, motivates the workers to join TUs?

4.5.1 What factors discourage the workers from joining TUs?

4.6 What measures do you suggest for increasing membership of TUs?

4.7 Apart from formal membership, are you satisfied with the actual participation of the workers in the activities organised by your TU? Highly satisfied/Satisfied/ Dissatisfied/Highly dissatisfied

4.7.1 Did your TU participate in any strike or agitation during the last three years? No/Once/Twice/Three times or more.

4.7.2 What was the proportion of membership participating on the last such occasion? All or most/Three-fourth/One half/A quarter or lesser.

4.7.3 What measures do you suggest for increasing existing member participation in TUs?

4.8 List three things which you think an ordinary TU member must do to help strengthen TUs.

4.9 Do you think any group of members in your TU is indulging in factionary or disruptive activities? Yes/No

4.9.1 If yes, what group and why?

4.10 How do you come to know the TU member grievances?

5.0 Block 6 :	Attitude

5.1 Why did you decide to work in TU movement?

5.2 Are you satisfied with your present and past services to the TU movement? Highly satisfied/Quite satisfied/ Dissatisfied/Highly dissatisfied

5.2.1 Why?

5.3 What is your main source of news about TU affairs?

5.3.1 What newspapers/magazines do you generally read?

5.4 Please rank the following political parties in order of their favourable / hostile attitude towards TUs:

Party	Ranking	Party	Ranking
Akali Dal(Sant group)		Congress	
Akali Dal(Tara Singh)		Jan Sangh	
CPI (left)		PSP	
CPI (M)		SSP	
Swatantra			

5.5 Please name your most favourite TU leader, past or present, at all India level and at state level. Also please mention three of his qualities.

Level	Name	Qualities
State		
National		

5.6 Have you ever been abroad? Yes/No

5.6.1 If yes, please name the countries and purpose of visit :

5.7 Please give yourself marks on the following attributes. You can have a maximum of five and a minimum of one on each count. (5) = Highly satisfied; (4) = Satisfied; (3) = In between; (2) = Dissatisfied; (1) = Highly dissatisfied.

Attribute	Marks	Attribute	Marks
Correspondence		Court work	
Decision-making		Dedication to the cause	
Exercising control		Honesty	
Initiative		Intelligence	
Making Speeches		Leadership	
Organising agitations and demonstrations		Persistence	
		Persuasiveness	
		Self-confidence	
Resourcefulness		Skill in negotiations	

5.8 Your future aspirations. What do you wish to achieve for :

5.8.1 Yourself :

5.8.2 Your TU :

5.8.3 Your Country :

5.9 Do you think you can serve the TU movement better in any other capacity, apart from being a Union leader? (E.g. being elected as an MLA or MP)? Yes/No

5.10 If you have any further comments and suggestions kindly state the same.

THANK YOU!

Bibliography

Acton, Siaren, Robert Miller, John Maltby and Dierdre Fullerton, *SPSS for Social Scientists*, Palgrave Macmillan, Hampshire, 2009.

Adams, John, *Research Methods for Graduate Business and Social Sciences*, Sage Publications, New Delhi, 2007.

Ahuja, Ram, *Research Methods*, Rawat Publications, Jaipur, 2005.

Arlene, Fink, *The Survey Kit*, Sage, London, 2002.

Antonius, Richard, *Interpreting Quantitative Data with SPSS*, Sage Publications, New Delhi, 2004.

Babbie, Earl, *The Practice of Social Research Methods*, Wadsworth Thomson Learning (USA).

Bell, Judith, *Doing Your Research Project*, McGraw-Hill Education, London, 2007.

Berg, Bruce L., *Qualitative Methods for the Social Sciences*, Pearson Education, New Delhi, 2008.

Bhattacharya, Deepak Kumar, *Human Resource Research Methods*, Oxford University Press, New Delhi, 2007.

Blaikie, Norman, *Designing Social Research*, John Wiley, New Delhi, 2009.

Boeije, Hennie R., *Analysis in Qualitative Research*, Sage Publications, New Delhi, 2009.

Bradburn, Norman K. and Seymor Sudman, *Asking Questions: Definitive Guide to Questionnaire Design*, Jossey-Bass, San Francisco, 2004.

Bryman, Alan, *Social Research Methods*, Oxford University Press, New Delhi, 2004,

Bradburn, Norman K. and Seymor Sudman, *Polls and Surveys: Understanding What They Tell Us*, Jossey-Bass, San Francisco, 1988.

Bryman, A., *Quantitative Data Analysis in Social Sciences*, Oxford University Press, New Delhi, 2008.

Coltoj, David and Robert W. Covert, *Designing and Constructing Instruments for Research and Evaluation*, Jossey-Bass, San Francisco, 2007

Cooper, Donald and Pamela Schindler, *Business Research Methods*, Tata McGraw-Hill, New Delhi, 2005.

Davies, Brett Martin, *Doing Successful Research Project*, Palgrave Macmillan, Hampshire, 2007.

Denscombe, Martin, *Ground Rules for Social Research-Guidelines for Good Practice*, Mc-Graw Hill Education, London, 2002.

Denscombe, Martin, *The Good Research Guide for Small Scale Social Research Projects*, McGraw-Hill Education, London, 2007.

de Vaus, David A., *Design in Social Research*, Sage, London, 2002.

Dorsten, Linda E. and Lawrence Hatchkiss, *Research Methods and Society: Foundations of Social Inquiry*, Prentice-Hall, New Delhi, 2005.

Fife, Wayne, *Doing Fieldwork: Ethnographic Methods for Research in Developing Countries*, Palgrave Macmillan, New Jersey, 2005.

Fink, Arlene, *Conducting Research: Literature From the Internet to Paper*, Sage, New Delhi, 2005.

John, Gill and Johnson Phil, *Research Methods for Managers*, Sage Publications, London, 2003.

Gina, Wisker, *The Undergraduate Researcher*, Palgrave Macmillan, 2009.

Gomm, Roger, *Social Research Methodology*, Palgrave Macmillan, Hampshire, 2008.

Graziano, Anthony and Michael L. Paulin, *Research Methods: A Process of Inquiry*, Pearson Education, Hongkong, 2010.

Harkness, Janet A., *Cross-Cultural Survey Methods*, Addison-Wesley, Singapore, 2002.

Haslam, S.A. and C. McGarty, *Research Methods and Statistics in Psychology*, Kogakusha, Tokyo, 2003.

Henn, Matt, *A Critical Introduction to Social Research*, Sage Publications, New Delhi, 2006.

Heise, David R., *Surveying Cultures: Discovering Shared Conceptions and Sentiments*, Wiley Publishers, New Delhi, 2000.

Heise, David R., "The Semantic Differential and Attitude Research", in Gene F. Summer, *Attitude Mesurement*, Rand McNally, Chicago, 1970.

Hesse, Biber et al., *The Practice of Qualitative Research*, Sage, New Delhi, 2006.

Hontrais, Linda, *International Comparative Research: Theory and Practice*, Palgrave Macmillan, Hampshire, 2008.

Jelke, Bethlehem, *Applied Survey Methods: A Statiscal Perspective*, Wiley, Singapore, 2009.

Kumar, Ranjit, *Research Methodology: A Step by Step Guide for Beginners*, Sage Publications, New Delhi, 1999.

Kundu, Abhijit, *The Social Sciences Methodology and Perspective*, Pearson Education India, 2009.

Law, John, *After Method: Mess in Social Science Research*, Routledge, London, 2004.

O'Leary, Zina, *The Essential Guide to Doing Research*, Sage Publications, London, 2004.

Ramler, Dahlia K., *Research Methods in Practice : Strategies for Description and Causation*, Sage Publications, New Delhi, 2010.

Ramsey, Sally, *How to Find Information*, McGraw-Hill Education, London, 2008.

Richard, Antonius, *Interpreting Quantitative Data with SPSS*, Sage Publications, New Delhi, 2004.

Richard, John M. (ed.), *Handbook of Qualitative Social Research for Psychology and Social Sciences*, Wiley, New Delhi, 2009.

Robert M. et al., *Survey Methodology*, Addison-Wesley, Singapore, 2009.

Ruane, Janet M., *Essentials of Research Methods*, John Wiley, New Delhi, 2004.

Rubin, Allen and Earl Babbie, *Research Methods for Social Work*, Wordsworth Florence, USA, 2007.

Ruegg, Gordon and Marian Peter, *Research Methods*, McGraw-Hill Education, London, 2006.

Sapsford, Roger, *Survey Research*, Sage Publications, New Delhi, 2006.

Silvan, D. et al., *Qualitative Research Design for Software Users*, McGraw-Hill Education, New Delhi, 2009.

Singh, Kultar, *Qualitative Social Research*, Sage Publications, New Delhi, 2007.

Smith, Herman W., *Strategies of Social Research: The Methodological Innovation*, Prentice-Hall, New Delhi, 1981.

Smith, Roger, *Doing Social Work Research*, McGraw-Hill Education, London, 2007.

Somekh, Bridget, *Research Methods in the Social Sciences*, Sage Publications, New Delhi, 2004.

Sotiorios, Saratakos, *Social Research*, Palgrave Macmillan, Hampshire, 2005.

Stolzenberg, Rose (ed.), *Sociological Methodology*, Blackwell, Washington DC, 2002.

Sve, Heath and Fiona Devine (eds.), *Doing Social Sciences: Evidence and Methods in Empirical Research*, Palgrave Macmillan, Hampshire, 2009.

Taslokori, Abbas, *Handbook of Mixed Methods in Social and Behavioral Research*, Sage Publications, New Delhi, 2010.

Thomas, Alexander, *Spotlight on Social Research*, Prentice Hall, New Delhi, 2002.

Tacq, Jaques, *Multivariate Analysis Techniques in Social Sciences: From Problem to Analysis*, Sage Publications, New Delhi, 1997.

Weathington, Bart L., et.al, *Research Methods for the Social and Behavioral Sciences*, John Wiley & Sons, New Delhi, 2010.

Willis, Paul, *The Ethnographic Imagination*, John Wiley & Sons, New Delhi, 2000.

Wineberg, David (ed.), *Qualitative Research Methods*, John Wiley & Sons, New Delhi, 2001.

Index